2

Praise for *The Financial Crisis and the Free Market Cure*

"John's book should be required reading for all future business leaders. This book shows how our economic crisis was a failure, not of the free market, but of government (and of businesses profiting politically rather than by satisfying their customers). One need look no further than John's principled leadership of BB&T—and the company's resulting accomplishments—for validation of the theories he presents in this timely, insightful book."

—**Charles Koch**, Chairman and CEO, Koch Industries, Inc.

"John Allison is America's leading business defender of the morality and philosophy of capitalism, and he was also the longest standing CEO of a major financial institution. His take on the financial crisis is not to be missed."

—**Tyler Cowen**, General Director, Mercatus Center, and Professor of Economics, George Mason University

"John Allison provides an invaluable lesson based on unique insights. His astute understanding of finance, economics, history and philosophy combine to provide a must read for business leaders, and more important, policy makers, if we are to avoid a cataclysmic economic collapse."

—**Robert A. Ingram**, former Chairman and CEO, Glaxo Wellcome

"No one is better qualified to review the events that lead to one of our nation's worst financial collapses than John Allison. A student of finance, philosophy and government, he opens our eyes to much needed changes in how we run our country. John shares with us a glimpse of what it was like to be behind closed doors with the leaders of American finance at the time of crisis during our financial debacle in 2008. Fascinating, informative, and shocking. *All will benefit by John's great work.*"

—**James Maynard**, Chairman, Golden Corral Corporation

"John Allison has the intellect and the experience to dissect complex matter and to interpret it in useful and practical ways. His insights in this book are informative and his arguments are persuasive. As a successful leader of a major corporation, he inspired audiences everywhere with his reasoned thinking and enlightened analysis. This is a thought-provoking read. Highly recommended."

—**Nido Qubein**, President, High Point University, Chairman, Great Harvest Bread Company, and author of *How to Be a Great Communicator*

"John Allison lucidly depicts how government and private institutions helped create the biggest financial debacle of our times. This book persuasively debunks the conventional wisdom!"

—**Tom Stemberg**, Managing General Partner, Highland Consumer Fund, Chairman Emeritus, Staples, Inc.

"For 20 years, John Allison supplied real leadership, including through the turbulent times of the banking crisis. He understands what caused the collapse and what we need to do going forward to ensure our financial future. His arguments are clear and compelling, and he has a gift for taking complex financial issues and making them understandable. I believe his blueprint is the roadmap for our economic success both now and in the future."

—**Fran Tarkenton**, NFL Hall of Fame Quarterback, Chairman, OneMoreCustomer.com, and author of *Every Day is a Game*

"John Allison's book provides real clarity to who and what caused the financial meltdown of 2008 from a person who successfully navigated his bank through the crisis. His willingness to call out institutions and individuals who were responsible is refreshing. He takes a highly complex subject and makes it understandable through the use of simple examples. If you have been puzzling over what happened, this book will set it straight. He also makes a strong case that more of the same is ahead if we continue to pursue the same destructive government policies that brought us to this point."

—**Stephen Zelnak**, Chairman, Martin Marietta Materials

"John Allison's *The Financial Crisis and the Free Market Cure* is more than extraordinary. His explanation of the financial collapse rests on a values-rich, free-market foundation. The account is enlightened by decades of experience as CEO of one of the nation's largest and most successful financial institutions. Allison was in the room when it happened. But while these two features of the book make it extraordinary, it is the last feature that carries the book beyond extraordinary. This is his identification and treatment of the way government policies led to the misallocation of trillions of dollars of resources and to the ruin of institutions that unfortunately responded to the policy incentives. John Allison proves there is room on the shelf aplenty for a market-based book on the financial collapse."

—**Bruce Yandle**, Dean Emeritus, College of Business and Behavioral Science, Clemson University

"If you only read one explanation of the Great Recession, make it this one. John Allison soundly analyzes its origin, debunks the prevalent myths, and illuminates the only path that can prevent the next one. I haven't found myself exclaiming 'Amen!' this many times since I first read the Declaration of Independence fifty years ago."

—**Lawrence W. Reed**, President, Foundation for Economic Education,
and author of *A Republic—If We Can Keep It*

"This book is a brilliant analysis of America's current economic woes. What makes it unique is the combination of John Allison's first-hand experience with the economy as one of America's top bankers with his deep philosophical reflection of the underlying causes of the financial crisis. More important, Allison provides a roadmap for saving the American economy and restoring the principles that once made it great. *The Financial Crisis and the Free Market Cure* is a game changer."

—**C. Bradley Thompson**, Professor of Political Science,
Clemson University, Executive Director,
Clemson Institute for the Study of Capitalism,
and co-author of *Neoconservatism*

"You will not find a more readable and straightforward explanation of how government policies are the cause of both the Great Recession and the slow recovery than John Allison's *The Financial Crisis and the Free Market Cure*. But Allison's story is not limited to a diagnosis of how government intervention throughout the economy, and in particular in the financial sector, turned the inevitable market correction to distortions caused by previous government interventions into an economy-wide crisis due to additional government interventions; he informs his readers in just as clear a way how to get out of our current morass through the consistent and persistent application of free market principles to questions of public policy. Allison's work is grounded in up close and personal experience in the banking industry plus years of serious study of economics, history, politics, and philosophy. Allison's clarity of vision and message is sorely needed in the day and age of politicized political economy."

—**Peter Boettke**, University Professor of Economics
and Philosophy, George Mason University

"*The Financial Crisis and the Free Market Cure* is a sophisticated yet accessible analysis of the causes and solutions to America's financial meltdown. Allison possesses an encyclopedic knowledge of banking and financial regulations. A clear and forceful writer, he makes a compelling case for a true free market in financial services based on sound philosophic principles."

—**Ed Crane**, President Emeritus of the Cato Institute

"In his new book *The Financial Crisis and the Free Market Cure*, John Allison provides an indispensable contribution to the debate about the future of the American economy. He persuasively argues that 'crony socialism,' not free markets, laid the groundwork for America's economic crisis, and shows how redoubling our commitment to free enterprise and limited government will lead our nation back to greatness."

—**Arthur Brooks**, President, American Enterprise Institute,
and author of *The Road to Freedom*

"The author of a book on the free market and today's financial crisis must be someone with real-world experience, maturity, and the ability to offer the best solutions. John Allison is that author, and this is the right book to learn about the importance of capitalism in America. No one is better equipped to understand what is going on today and the causes of the financial crisis. Please pay attention to what he says here."

—**Bernie Marcus**, Chairman, The Marcus Foundation,
and co-founder, The Home Depot

"John Allison explains the unintended consequences of government policies and their impact on the financial crisis, and recommends practical steps to improve the economy and individual liberty."

—**James M. Kilts**, former Chairman and CEO,
The Gillette Company and
author of *Doing What Matters*

"John Allison is uniquely qualified to explain the causes and consequences of the financial crisis: he was CEO of one of the largest yet healthiest financial institutions in the United States; he has a deep understanding of economics and the way it plays out in the business and political world; and he has an understanding of how fundamental, philosophical ideas shape a culture. In this book, Allison brilliantly integrates all of these perspectives into the best, deepest explanation of what caused the crisis and the consequences of our government's response to it."

—**Yaron Brook**, President and Executive Director,
The Ayn Rand Institute,
and author of *Free Market Revolution*

"John Allison is superb with his comprehensive and thought-provoking explanation for our current economic crisis and a clear and compelling path to a brighter future."

—**Steve Reinemund**, Dean, Wake Forest University
Schools of Business,
retired Chairman and CEO, PepsiCo

The Financial Crisis and the Free Market Cure

Why Pure Capitalism Is the World Economy's Only Hope

John A. Allison

New York   Chicago   San Francisco   Lisbon   London
Madrid   Mexico City   Milan   New Delhi   San Juan   Seoul
Singapore   Sydney   Toronto

1 2 3 4 5 6 7 8 9 0   DOC/DOC   1 8 7 6 5 4 3 2

ISBN   978-0-07-180677-0
MHID   0-07-180677-6

e-ISBN 978-0-07-180678-7
e-MHID   0-07-180678-4

This book is printed on acid-free paper.

Contents

Introduction

THE PURPOSE OF THIS BOOK IS TO PROVIDE AN INTEGRATED INSIDER's perspective on the recent financial crisis, the related Great Recession, and why a meaningful economic recovery has not occurred. It will also define the dire consequences if we do not change directions, along with the fundamental long-term cures for our economic problems.

The financial crisis is the most important economic event in 80 years. It will have a significant impact on the quality of your life and that of your children. The vast majority of the explanations for the crisis and the ensuing recession presented in the popular press are not true. Destructive policy decisions are being made based on this misidentification of the causes of our financial problems. If you misidentify the causes, you will, of necessity, propose the wrong cures. The Great Recession and the failed recovery (this is the slowest recovery in American history) are best explained by understanding the impact of all types of incentives on the behavior of business leaders, who are the ultimate job creators.

As the longest-serving CEO of a top 25 financial institution, I had a special inside view of the factors leading to the financial crisis. I served as chairman and CEO of BB&T Corporation from 1989 to 2008. During my 20-year tenure, BB&T grew from $4.5 billion to $152 billion in assets and became the tenth largest financial services holding company headquartered in the United States We also grew our insurance business from a small local agency to become the seventh largest insurance broker in the world.

BB&T's strengths are a clearly defined culture based on fundamental principles, outstanding client relationships, and a fundamental commitment to employee education, resulting in the lowest employee turnover rate of a large financial institution. BB&T has maneuvered through the financial storm extraordinarily effectively without experiencing a single quarterly loss. We avoided all the major excesses and irrationalities of the industry. Of course, BB&T has been negatively affected by the economic environment, as banks reflect the financial health of their clients and BB&T's core business is real estate related. However, we have nothing for which we need to apologize. I was in charge of BB&T's lending business during the significant recession of the early 1980s and CEO during the last major real estate correction in the early 1990s. BB&T weathered both of these storms extremely successfully. The reason for providing this background is to create a sense of credibility concerning my insight into the causes and consequences of government policies and the decisions of individual financial firms. By objective standards, I am an expert on the financial industry.

I also have an unusual hobby: studying philosophy and economics (including economic history). We have failed to learn from economic history because of many misinterpretations of the causes of and cures for past economic problems. In addition, the deepest causes of the financial crisis and the ensuing Great Recession are philosophical. In the later chapters of the book, these fundamental philosophical causes will be integrated with the economic consequences.

This is not a book with a focus on numbers and mathematical formulas. It is a study of the impact of the incentives created by various government policies on the actions of business leaders, especially those in the financial industry. In the end, the laws of human nature drive all economic activity. This book is about the impact of government incentives on the decisions of "real-world" decision makers, that is, human action.

The CEOs of large financial firms, including those companies that experienced severe problems, were intelligent, highly educated, and experienced, and in most cases they had been successful for many years. Obviously, a number of these individuals made irrational decisions, but the argument that there was a sudden burst of greed on Wall Street is childish. Yes, there are always individuals and firms on Wall Street that have a desire for the unearned. In my almost 40-year career in banking, there has always been greed on

Wall Street. However, we did not have a sudden burst of greed that created the financial crisis. The causes are far deeper, longer-term in nature, and far more destructive. Our educational system, especially our "elite" universities, played a far more significant role in the destruction of wealth than greed on Wall Street did. The ideas that these elite universities are currently teaching our future leaders pose a fundamental threat to our long-term prosperity.

Understanding all the causes and consequences of the financial crisis is a complex subject. Unfortunately, both the popular press and many academics have provided arguments that lack basic understanding, ranging from the simplistic greed on Wall Street argument to the idea that complex derivative instruments such as CDOs, SIVs, and CDSs (the "shadow banking system") caused the crisis. Much of the information has been presented in "sound bites" by commentators, who do not understand economics, or academic articles by professors, who have never been in business and do not understand how government policy incentives affect human behavior. The effect has been to create misunderstanding and confusion.

The goal of this book is to deal with the fundamental causes, that is, to focus on essentials. After you read this book, you will have an integrated understanding of the economic and philosophical causes of the financial crisis, the negative consequences of the policy decisions we are making today, and what the proper answers are for future economic success. Also, you will grasp how the correct philosophical principles will lay the foundation for individual, organizational, and societal success and, most important, personal happiness.

In the end, this is a book about how the pursuit of happiness (in the Aristotelian understanding of this concept) is the foundation for societal well-being. Furthermore, a free society is essential if any individual is to achieve personal self-fulfillment and true happiness.

Fundamental Themes

THERE ARE SIX FUNDAMENTAL THEMES THAT REFLECT THE BASIC causes, consequences, and cures of the financial crisis and the ensuing Great Recession. These themes outline the essential ideas that must be understood and that will be discussed in detail in the following chapters.

1. *Government policy is the primary cause of the financial crisis.* We do not live in a free-market economy in the United States; we live in a mixed economy. The mixture varies significantly by industry.

Technology is one of the least regulated industries in the United States. It should be noted that technology continued to perform well in the difficult economic environment.[1]

Financial services is a very highly regulated industry, probably the most regulated industry in the world. It is not surprising that a highly regulated industry is the source of many of our economic problems. By the way, if you do not believe that financial services is highly regulated, obtain a copy of the state banking, Federal Deposit Insurance Corporation (FDIC), Office of the Comptroller of the Currency (OCC), Federal Reserve, Securities and Exchange Commission (SEC), or other agency regulations document that affects the industry. The claim that the financial industry was deregulated is a myth that will be discussed in Chapter 13.

Not only did government policy create the financial environment for a significant economic correction, but government policy makers unnecessarily turned a challenging economic environment into a crisis.

2. *Government policy created a bubble in residential real estate.* A bubble is an irrational, excessive investment of capital and human resources. The real estate bubble burst, as all bubbles do. The loss of wealth from the declining values in residential real estate was transmitted to the capital markets, destroying more wealth and leading to a significant reduction in economic activity, that is, to negative real growth and the destruction of millions of jobs.

The recent roots of the government policy incentives that created the bubble in housing can be traced to Lyndon Johnson's "Great Society" of the late 1960s. The errors multiplied and went exponential over about a period of 10 years ending in 2007.

Unfortunately, another of Johnson's Great Society programs, Medicare/Medicaid, will go exponential in less than 10 years and will be far more damaging than the housing bubble if the direction is not changed. (*Going exponential* means increasing at a mathematically accelerating pace.)

3. *Individual financial institutions (Wall Street participants) made very serious mistakes that contributed to the crisis.* These institutions should have been allowed to fail. (In Chapters 17 and 19, we will discuss the consequences of not letting companies fail.) However, any errors by these institutions, individually and collectively, are far less important than government policy mistakes, and almost all the errors were the direct result of government policy incentives.[2] It is important to note that many of the financial institutions that should have been allowed to fail had a history of being crony capitalists; that is, these companies did not advocate limited government but instead sought special favors for themselves. Goldman Sachs, Citigroup, and Countrywide are examples of crony capitalists. Crony socialist is probably a better name for these individuals and firms. If the United States had separation of "business and state" as it does separation of "church and state," crony capitalism (or crony socialism) could not exist.

4. *Almost every governmental action taken since the crisis started, even those that may help in the short term, will reduce our standard of*

living in the long term. If you misidentify the fundamental cause of a problem, you will almost certainly recommend the wrong solution. If your doctor treats you for cancer when you have heart disease, the outcome will not be good.

In addition, some of the primary culprits who caused the financial crisis, such as Bernanke, Geithner, Frank, and Dodd, are the people who developed the "solution." How realistic is it to expect that they would identify the cause as their own actions and suggest cures accordingly?

5. *The deeper causes of our financial challenges are philosophical, not economic.* All of the destructive government policies are based on philosophical ideas taught in our elite universities to future elitist leaders.[3] These ideas are inconsistent with the founding principles that made America great. They are also inconsistent with individual rights, especially property rights. At a deeper level, these ideas are inconsistent with humans' fundamental nature as thinking beings who must make independent judgments that are based on the facts and that use their ability to reason.

Academics purport to defend academic freedom. They are right to do so. However, when put in government policy positions, the same academics somehow believe that businesspeople can continue to innovate and create wealth despite the ball and chain of government regulations. In reality, government regulations prevent businesspeople from being innovative and from thinking creatively. In my career, I have seen a number of significant opportunities to add products and services that would unquestionably benefit our clients, and yet some law made this impossible. All human progress is, by definition, based on creativity, because anything that is better is different. Creativity is possible only for an independent thinker. Someone who is not creative, who cannot innovate, cannot contribute to human progress. Government policies often provide incentives for destructive activities and prevent productive innovations. In a broader context, our lives ultimately depend on our individual ability to make independent judgments based on our assessments of the consequences of our actions for us.

These regulatory policies are typically based on a fundamental misunderstanding of human nature, the means of human survival, and the nature of the production process. Ideas have consequences.

We need to ensure that our future leaders are taught ideas consistent with the laws of nature and human nature, which are the foundation for a successful society and individual happiness.

Intentions that are called "good" often do not produce favorable outcomes. This is particularly true when these good intentions are based on false premises and a lack of understanding of what motivates human actions. Sometimes, unfortunately, the so-called good intentions actually reflect a lust for power, the desire to control others, and the belief that you are smarter than the people you are going to "save." Chapters 21 through 25 are the most important in the book because they deal with the philosophical issues. However, the preceding chapters make concrete the effect of the philosophical ideas expressed in these chapters and therefore are very helpful to an understanding of these concepts.

6. *If we do not change direction soon, the United States will be in very serious financial trouble in 20 to 25 years.* The economic forces that have now been set in motion are laying the foundation for a long-term disaster. Social Security deficits, Medicare deficits, unfunded state and local pension liabilities, government operating deficits, retirement of the baby boomers, and a failed K–12 education system are huge issues.

Countries do not go bankrupt the way businesses do. They typically hyperinflate—that is, print valueless money—and move to some form of authoritarian government. In 1920, the United States and Argentina had the same standard of living. Argentina, through authoritarian government policies, has made itself into a third-world country despite having vast natural resources. The United States will be the next Argentina if it does not change direction soon. It is not too late for us to deal with our fundamental problems, but time is running out.

Chapters 17 through 20 will clearly outline the fundamental economic solutions to our financial problems consistent with the philosophical principles covered in Chapters 21 and 22.

2

What Happened?

THE PRIMARY CAUSE OF THE GREAT RECESSION WAS A MASSIVE MIS-investment in residential real estate. We built too many houses, too large houses, and houses in the wrong places. The overinvestment in residential real estate was more than $3 trillion (and possibly as much as $8 trillion, based on the decline that has occurred since the bubble burst).[1]

Underlying this massive misallocation of capital to residential real estate was a belief that home prices appreciate forever and that housing is a great investment. This false belief was based on a long-term trend of home appreciation that was driven by a long history of government policies supporting investment in the housing market, which we discuss in future chapters.

In economic terms, spending on housing is consumption, not investment. We live in a house, and therefore we consume the house. Houses are not used to produce other goods. A manufacturing plant that makes computer parts is a production investment. Thus, the misinvestment in housing shifted resources from production to consumption. You can spend your money only once. If you spend it on houses, you cannot spend it on manufacturing plants. While houses create jobs while they are being built, once they are built, they do not create jobs going forward. A manufacturing plant creates jobs when it is being built, but, more important, it continues to create jobs as long as it operates. In fact, it is jobs that create houses, not houses that create jobs.

When you shift capital (money) from production to consumption, you reduce your future standard of living. This may be a good decision for an individual (or an economic system) because we may want to or need to consume today. However, if artificial incentives cause this redistribution from production to consumption, our future standard of living will be permanently reduced. In other words, by investing too much in housing, we invested too little in manufacturing capacity, technology, education, agriculture, and other such areas. Also, we saved too little and borrowed too much from foreigners, which will have to be repaid. This is analogous to having partied for years in the Caribbean and now finding that we have a really bad "hangover" and a giant credit card bill.

This type of misinvestment has many destructive effects. For example, numerous workers developed skills in building houses, but these skills are no longer needed or valuable. The workers could have been developing skills in running machines that manufacture advanced medical products. These construction workers will need to be retrained to do useful work. Retraining is expensive, and some older workers may not be retrainable.

However, there is a bigger problem. Since we did not build the manufacturing plants, the jobs do not exist even if the worker is retrained. Also, construction jobs are competitive with manufacturing jobs, and so as the excessive construction of houses continued, construction wages rose rapidly and created upward pressure on manufacturing wages. As these manufacturing wages rose in the United States, jobs were driven overseas because U.S. manufacturers could not be competitive. At first, the workers in India and China were not skilled. However, the Indians and Chinese have become skilled and are highly productive at relatively low wages, making it difficult for us to get the jobs back.

We cannot afford to build the manufacturing plants now because we wasted our capital building houses that we did not need. In addition, the government is taking the capital that we do have and spending it on pork barrel projects or projects that are not economically justified (clean energy), so these good jobs may never be created.

Also, these former construction workers are accustomed to being paid a healthy wage rate because of their construction skills, but the new manufacturing plants cannot afford to pay that high a wage because the workers, even after being retrained, still have a great deal to learn. Unemployment insurance provides an incentive for workers not to take a lower-paying job. Also, the minimum wage law keeps small businesses from hiring low-skilled workers at a wage rate that would allow their businesses to be profitable, so entry-level workers cannot gain the skills to become more productive and thereby paid at a higher level.

The ripple effect continues. Manufacturing is a primary industry. The manufacturing workers, if they had jobs, would be able to buy more food, clothes, and other things, creating other jobs in other industries. (By the way, this is not an argument for manufacturing vs. service jobs; it is just easier to understand the manufacturing example.)

Of course, the impact of this overbuilding is not limited to construction workers. Real estate agents, attorneys, mortgage lenders, and other such groups also developed skills that are no longer needed. They will have to be retrained and will be less productive for years than they would have been had they not participated in the residential construction industry.

Commercial real estate tends to follow residential real estate, especially shopping centers, retail stores, office buildings, and even hotels. After all, if there are many new houses being built, and numerous consumers are expected to be living in these homes, will there not be a need for a shopping center? This secondary misinvestment has the same ripple effect on commercial construction workers, commercial real estate brokers, and other such groups that we discussed earlier for residential real estate. It should be noted that the bubble was at least 10 years in the making, which means that millions of workers in multiple industries learned the wrong skills.

There is another important consideration. When many (or most) individuals started viewing homes as investments, instead of as consumption, and also believed that these investments would continue to appreciate indefinitely in the future, they adjusted down their savings because they thought that "investing" in a house was a form of saving (when in reality it is consumption).[2] People today are coming to realize that housing is consumption, not investing, which encourages them to save more in other areas. This is likely to have a permanent impact on housing consumption.

Why did so many people make such bad financial decisions? The press likes to indicate that it was greed. Well, there certainly were some people who were greedy (that is, who made irrational, risky financial decisions). However, this group was relatively small. Many honest, intelligent people were simply mistaken, primarily because of the misinformation provided by government policy actions. After all, the government (both Democrats and Republicans) has been supporting housing for many years, and home prices have had a steady upward trend for many years. Every time prices started to decline, the government, in one way or another, stepped in to protect home values.[3] Housing was an "investment" with upside potential and no downside risk.

Residential developers and contractors were also misled by the same policies. Assume that it is the spring of 2005, and you are in the business of buying land, converting it into lots, and constructing residential buildings. Your business is excellent, and has been for many years. The economic forecasters, including the Federal Reserve economists, are projecting good times ahead. You are worried about running out of building lots several years in the future. Unfortunately for you, your business is in a market where the local government zoning laws make it very difficult to get land zoned for residential development. Because of the long time frame involved, you have to buy the lots many years in advance to get them approved for zoning. In addition, land values have skyrocketed because the county will approve only a few lots per year, less than the market demand. You know you may have to make some significant contributions to local politicians if your lots are have a chance of being considered, and maybe be "generous" to the local building inspectors once you start development. You go ahead and purchase the lots long before you need them and at a higher price than you feel comfortable paying, because if you do not buy those lots and get them zoned by the spring of 2007, you will be out of business. Also, after all, the government always supports the housing market. It will not let prices fall.

How about bankers? Let me share with you my personal experience. Among BB&T's core businesses are residential construction and development lending and home mortgage finance. BB&T is organized conceptually as a group of community banks, and our focus is on local small and midsize businesses. Residential builders and developers fit into this category. We have been in this business for many years, with outstanding results—low loan losses and excellent economic returns. The bank even weathered the significant real estate corrections in the early 1990s.

Even with this very positive historical pattern, in the summer of 2005, our management team was becoming concerned about the residential real estate market. House prices were rising too rapidly. It was obvious that "get rich quick" speculators were taking a bigger role in the market. In some communities, home prices had gone above affordability. What should we do? Would it be fair to our builder customers to just stop providing financing, which would put them out of business? If their business was doing well, how could we convince them that times might get tough? How about our residential lenders who work for the bank? They do not want to make their builder clients unhappy. In many cases, the clients are also friends, as BB&T is a local institution for which personal relationships matter. Also, of course, our lenders' performance evaluations are partially based on production goals. Were the bank's lenders going to be unfairly evaluated? A lender could easily leave BB&T and go to work for a competitor bank that had not tightened its standards and potentially move our clients' business to that competitor bank.

What about shareholders and financial analysts? If the bank does not keep making these loans, current earnings will be lower and the stock price will decline. Since economists are all predicting good times ahead and almost no one is seeing problems in housing, the analysts are going to be critical of the pullback strategy.

But what really made the decision tough was that in the back of my mind, I knew that the housing market should have been correcting all along. However, every time a correction would have been natural in a free market, various government agencies took some action to support the market. If BB&T were to exit the market too soon based on a rational analysis of economic factors, government policy could make our decision appear to be mistaken by bailing out the housing industry one more time.

At BB&T, we decided to tighten our residential construction lending standards, and we tried hard to coach our builder and developer clients to be more conservative. However, the knowledge that government policy makers could act in an aggressive manner to save the housing market made us significantly less willing to act to reduce risk than we would have been had the economy been a free market where we knew that market forces, not government action, would drive the results.

Business leaders are often accused of being short-term-oriented. Sometimes this is a valid criticism. However, businesses must be successful in the short term if they are to be in business in the long term. Therefore, even long-term-thinking CEOs must take actions to stay in business in the short term.

Government incentives (which we will discuss) caused a massive reallocation of resources from savings (investment) to consumption (primarily in housing). Because investment in capital stock increases our productivity, when we underinvest (or save too little), we lower our long-term standard of living. Using a farming analogy, we ate our seed corn. We have had to borrow from our neighbors (that is, foreigners, especially the Chinese and Japanese) in order to plant a corn crop, and we will have to pay them back in the future.

For a $3 trillion (or greater) misinvestment to occur, it takes government action. Private markets are constantly making mistakes and then correcting. However, private markets will not make a mistake of this magnitude without significant incentives from government policy makers.

The primary sources of the massive misallocations of resources (both capital and labor) are:

1. The Federal Reserve (Fed)
2. The Federal Deposit Insurance Corporation (FDIC)
3. Government housing policy, primarily carried out by Fannie Mae (created in 1938) and Freddie Mac (created in 1970), the giant government-sponsored enterprises
4. The Securities and Exchange Commission (SEC)

A number of other government agencies (programs) made matters worse, including the Department of Housing and Urban Development

(HUD), the Federal Housing Administration (FHA), local government zoning restrictions, and so on. However, the Fed, the FDIC, Freddie, Fannie, and the SEC were the primary drivers of this destructive misinvestment.

In the following chapters, we will discuss the role of these four culprits and illustrate how they effectively magnified one another's mistakes. Please note that neither Bush, Obama, nor Congress has proposed any serious effort to deal with the actual sources of the problem. Indeed, these four culprits have received even greater resources and powers.

3

Government Monetary Policy: The Fed as the Primary Cause

IN A SIMPLE (BUT FUNDAMENTAL) SENSE, THE ONLY WAY THERE could have been a bubble in the residential real estate market was if the Federal Reserve created too much money. It would have been mathematically impossible for a misinvestment of this scale to have happened without the monetary policies of the Fed.

In 1913, the monetary system in the United States was nationalized. The federal government owns the monetary system. We do not have a private monetary system in the United States. Problems in the monetary system were the source of the current Great Recession. If there are problems in the monetary system, they are, by definition, caused by the federal government, because the federal government owns the monetary system.

If interstate highway bridges were falling down, most people would realize that since the interstate highways are owned by state and federal governments, the problem was essentially caused by government decisions. Even if a bridge contractor did not use the right materials, government highway agencies select the contractor, inspect the materials, and so on. This would be particularly true if many bridges were falling down and these bridges had been built by different contractors.

It would then be clear that something was wrong with the government highway agencies' specifications, selections, procedures, inspections, and other actions. In the last several years, monetary highway bridges have been falling down all over the place.

The Federal Reserve owns and controls the monetary system in the United States. The Federal Reserve is theoretically an independent government agency. However, the president appoints the members of the Federal Reserve Board with the approval of Congress. While some members of the board are qualified, many appointments are driven primarily by political considerations. As with many government appointments, it is very unlikely that an individual who does not fundamentally agree with the existing role of the Fed will be appointed. This makes it difficult for the board to have a broad base of different economic perspectives and means that the board is strongly influenced by the political environment. Many members of the board (regardless of their professional backgrounds) are political in nature or they would not have gone through the political process necessary for their appointment. The banking industry has one appointment position on the board. In my 40-year career, the industry has never been represented by the best and brightest bankers. The industry is typically represented by politically connected bankers.

While in theory, the Fed has a dual role of maintaining both stable prices and low unemployment, I have had numerous private conversations with board members over the years in which they readily admitted that the political pressure is to maintain low unemployment, not stable prices. We will discuss the significant long-term implications of this political pressure.[1]

In theory, the Federal Reserve was created to reduce volatility in the economy. In fact, the Federal Reserve reduces volatility in the short term, but increases volatility in the long term. In a free market, because human beings are not omniscient, markets are constantly correcting. Poorly run businesses, or businesses for which customer demand has changed, go out of business, and new businesses that do a better job of meeting consumer demand are created. A free market is in a constant correction. It is always searching for the best way to produce goods and services at the lowest cost and of the best quality.

When the Federal Reserve steps in and uses monetary policy to stop the downside correction process, all it achieves is to defer problems to the future and make them worse. Its action delays and distorts the natural market correction process, thereby reducing the long-term productivity of the economic system by encouraging a misuse of capital and labor. One of the best ways to view free markets is as a great number of experiments that are being conducted simultaneously. Most of the experiments are failures. However, every failure contributes to the learning process. Thomas Edison noted that the 1,000 apparently failed experiments that led to the lightbulb were, in fact, absolutely necessary. For every Google or Microsoft, there are 1,000 failures, all of which are in a certain sense necessary.

By the way, the argument for the Federal Reserve is that there were significant economic corrections in the 1800s and government needed to provide stability to banking. Interestingly, the United States created two quasi-central banks in the 1800s, both of which effectively failed. (One of the great debates at our founding was between Jefferson and Hamilton on this issue.) Most banks, however, were state-chartered.[2] The state banks were not any less political than the federally regulated banks. One of the major reasons for failures of state-chartered banks was that they were required to purchase state-issued bonds that typically financed the expansion of railroads.[3] Many of the railroads were built by crony capitalists who had powerful political contacts and did not know how to run a railroad. The railroads failed, then the state bonds failed, and then the banks failed. Still, U.S. government surpluses were the norm during this period, and the national debt declined steadily from 30 percent of GDP in 1869 to just 3 percent in 1913. Downturns during the Gilded Age (1865–1913) were less common and less severe than economists once believed.

Before the Federal Reserve, and despite these problems, in the late 1800s and early 1900s, the United States experienced a phenomenal growth rate while absorbing a huge inflow of immigrants with very limited skills. Most economic corrections during this period, while sometimes deep, were short, and the economy quickly regained steam.[4] Government debt was low, and the future was not mortgaged (as it is today). There was nothing close to the economic devastation of the Great Depression. It is interesting that the Federal Reserve will now, finally, admit that its policies played a significant role in causing the Great Depression,[5] even though this fact was established decades ago by Milton Friedman.[6] In other words, without the Federal Reserve, we would not have had a Great Depression.[7]

Individual market participants are always making mistakes. However, not all competitors make the same mistake, and different parties often make counterbalancing mistakes unless "Big Brother," in this case the Federal Reserve, drives almost all market participants in the same wrong direction.

Let us return to basics and discuss the purpose of money. Money is a standard of value that allows exchange to take place. Before money, people had to barter 1 cow for 12 pairs of shoes. But the cow owner did not need 12 pairs of shoes, so he had to trade those that he didn't need for the things he really needed, and so on, which is a very inefficient system. The reason we accept money for our production is that we can trade it for other goods. For money to accomplish this purpose, its value must be trustworthy; that is, it must not change arbitrarily.

While many items have served the role of money, modern economic systems evolved primarily using a gold standard (sometimes silver). Gold was selected because it is limited in quantity, hard to find, and suitable for conversion into coins. Also, the quantity of gold increases as it is dug out of the ground, but at a low rate. The speed with which gold increases is dependent on its price, and also on chance discovery. (It is believed that the discovery of the New World affected the quantity of gold and created a destructive inflationary spiral in Spain. Discoveries of new worlds are rare and not likely to be a problem today.) Even today, after five centuries, our new yearly gold supply from mines constitutes only 2 to 3 percent of the aboveground gold stocks—a steady growth in the money supply that modern-day central bankers have failed to replicate.

The best way to think of money is to use an analogy with a yardstick in engineering. To properly design a structure, an engineer must know that a yardstick will always be 36 inches. If one day it is 28 inches and a few months later it is 38 inches, the engineer cannot design or build a building.

Money serves the same role. In order to make economic calculations, business decision makers must know that the value of money will be the same from one day to the next. Of course, this does not mean that the price of any individual item will not change, because people are constantly changing their preferences, factors of production are changing, substitute products are being produced, capacity is expanded or contracting, and so on. In other words, the prices of individual goods will be constantly changing, but the price of all goods should not be changing because someone is arbitrarily increasing the amount of money (in effect, varying the length of the yardstick). Even governments cannot manipulate the quantity of gold, which is why politicians and government bureaucrats do not like gold standards. They can manipulate the quantity of paper money, which is why politicians and government leaders like central banks that print paper (fiat) money.

The very existence of the Federal Reserve enhances the ability of the federal government to borrow and has allowed politicians to substantially increase the debt leverage in the U.S. economy. Before the Fed existed, the federal government operated with a low level of debt, except during wars. Central banks were founded and still exist today not primarily because they stabilized the banking system or the business cycle, but because they facilitate government finance.[8]

One reason that federal debt was limited before the Federal Reserve was created was market discipline, which meant that the federal government was in a position similar to that of state governments today. A state can borrow substantial amounts based on its ability to tax. However, there is a limit to a state's ability to borrow, as California discovered. In fact, if the markets had not thought that the federal government would support California, the state would probably not have been able to borrow in 2008–2009. However, the U.S. Treasury can borrow much more, because not only can it tax, but it can also "print" money. A lender knows that the U.S. government will not default because all it has to do is print more money to pay its debts. Of course, if it prints too much money, that money will be of limited value to whoever receives it, because the value of money is in its scarcity. However, at least the federal government can pay its debts, so it can borrow almost without end. However, if the market believes that the U.S. Treasury will be paying its debt with inflated currency, interest rates will rise, reflecting expected inflation.

If you owe a great deal of debt (like the U.S. Treasury), it is to your advantage to have inflation, because you are paying back your debt with "cheaper" money. Since the federal government owes a huge amount of debt and the Federal Reserve is controlled by the federal government, the Federal Reserve decision makers believe that some inflation is good. This is one reason why the Fed becomes so panicky if there is the slightest risk of deflation (declining prices). If you own a bond and the value of money is appreciating (which is deflation, that is, a dollar will buy more widgets than before), you are economically better off. However, if you are a debtor (especially a very big debtor like the U.S. government), deflation is tough because you have to pay your debts with more valuable dollars.

The fact that the federal government (via the Treasury and the Federal Reserve) can "print" money allows Congress to undertake many programs that accumulate debt (and buy votes) and motivates the Fed to constantly try to inflate the money supply, undermining the trustworthiness of the value of money. Markets are always aware of this risk and are constantly trying to figure out when the Fed will begin to debase the currency again. The fact that the Fed can debase the dollar anytime it wants to makes investing in dollar-denominated assets more risky. If a business undertakes the development of a long-term project, it may face higher input costs than it expects if the Fed decides to start inflating the currency. The business cannot know which will rise more, its cost of production or the sales price of its products, because inflation does not affect all prices evenly.

This has been a particularly significant problem in recent years because the Federal Reserve has undertaken a massive expansion of the money supply.[9] If the economy begins to improve and the Fed does not withdraw the tremendous reserves it has created from the banking system, rampant inflation will follow. If it does withdraw the reserves quickly, interest rates will rise rapidly. This situation makes economic calculations extremely difficult and makes businesses less willing to invest, especially for the long term. If business owners could fully trust the Fed, this would not be an issue, but we have all been burned too many times to trust the Fed.[10]

The primary means by which the Fed controls the monetary supply is through the banking system. If the Fed wants a little inflation, it needs to increase bank reserves and encourage banks to lend more money. The banks can increase their capital to maintain the same capital cushion percentage as protection against losses. However, some banks resist raising more capital, as capital is expensive. If the

Fed allows or encourages banks to lower their capital percentage (increase their leverage), the banks will be more willing to lend the extra reserves because they do not have to raise more expensive capital. One way the Fed can have a systematic effect in the direction of this objective is to allow the largest banks to increase their leverage. The smaller banks will eventually follow; if they do not, they will end up with lower returns on equity than their bigger competitors and will be vulnerable to being acquired. The larger company can simply leverage the "excess" equity in the smaller company, acquiring it.

Also, anytime there is a downturn in the economy, the Fed consistently "saves" the very large banks, creating an unbalanced risk/return trade-off. If you manage a large financial institution, why not be leveraged, which increases your profits in good times, because the Fed will always bail out your company during bad times? During my career, the Fed has systematically effectively encouraged banks to increase their leverage (sometimes intentionally, sometimes not).

In a free market, where the economic system is in a constant correction process, individuals are aware of risk. Because they realize that risk exists and that no one will bail them out during the down times, they save for those risky times. Individuals save for the future, but they also save to deal with unknown risk. If the Federal Reserve eliminates the downside risk in difficult times, individuals will reduce their savings rate, which is exactly what happened to the U.S. economy. (Of course, individuals also misconceived their homes as investments [savings] instead of consumption.)

From the early 1990s until 2007, the U.S. economy experienced only a minor economic correction. One of the main reasons was that every time there was a problem in the economy, the Fed would act aggressively to eliminate the downside. This encouraged all of us in business to believe that the Fed had the ability to eliminate downside risk.[11] In the stock market, this psychology became known as the Greenspan "put." If things went bad, you could depend on Greenspan to print money, cut interest rates, and save the economy and the stock market. By 2007, BB&T (and all other banks) had business and consumer lenders with more than 10 years' experience who had not seen the impact of a major national economic correction, especially in the real estate markets. It should not be surprising that many of these lenders were overly optimistic. One factor that helped BB&T was that our executive management team had come together during the severe economic correction of the early 1980s, and I had been CEO during the real estate bust of the early 1990s. Most of the CEOs of major banks in 2007 had not been CEO in 1990 and did not know how bad business can get. However, even experienced CEOs (such as myself) were lulled to sleep by the Greenspan Fed.

In the early 2000s, the Federal Reserve made the same conceptual error that it made in the late 1920s. When there are massive improvements in the production process, prices should be falling.[12] In this environment, stable prices actually reflect a significant amount of underlying inflation. To understand this concept, let's return to the concept of money as a yardstick of value. Suppose you are laying copper cable for telephone communications. Copper is expensive and rare and can carry only a limited number of phone calls. Someone invents fiber optic cable. Fiber optic cable is made of silicon (sand), which is very common (cheap), and it can carry many, many more calls. Other things being equal, the cost of phone calls will fall.

On very rare occasions, there are an extraordinary number of major inventions all at once, such as during the 1920s, with automobiles, oil, electricity, telephone, and radio (that is, major advances in transportation, energy, and communications). During this period, overall prices (not just individual product prices) should have been falling. This is because the same quantity of gold could buy many new and/or better products. Of course, if prices are not allowed to fall, producers get the wrong message and overproduce, thereby misallocating capital and human resources. Overoptimism prevails, and then consumption gets out of line with savings and investment.

This happened in the 1920s, as the Fed effectively expanded the money supply to keep prices stable when prices should have been falling. In the early 1930s, the Fed doubled its folly by allowing the money supply (which it had arbitrarily inflated) to contract rapidly. The Fed had allowed the yardstick to grow to 45 inches, then suddenly contracted it to 25 inches. This Fed action was a significant cause of the Great Depression. Of course, Hoover and Roosevelt piled on with higher taxes, trade tariffs, massive regulatory schemes, and other such actions, which greatly magnified the impact of the Fed error.

There is an interesting analogy between the 1920s and the early 2000s. Instead of a large number of technology advances, as in the 1920s, there was one major game changer: the introduction of free-market policies in China and India. This fundamental policy change brought into the global production process billions of people who had been enslaved by their own governments. Many of these individuals are energetic and hardworking. They have been able to produce a great deal. While this sea change had started earlier, it began to mature in the late 1990s and early 2000s.

Because of the willingness of the Chinese (and Indian) workers to work harder and more productively for less pay, there was a fundamental shift in global productivity. Since we could now buy more goods with the same quantity of our work, prices should have been falling. However, Greenspan did not want prices to fall. Remember, he represented the federal government, and it owed a lot of money. Deflation is hard on big debtors. Since he was effectively printing money (that is, lengthening the yardstick), individuals had more money to spend. They decided to spend it on housing (that is, to consume instead of to save) for reasons that we have already discussed.

The mistake this time was particularly destructive because the Chinese government made problems worse. For political reasons, it was interested primarily in unemployment in China. Therefore, the Chinese government was providing incentives for producing goods to be used in trade and trying to hamper domestic consumption. One way it did this was by becoming a major investor in U.S. government debt, holding down interest rates in the United States. If the Fed had allowed the U.S. economy to adjust by having prices fall, the Chinese would not have been able to export to the United States profitably. They would have been forced to readjust more toward domestic consumption, which would have been healthy for U.S. exporters. By not allowing the U.S. economy to react as it would have done if it had had sound money, Greenspan was effectively encouraging the Chinese to expand their manufacturing capacity, driving manufacturing jobs out of the United States and into China.

This type of error would not happen in a private banking system based on a market standard (probably gold). The amount of gold would not have changed because the Chinese had dramatically increased their productivity. If the amount of gold had remained relatively fixed while the quantity of goods increased significantly, prices would have fallen. This would have sent a signal back to the Chinese to rethink their expanding capacity. Also, since the U.S. government would not have been creating huge amounts of debt, the Chinese might have invested their excess savings in U.S. industries that produce goods (and create jobs) or chosen to consume more in China. It is sad that such a major improvement in the world's standard of living helped create a financial crisis in the United States. This result would not have occurred without the actions of the Federal Reserve.

In addition, there are fundamental problems with the way the CPI (Consumer Price Index) is calculated that made the Fed's mistake even worse. The Fed uses the CPI as one of its key measures of inflation. (Often it quotes the core CPI; this excludes gasoline and food, which are somehow not supposed to be core.) The CPI measures cost of living changes based not on house prices (even though two out of three people live in houses), but on apartment rental rates. During the run-up to the financial crisis, rental rates were not rising, since individuals were moving out of apartments into houses, reducing the demand for apartments and therefore reducing apartment rental rates. The government's method of calculating the CPI significantly underestimated the true rate of inflation. Anybody who bought a house knew that this was happening (and there were many people who bought homes during this period). Unfortunately, the Federal Reserve apparently did not. Is this a case of one government bureaucracy (CPI comes from the Government Accountability Office) misleading another government bureaucracy?

The most destructive decisions that Greenspan made took place during the period 2000–2003. During this time, the Federal Reserve created a structure of negative real interest rates. Financial investors could borrow at 2 percent, and inflation was 3 percent. (Inflation was actually probably higher, as outlined previously.) This creates a huge psychological and economic incentive to borrow. I remember discussing this situation with other bankers. The message was clear: make as many loans as possible. It was particularly tempting to finance the residential market, where houses were appreciating at

5 percent or better. The borrower would almost certainly be able to pay you back because his interest rate would be below the inflation rate. How could the bank or the borrower lose?

It is important to note that Greenspan changed the CPI calculation, including using apartment rentals instead of house prices. He also made a more fundamental change by trying to adjust for qualitative improvements in products. For example, a new car has better equipment than last year's car, so the change in price for the new car reflects both inflation and the cost of the better equipment. Therefore, the CPI needs to be adjusted downward because of the qualitative improvement.

While this idea sounds appropriate, it is a complex concept that is difficult to execute because defining how much of the increase in the cost is really the result of the better equipment is often subjective. Also, there is a major risk of double-counting the quality improvements and the cost impact. The primary driver of improvement in automobiles has been advances in computer technology. If you count both the fall in the cost of computer technology and the quality improvement in the automobile, it is easy to double-count falling cost components. Also, an individual still has to buy a car. Even though the new car may be better, she still has to pay for it, and many times she does not have the option of buying a cheaper car without the improvements. This is one reason that the vast majority of consumers think inflation is greater than the CPI indicates.

The inflation rate using the "old" CPI is significantly higher than that using Greenspan's calculation.[13] Could the Fed be making improper decisions based on miscalculating the CPI? At best, the calculation of the CPI is more art than science.

After he became chairman of the Federal Reserve in early 2006, Bernanke rapidly raised interest rates and created an inverted yield curve. An inverted yield curve is one in which short-term rates are higher than long-term rates, and even Fed researchers acknowledge that an inverted yield curve tends to trigger recessions.[14] Because bankers had been misled by Greenspan's often-spoken concern about deflation, many of them had extended their bond portfolios, as this was one of the few areas where they could make long-term profits based on Greenspan's deflation scenario. (Greenspan based his assumptions on his belief in "excess" global savings driven by the

Chinese.) When Bernanke raised interest rates rapidly, banks started incurring significant losses in their bond portfolios. In order to offset these losses, they were motivated to make high-risk investments with potentially higher returns.

At BB&T, we had been very concerned about Greenspan's money-printing spree. However, we finally became convinced that even though economic reality would prevail in the long term, Greenspan might make his low-rate/deflation projections come true for several years. We ended up extending the maturity of our bond portfolio shortly before the Fed started its dramatic increase in interest rates.

This experience highlights a major general issue that the existence of the Federal Reserve creates. Bankers have to engage in economic forecasting in order to manage their interest-rate risk position. In a global economy, this is a very difficult task. However, the difficulty of the task is doubled when, in addition to trying to examine real economic activity, one has to speculate on the whims of the chairman of the Federal Reserve. Also, it is easy to get lulled into believing that the Fed is telling the truth, and we are surprised when it radically changes direction. Go back to 18 months before the Fed started its dramatic increase in interest rates and read its comments. There was absolutely no evidence that would have led bankers to anticipate a 425 percent increase in interest rates in two years. A 425 percent increase in input cost in two years is extraordinarily difficult for any business to manage. For a long-term-investment-based business like banking, this is a dramatic event. The rapid increase in interest rates was far more destructive than the level of rates. Also, the unanticipated pace and magnitude of rising interest rates left bankers in a very difficult position.

Inversions of yield curves are an unusual phenomenon. Typically, investors will invest for a longer duration only if they can earn a higher interest rate, because, other things being equal, the longer the investment, the greater the risk and the lower the liquidity. Markets practically never invert yield curves.

It is interesting that Bernanke's decision to both raise short-term interest rates (to a peak of 5.25 percent) and invert the yield curve must have reflected his realization that Greenspan's policies had been inflating the economy and leading to misinvestment (overinvestment in housing). Greenspan himself seemed to have realized it, since as chairman he had raised the fed funds rate from 1 percent in 2004 to 4.5 percent before leaving office in early 2006. Why would these men have acted as they did if they were not concerned with the real inflation rate? Of course, both men now insist that the Fed did not err in the early 2000s. This is a scary case of evasion that should make all of us concerned about Bernanke's future actions. When a decision maker cannot admit his mistakes, he can be dangerous.

What is sad, however, is that even though at some level Bernanke knew that the Fed had made major mistakes, this is not what he discussed publicly. He said repeatedly that the inverted yield curve would not cause a recession, but would simply slow the rate of inflation. While he mentioned the housing market occasionally, mostly by claiming that there was no bubble,[15] his focus was primarily on commodity prices. He held the inverted yield curve for more than a year (from July 2006 to January 2008), one of the longest yield-curve inversions ever. The subsequent Great Recession, which lasted through June 2009 (and, practically speaking, continues in December 2011), began in December 2007. As mentioned, history reveals that there is a very high correlation between inverted yield curves and recessions. Bernanke denied this correlation and was adamant that things were different this time because of globalization. He was right in a certain sense. Things were different because of globalization, but in exactly the opposite way from what he expected. The Chinese were making things worse by constantly buying long-term U.S. government debt and holding down long-term interest rates, helping to provide incentives to the housing market.

If you are managing a financial intermediary (especially a commercial bank), an inverted yield curve is a disaster. Banks borrow short (at lower interest rates) and lend long (at higher interest rates). If short-term rates are higher than long-term rates, banks are faced with negative margins. This is similar to buying a watermelon for $10 and selling it for $8. Not much fun. Of course, banks can variably price some loans, but clients can move their money to the capital markets and obtain lower long-term interest rates. In fact, large amounts of financing left the banking industry for the capital markets and the so-called shadow banking system. The inverted yield curve played a major role in shifting lending out of the regulated banking industry.

It is ironic to hear the Fed complain about the growth rate of the shadow market when it played a major role in creating this market. (Regulatory cost created by the Fed on traditional banks was an even bigger factor in growing the shadow banking system, as will be discussed later.) If the Fed did not know that it was driving lending, especially traditional commercial loans, outside the banking system, we in the banking business were fully aware of this fact. Two important trends were magnified by the inverted yield curve.

First, banks had to lend to clients that did not have access to the capital markets, were willing to pay variable interest rates, and needed to borrow money. The residential construction and development sector clearly met these criteria. Second, one way to get higher returns is to take more risk. Faced with negative margins, many financial institutions started taking more risk because taking risk was the only way in which they could sustain their profitability. They were also trying to offset the Greenspan-created losses in their bond portfolios, which we discussed previously.

During this whole period, the Federal Reserve was not predicting a recession (much less a Great Recession). In fact, Bernanke was adamant that there would not be a recession.[16] Why not believe the Fed? Times had basically been good since the early 1990s. Every time something negative had happened, the Fed had stepped in to save the economy. House prices had been rising consistently for many years. The government had always protected the housing market. Why not take more risk and get higher returns?

From a personal level, I can appreciate the power of these incentives. Even if you have been a CEO for a long time, and even if you know that the Fed cannot simply print money to make the economy healthy, it is incredibly difficult to go against the tide. In the previous chapter, I outlined BB&T's decision to be more conservative, but not to react anywhere near as strongly as we would have done had Greenspan not lulled us to sleep and had Bernanke not forecast good times in the future. Business leaders must make difficult decisions based on many unknown factors. However, even when you understand that the long-term consequences of policy decisions will be destructive, it is impossible to predict the timing, especially when the outcome will be driven by the whim of government bureaucrats (Greenspan's negative real interest rates; Bernanke's inverted yield curve). Free markets represent the insights of millions of market participants, who get to vote based on their past successes (how much wealth they have earned). This does not make markets always right, but it dramatically improves the odds.

The free-market economist and Nobel laureate Friedrich Hayek highlighted a concept that he termed *fatal conceit*. This is the belief on the part of elitist intellectuals that they are smarter than the reality of markets and in fact are smarter than the accumulation of all human knowledge over many centuries.[17] It is irrational to believe that these elitists somehow know the individual capabilities and goals of billions of people and can "fairly" determine how production should be created and wealth distributed. The key decision makers in the Federal Reserve are highly educated and intelligent. They use massive mathematical models (all of which failed). However, no matter how smart you are or how many mathematical models you use, it is impossible to integrate and evaluate the collective economic decisions of 7 billion people on this planet.

In my career, the Fed has a 100 percent error rate in predicting and reacting to important economic turns, which is not surprising. It is trying to arbitrarily set the single most important price in the economy—the price of money. This price affects every economic decision. What is interesting is that the economists at the Fed know that bureaucratic price setting is a total failure. They have observed this phenomenon in all socialist and communist economies. They would not claim the ability to set the right price for an automobile, but they somehow believe that they can establish the proper interest rate for a highly complex economy in a globally integrated environment.

On several occasions, I have asked members of the Fed Open Market Committee (who set interest rates) whether they believed in price fixing. They all emphatically said no. Then I asked them why they believed that they had the ability to set the price of money. Their response was effectively that the price of money (interest rates) is different. Why? No answer. I said earlier that the Federal Reserve economists are intelligent. They are, but they have a specific kind of intelligence. They have a detached-from-reality, academic, floating abstraction form of intelligence. This type of intelligence thrives on mathematical reasoning, but has difficulty dealing with nonmathematical phenomena, such as the impact of intangible incentives on human actions. They are surprised (continually) that individuals do not act the way their models say they should. Of course, if they were truly intelligent, they would realize that their task is impossible and recommend a market-based monetary system.

One reason for this phenomenon is that being a key decision maker in the Federal Reserve is intoxicating. After all, the Fed is one of the most powerful economic bodies in the world. Alan Greenspan is a classic example. Before he became chairman of the Fed, he argued in *Capitalism: The Unknown Ideal* that the Fed should be abolished and the United States should go to a gold standard. Once he became chairman, he was seduced by the office and became the maestro of Fed policy. Power corrupts. It is sad to hear Greenspan argue that the Fed (he) did not fail, markets failed. When it appeared that the economy was doing well, he was clearly enjoying being the hero. Unfortunately, in Greenspan's case, power not only corrupted him, but also destroyed his integrity.

The "success" of the Fed's efforts to prevent significant market corrections from the early 1990s to 2007, which was achieved at the expense of a massive misallocation of capital (especially to the housing market), laid the groundwork for the Great Recession. The Fed not only provided the money for the misallocation from savings and investment to consumption (housing), but created a false sense of security (low risk) that fooled many financial institutions, residential builders and developers, and home purchasers. As I noted earlier, in a fundamental sense, there could not have been a bubble (misinvestment) in the housing market if the Fed had not expanded the money supply (that is, printed money) to finance the bubble. The fundamental cause of the financial crisis is mistakes by the Federal Reserve—a governmental entity.

Figure 3-1 shows the interest rates driven by Federal Reserve policy: the fed funds rate, the prime rate, and the 10-year bond rate from 1990 to 2008. Focusing on the period from 1998 to 2008, let me share with you an important observation. During this period, I met periodically with other large bank CEOs in forums such as the Financial Services Roundtable. At these forums, we would always discuss the economy and the level of interest rates. We would also meet with officials from the Federal Reserve.

FIGURE 3-1 Effective Federal Funds Rate and 10-Year Treasury Constant Maturity Rate

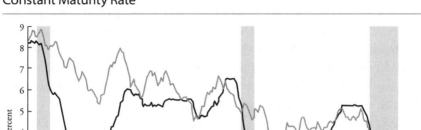

Shaded areas indicate U.S. recessions.
2011 research.stlouisfed.org

— FEDFUNDS
···· GS10

At many of these meetings, I believe there were enough CEOs from large financial institutions to represent a proxy for the capital markets. While this idea is certainly arguable, if the 25 largest financial institutions were acting in a certain manner, it is hard to believe that in a private market, these actions would not have had a significant impact on interest rates. Of course, in a government-regulated market, the Federal Reserve drove interest rates; this was not limited to short-term rates, but through inflation expectations, the Fed had a fundamental impact on long-term rates (which it does not technically manage).

Based on these numerous conversations, and to the degree that these large banks are a proxy for the capital markets, I am convinced that in a market-based monetary system, interest rates would not have been as low as Greenspan drove them in the period from 2000 to 2003, when he was laying the foundation for the housing bubble. Also, rates would not have risen as fast as Greenspan and Bernanke raised them (partially because they would not have been as low at the beginning). I am also certain that the capital market would never have inverted interest rates.

In retrospect, the interest-rate variation created by free-market phenomena would have been significantly less volatile than that created by the Federal Reserve, and there would have been less variation in the economy. The Great Recession would never have occurred, although we would have almost certainly experienced modest slowdown(s). The economy would be in better condition today and our future brighter if the free market had been setting interest rates instead of the elitist experts at the Fed.

It is important to understand that I am not arguing that CEOs sitting in a back room trying to optimize the so-called public good (as the Fed does) would have made better decisions. My argument is fundamentally different. My argument is that if each of the CEOs had been making independent decisions for the sole purpose of maximizing her individual firm's profit (while controlling the risk of failure), with no concern for the so-called public good and in competition with other CEOs, they would not have driven rates as low as Greenspan drove them, raised rates as fast as Bernanke did, or created a very destructive inverted yield curve.

That free markets would make better price decisions than elitist central planners (members of the Federal Reserve) should not be a surprise. Ludwig von Mises proved the futility of central planning in his numerous books, including *The Theory of Money and Credit* (1913), *Socialism* (1922), and *Human Action* (1940). Of course, reality has proved the correctness of von Mises's theory, as seen in the economic failures of the Soviet Union, East Germany, Eastern Europe, North Korea, Cuba, and other such countries. Only when economies start using market-based price information (from freer markets), as the Chinese have relatively recently chosen to do, can proper resource allocation decisions be made.

It is curious that we both know that central planning of prices does not work (price controls fail) and know that the Fed has consistently mismanaged interest rates in its efforts to centrally plan the most important single price in the economy, and yet most people still support the Fed. Strange indeed!

One reason is that the Fed either currently employs or has employed the vast majority of monetary economists in the United States. It is an extreme career risk for a professional economist to be opposed to the existence of the Fed. Also, the Fed regulates the banking industry, so it is risky for a banker to be opposed to the Fed (writing this book is risky). The same phenomena have been identified in the so-called scientific study of weather. If you are opposed to the theory of global warming, you will not get a job. See *Meltdown* by Patrick J. Michaels.

At a deeper level, government and academic elitists need to believe that they are smarter than markets (that is, than not so highly educated decision makers). Also, government and academic elitists have a high need for control. Politicians know that without the Fed to print money at their whim, they could not dole out the "goodies" that get them elected. These are the political reasons that the Fed continues to exist despite the contrary evidence.[18]

It is also important to recognize that by holding interest rates below the rate that the market would set, an unelected group of bureaucrats at the Federal Reserve is creating a massive reallocation of wealth. For example, my 85-year-old mother has been living on her interest income. Because Bernanke has chosen to hold interest rates below their natural level, she is not receiving enough interest income to cover her expenses, so she has to consume her principal. While she objectively should not be worried because I can afford to take care of her, she does not want to have to rely on me and is worried. Even if Bernanke's interest-rate policy works, given her age, it is impossible for her to recover economically in her lifetime. Bernanke is redistributing wealth from savers to borrowers (including speculators); that is, he is stealing from many old people, such as your mother. While many people do not fully understand this process, they do know that this arbitrary and unjust redistribution is happening, and this affects their willingness to make long-term economic decisions.[19]

FDIC Insurance:
The Background Cause

THE FEDERAL DEPOSIT INSURANCE CORPORATION (FDIC) WAS launched in 1934, after the banking collapse that began in 1930, to protect small depositors in commercial banks, even though FDR, while signing the bill, conceded that in the future, it would "place a premium on unsound banking" and "involve the government in probable loss." (He was correct.)[1] Over the years, the amount of deposit insurance coverage has been increased until at the beginning of the financial crisis, the insurance coverage was at $100,000. In addition, a family of four could use a variety of techniques to increase its coverage to more than $500,000. The Troubled Asset Relief Program (TARP)—which I will discuss later—raised the coverage to $250,000 (and pooled coverage to over $1,000,000) and provided unlimited coverage for demand deposits.

The FDIC is an insurance pool that banks pay into to insure their deposits and the deposits of their competitors. There is a backstop from the U. S. Treasury. The taxpayers had substantial losses (more than $300 billion) from a similar insurance program (the Federal Savings and Loan Insurance Corporation, or FSLIC) related to the failure of the savings and loan industry. FSLIC was merged into the

FDIC, with banks that had purchased savings and loans having to pay a portion of the losses incurred by FSLIC through extra premiums to the FDIC. The taxpayers have never had to cover any losses in the bank fund (FDIC), even though they did pay substantial costs in the FSLIC (savings and loan) fund. To date, banks have fully paid their way. However, the backup from the U.S. Treasury (that is, the taxpayers) is vital to the perception of the fund.[2] Low-risk, well-run banks have to pay for losses by poorly run banks. Healthy banks cannot determine who is allowed in the insurance pool or what risk the participants in the pool decide to take. Government bureaucrats at the FDIC make these critical decisions. BB&T has been paying into the FDIC fund since 1934 and, of course, has been paying for the failures of our worst (that is, most irrational) competitors.

There are several serious problems with the FDIC insurance concept. First, FDIC insurance destroys market discipline. A typical individual depositor does not worry about the safety and soundness of her bank, because she believes that the federal government is insuring her deposits. Therefore, until there is some extremely visible problem with the bank, individual depositors do not even attempt to research the strength of the financial institution in which they are investing their savings. Many depositors shop for the highest certificate of deposit (CD) rates and assume that the risk among financial institutions is equal. Of course, the banks that pay the highest CD rates are the most risky.

The existence of the FDIC provides incentives for taking large risks, which lead to bank failures. New banks are opened by local investors, typically led by individuals who have sold a previous bank to a larger institution. Often the plan is to run the bank for a few years and then sell it to another regional bank. The local investors put in a small amount of capital, and the bank is able to leverage this capital quickly by paying above-market interest rates for certificates of deposits. The bank then makes high-risk loans, often to friends, family members, and business associates of its board members and investors. The new bank often attracts this business by offering to make higher-risk loans than other banks will make, by offering more liberal terms, or by cutting the interest rate on the loans below the market rate.

There were a large number of start-up banks of this nature in the Atlanta, Georgia, market where BB&T operates. A number of these banks have failed, and more are likely to fail. BB&T took over one of these failed banks with the assistance of the FDIC. This was a typical example; a relatively small number of investors raised a small amount of capital, leveraged the capital by paying above-market rates on CDs, and then used the capital to make risky motel loans. The FDIC lost almost 50 cents on the dollar. Of course, the loss was paid for by healthy banks (including BB&T) through the increased cost of deposit insurance.

The vast majority of these start-up banks would not exist in a free market. They exist only because of a massive subsidy (relative to their size) from FDIC insurance. BB&T has been in business since 1872. Would a rational consumer move his life savings from BB&T to a start-up bank for 0.25 percent more in interest without FDIC deposit insurance? Of course not.

The secondary impact of these high-risk-taking banks is equally significant. They poison the market for other banks by degrading the risk standards of all the financial institutions in the market. Being a relative newcomer to the Atlanta market and having a community bank focus on lending to the residential real estate market, BB&T had to compete against these irrational bankers who were taking excessive risk and underpricing the risk they were taking. In retrospect, it is easy to say that we should have ignored their activities. However, had we done so, we would have been out of business in Atlanta.

BB&T chose to be more conservative than these banks, but we took more risk than we would have if these (government-subsidized) banks had not existed. The impact, however, is even more subtle. Even if BB&T is being more careful with its borrowers, these high-risk (government-subsidized) banks are funding projects that should not be created. These projects will overbuild the whole market, bringing down even the rational projects. There is no question that these start-up lenders at the margin created a huge overinvestment in the Atlanta real estate market that broke even the best residential builder/developers.

On a bigger scale, government deposit insurance played a major role in the economic waste created by the failure of a number of large financial institutions. IndyMac, Golden West, Washington Mutual, and Countrywide were all large financial institutions that effectively failed. In all cases, the companies funded high-risk loan portfolios by paying above-market interest rates for certificates of deposit using FDIC insurance. All these companies were major players in the high-risk home-lending business and played a significant role in lowering lending standards in the home mortgage market (with major help from their friends, the giant government-sponsored enterprises [GSEs], Freddie Mac and Fannie Mac, which we will discuss in the next chapter).

Again, BB&T had to compete directly with these financial institutions. While we did not lower our standards to their level, we did take more risk than we ideally would have in order to stay in business in the short term. It is not practical to completely ignore the risk and pricing strategies of major competitors. Interestingly, these companies locked themselves into a self-destructive pattern. They had attracted deposit clients who were price-driven. These clients would have moved their deposits if Washington Mutual and the others had not paid above-market interest rates for CDs. The only way to pay for the high deposit cost was to make more and more risky loans on which they could charge higher interest rates. This destructive cycle was rapidly accelerated when the Federal Reserve (Bernanke) inverted the yield curve and destroyed bank lending margins. Countrywide and the others like it had to move even further up the risk curve in order to remain in business in the short term.

In a free market, without government-subsidized deposit insurance, these large banks could not have raised the funds to finance these high-risk loan portfolios. Investors would have asked tougher questions. In addition, the impact of the FDIC was magnified in the case of these larger financial institutions in two ways. Bond investors believed that the government regulators (the FDIC, the Office of the Comptroller of the Currency [OCC], the Office of Thrift Supervision [OTS], and the Federal Reserve) were in fact regulating these institutions and would not allow them to take on too much risk. After all, this was the primary role of this army of regulators. Furthermore, while the bondholders did not perceive these companies as necessarily being "too big to fail," they believed that in difficult situations, the regulators would take some actions to at least support these sizable financial institutions (which, in fact, the regulators did in several cases). Therefore, the market-distorting effect of FDIC insurance was magnified by the existence of regulators who were supposed to limit and control risk and by the backup support from the regulators, especially the Federal Reserve, that was perceived to be available.

Based on the information available, bond investors and uninsured depositors were taking a rational risk. They never would have funded Countrywide and the others without this governmental structure, and therefore the market for high-risk home loans would not have become anywhere near as large as it did. In addition, these high-risk financial institutions tainted the market for more rational competitors and forced them to take higher risk than they would have liked in order to stay in business in the short term.

Why did the regulators (FDIC, OTS, and the Federal Reserve) not identify these problem institutions earlier and take corrective action? In my career in banking, there have been very few, if any, occasions when the financial regulators identified a problem bank and acted in advance to correct the problems. In fact, in almost every case of bank problems or failures, government regulators have been the last people to know. They almost always "close the stable door after the horse has been stolen." The belief that regulators will somehow act differently in the future is extraordinarily naïve. It shows a deep lack of understanding of human nature and the power of incentives. It also reflects a lack of understanding of the information available to regulators to make decisions and their ability to integrate this information.

The bank regulatory agencies are dominated by lifetime government bureaucrats. The way to be successful in this environment is to follow the rules and not rock the boat. The environment is often routine, stifling, and anti-innovative. It is very process-oriented and mechanical. The best and brightest individuals tend to leave. Those who stay develop a more and more bureaucratic mindset over time.

The regulatory agencies have enormous power, and in a broad context they make the law. Congress often passes "sound-good, motherhood and apple pie" laws, which the regulatory agencies convert to the real law. The courts seldom override the decisions of the regulators. Even if it is fairly clear that the regulators have misinterpreted or simply made up a law, it could take years for a bank to prevail in court. In the meantime, the regulators can put the bank out of business. Very few banks (businesses) will go to court against their regulators on important issues, especially issues that affect only one or a few banks. Most legal battles are fought by some form of association.

The government regulators leave themselves tremendous leeway to interpret their own regulations. Sometimes they enforce a regulation; sometimes they do not enforce the same regulation. A very typical strategy is to enforce regulations after the fact. For example, regulation X42242 may prohibit certain activities, with a long list of subjective exceptions allowed. For years, the regulators, while auditing the bank, will ignore this regulation, especially when times are good. However, when the economic environment gets difficult, they will retroactively criticize bank management for not following a rule that they knew had not been followed for years.

The regulatory process is also extremely political, and therefore there is no objective rule of law for businesses that are subject to heavy regulation. BB&T experienced a classic example of this phenomenon after Bill Clinton was elected president. Clinton had been elected with strong support from the African American community. He wanted to reward that support by eliminating racial discrimination in bank lending. The problem was that there was practically no racial discrimination in bank lending. Banks are highly motivated to make all the good loans they can make. Also, there were laws against racial discrimination that had been in effect for years (the Community Reinvestment Act of 1977 and the Equal Credit Opportunity Act of 1974) and that were closely enforced, especially in lending.

The accusation that banks were racially discriminating was based on a totally misleading study by the Boston Federal Reserve bank.[3] Even the Fed currently acknowledges that this study was fundamentally flawed. The study compared debt-to-income ratios for various borrowers based on race. An African American was more likely to be turned down based on debt-to-income ratios (alone) than a white person. It was obvious that the Federal Reserve bureaucrats who did the study had never made a loan. There are many other characteristics that are considered in a loan decision, in addition to the debt-to-income ratio. One of the most important is the durability of the income. If your income has fluctuated over the last several years because you have changed jobs multiple times, your current income is more at risk.

Another factor is even more important. This factor is character. Some individuals pay their debts in difficult circumstances; some choose not to pay. The single most significant indicator predicting future behavior is past behavior. If you have acted a certain way in the past, you are likely (but not certain) to act that way in the future. Borrowers' past behavior is a very important consideration in loan decisions. Have they paid their past debts? If these factors are adjusted for, there is no evidence of racial discrimination in bank lending. In fact, if there is any discrimination, it is in favor of African Americans. This would not be surprising, given the many measures of the racial impact of their lending that banks have to report (and did even before Bill Clinton).

One reason for mentioning this background is that this flawed Federal Reserve study on racial discrimination in lending was a "milestone" in energizing the affordable-housing/subprime-lending efforts that subsequently destroyed the residential real estate market. These efforts, while theoretically targeted at all low-income borrowers, were in practice mainly designed to encourage lending to African Americans, a major constituency of the Democratic Party. Unreported by the Fed, the Clinton administration, or the GSEs in the late 1990s was the fact that homeownership among minorities was skyrocketing amid the economic boom of the decade. According to Harvard's annual study on U.S. housing,[4] between 1993 and 1998, the number of mortgages made to Hispanic applicants jumped 87 percent, while the number for African Americans increased 72 percent, the number for Asian Americans rose 46 percent, and the number for whites (non-Hispanic) advanced by just 31 percent. Homeownership rates for minorities remained lower than those for whites only because Hispanics and blacks tended to have lower credit ratings. The push to cure "racial bias" in mortgage lending was purely political—and bogus.

Back to the issue of the rule of law. Clinton wanted to find banks guilty of racial discrimination so that he could show his supporters that he was eliminating the alleged discrimination. He and his appointees to the regulatory agencies were certain that racial discrimination was prevalent, based on the Federal Reserve study. The regulators wanted to satisfy the politicians, so they designed a subjective test that enabled them to "prove" racial discrimination any time they wanted. They used a comparison technique that a tenth-grader could see was irrational. The comparison was not apples to oranges, but rather apples to mainframe computers.

In any event, a number of banks paid up under this regulatory pressure. From my experience in discussing this issue with the CEOs involved, they knew that their companies were not guilty of discrimination, but they also knew that there would be a high price to pay for fighting the regulators. The company would not be able to enter into mergers, which were a major issue in the consolidating banking industry. The more quickly the bank could get the problem behind it, the better. The actual fines were not significant. However, the press coverage was important to Clinton and his team, who were showing their voters they were making the evil bankers stop discriminating against minorities.

In this process, BB&T was accused of racial discrimination. When I first learned of the accusation, I was stunned. It was not just against our code of ethics, but also against the fundamental culture of our organization. We strongly believe in justice, which requires that individuals be judged on their personal actions, not their membership in a group. BB&T is a rigorously individualist company. My first question was, who did the discrimination, so that I could fire that person quickly. Well, it turned out that the regulators did not identify anyone who was guilty of discrimination. It somehow happened without any individual discriminating. Well, how about a bank process or procedure that was at fault? No, all our processes and procedures were fine. Oh, so no one did the discriminating and the processes were designed properly.

We then started examining the method that the regulators used to determine racial discrimination. They compared a loan to an African American borrower made (or turned down) by a lender in one market (often a rural market) with a loan to a white borrower made (or turned down) by another lender in another market (often an urban market), primarily based on debt-to-income ratios. When we started examining the loans, it became extremely clear that in every case, the loan decisions were appropriate. In fact, the local safety and soundness bank examiners (who knew that this was about politics, not discrimination) admitted that the minority loans that were turned down should have been turned down. Making the loans would have set these borrowers up for economic problems in the future (as subprime home lending did later).

Based on an objective examination of these facts, it was absolutely clear to us that BB&T had not racially discriminated. The examiners probably knew this by now, but they had a quota to fill from DC, so they would not back off. However, we were not going to agree to a fine over something we had not done wrong. Even though the amount of money involved was not material and we could get on with our business, this was an issue of principle for us. So we fought the regulators, with a number of our staff members working seven days a week for weeks. The examiners decided that there was "probable cause" that BB&T was discriminating, and they stopped all our mergers, providing a major incentive to settle. An interesting event then occurred. Two years into Clinton's term, the Republican revolution happened, with a landslide in Congress.

What was amazing was that the bank regulators involved in our racial discrimination examination went home the next day. I repeat, they went home the next day, and we never heard from them on this issue again. (They did ask us to make a token and confidential settlement with one borrower who was not part of the study.) This event crystallized to me that the regulatory process is highly political and that there is effectively no rule of law for regulated companies. (George Bush's "hot button" was the Patriot Act, which theoretically is supposed to reduce terrorism risk.) This fact is being demonstrated clearly in the current environment, in which regulatory enforcement has changed radically (without any change in the law) since Obama was elected president.

In a healthier economic environment, the political pressure on regulators is to let the banks alone. After all, bankers, especially community bankers, have political contacts. They know members of Congress. If you are a local bank examiner, and the economy is going well, why create problems for yourself by making the local banker unhappy with a bad examination report?

Suppose you work for the Office of Thrift Supervision. There are a small number of large companies that, through their regulatory fees, cover most of the cost of the OTS's operations. Those companies include Golden West, Countrywide, Washington Mutual, and IndyMac, all of which effectively failed. Those companies paid most of the cost of the OTS; that is, the companies paid the OTS employees' salaries. Some of the CEOs of these companies were politically connected to powerful congressmen and senators, such as the relationship between Angelo Mozilo, the CEO of Countrywide, and Chris Dodd, the senator from Connecticut.[5] Dodd also happened to be the chairman of the Senate Banking Committee. In good times, why would you make these companies unhappy?

In good times, the regulators tend to focus on politically driven areas such as racial discrimination, accounting fraud, or terrorist financing, depending on the whim of Congress and the president. In fact, regulatory scrutiny will increase in some politically correct areas (like Sarbanes-Oxley and the Patriot Act, as we will discuss later). After all, when George Bush is president, if the CEO of Countrywide is unhappy about the regulatory pressure created by the Patriot Act (antiterrorism), it just shows that you (the regulator) are doing your job well, even if a certain senator does not like the result. The senator is not going to raise a big issue about this regulatory issue because it is the politically correct focus of regulation at the moment. Regulatory focus fluctuates with the political wind. Regulators have been acting based on these political incentives for the 40 years I have been in banking. There is absolutely no reason to believe that giving them more authority (that is, adding more regulations) will make their behavior change.

In tough economic times, the regulators often become power-lusters. They had to be nice to the bank CEOs and others during the good times, and now it is their turn to be in charge. The humble bureaucrats are then energized with the moral certainty and clarity of the Gestapo.

There is a deeper reason why regulators do not act during good times. They do not see the bad times coming. They are not visionary, big-picture thinkers. The top regulators are political appointees. The rest are lifelong government bureaucrats. In good times, they are willing to rely on the optimistic projections of the Federal Reserve. In fact, the banking regulators were misled by the Fed, just like the rest of us. (See Chapter 3.) Also, most of the actual bank examiners are not experienced lenders and are unable to evaluate the risk at the time loans are being made. (They are excellent at second-guessing after the economy has collapsed.) Giving the regulators more regulatory authority will not increase their ability to see the future. In fact, it may give them incentives to become more conservative, which would stop a healthy economic expansion.

In 2009, BB&T took over a $26 billion failed bank (Colonial) with the assistance of the FDIC. The FDIC was not doing us a favor. Colonial was failing, and the FDIC needed a buyer. BB&T's purchase minimized the loss to the FDIC insurance fund. There is an interesting background to this acquisition. BB&T has grown rapidly over the years through mergers with community banks and thrifts. Based on its location and its apparent performance, Colonial appeared to be an excellent acquisition candidate. However, until the FDIC took it over, we had chosen not to pursue the acquisition of Colonial for several reasons. First, the CEO had a command-and-control mindset. He had an extremely difficult time attracting and retaining executive-level management because he wanted to make all the decisions. While Colonial had many excellent employees at the operating level (in its branches, for example), there was a significant weakness in upper management. As the company grew, this lack of executive-level management became a major problem. Also, the CEO had a hard time listening to negative feedback, which meant that he could not change direction when necessary.

The other important factor we observed in competing with Colonial was that it would take "hog shares" of large high-risk loans that did not meet our credit standards. It appeared that a major portion of Colonial's earnings came from high yields on risky loans that could become nonaccruals. Therefore, despite the fact that, on paper, Colonial looked like the kind of bank that BB&T might acquire, we chose not to seriously pursue an acquisition until we were able to obtain credit risk protection from the FDIC.

The interesting question is, "Why did the FDIC examiners not identify these problems years before they became fatal to Colonial?" As an outside competitor, we knew that Colonial had management problems and was taking on too much risk years before the FDIC acted.

There may be a number of reasons why this happened. The CEO of Colonial was very politically connected. It could have been risky to raise too many issues with the bank. Times were good, so how was the examiner to document his negative claims? Also, the "safety and soundness" aspects of the regulatory process had been materially reduced in importance. After all, times were good and were expected to remain good because Greenspan was the maestro at the Fed and would always thread the needle to future prosperity. (The bank examiners were misled by their fellow government bureaucrats.) Many of the examiners were focused on the politically correct Sarbanes-Oxley Act and Patriot Act (both enacted in 2002). Staff was being cut on the "safety and soundness" side of the FDIC, with many young examiners who had never seen bad times now being in charge.

Also, the examiners do not have a lot of "skin in the game." They would probably rotate to another bank before any issues surfaced at Colonial. Why make trouble? Also, even if Colonial had problems, maybe the examiners who failed to notice it would get a mild rebuke, but the FDIC would need all its examiners in bad times. It was not as if the examiners had guaranteed Colonial's debt, as BB&T and other banks had through the FDIC insurance pool.

There is every reason to believe that after a few years of good times, the same decisions will be made by bank examiners in the future. The incentives, the bureaucratic process, and the fact that they do not have special insights, information, or understanding ensures that the same type of mistakes will continue to be made until the process is fundamentally changed. Also, depositors and investors will continue to believe that the examiners understand the risks in banks and are making sure that those risks are managed. In fact, the regulators do not understand the risks and typically increase risk by their misconceptions.

There is a private solution to the issue of providing insurance to small individual depositors. Bert Ely, a consultant to the Financial Services Roundtable, designed a cross-guarantor insurance fund, with the banks guaranteeing each other's deposits, backstopped by insurance from large insurance companies.[6] The cross-guarantee pool would have a substantially higher reserve ratio than the FDIC maintains. The economic trade-off would be substantially reduced regulatory cost. Many regulations are based on the theory that the government is providing a subsidy to the banking industry by backing the FDIC fund. The concept is that the various regulatory bodies should or could eliminate many unnecessary rules, with material cost savings to the industry. Both the life insurance industry and security dealers have similar arrangements and have had substantially smaller losses than the FDIC has experienced.

The reason that the self-insurance pool could work is that the banks would have control of the underwriting standards. Instead of being forced to the lowest common denominator (that is, the highest risk taken), as tends to happen in good times with government regulators (who do not lose money when a bank fails), the healthy banks would impose tough standards on the insurance pool risk. Remember, if a competitor bank fails, the healthy bank pays. In addition, because the banks would have significant risk in the pool, their self-insurance fund would employ top-notch talent to investigate and understand the risk of individual institutions. This would include experienced bankers who had been through credit cycles. Probably bank capital requirements would be substantially increased, especially for start-up institutions. Also, instead of allowing depositors to be able to multiply insurance coverage, as is possible with the FDIC, the private insurance plan would have a fixed and limited amount, designed only to protect small depositors (as was the FDIC's original intent).

It is interesting that the opposition to the private insurance fund came not from government regulators, but from within the industry. (The regulators would have strongly objected, but we did not get that far.) The primary objections were from a few large institutions that knew that they would not be allowed in the insurance pool without raising far more capital. Also, small banks objected because government insurance is a clear subsidy to them.

There are many issues involved in finalizing the concept of a private cross-guarantee deposit insurance pool for the industry. However, the long-term benefits would be gigantic. If there had been a private deposit insurance program, the financial errors made by private banks that led to the financial crisis would have been far less significant. Numerous academic studies have demonstrated that government deposit insurance maximizes risk taking by financial intermediaries.[7] In fact, the larger the institution, the more risk it will be motivated to take, especially when, in addition to deposit insurance, the large institution has an implicit government guarantee. It is not surprising that Citigroup operates at the maximum risk position and has practically failed three times since 1970.

As an aside, there have been a number of articles recently about government employee compensation versus private compensation. The typical government employee earns about 25 to 50 percent more than a comparable private employee.[8] The public employee unions argue that this is because the government employees have more responsibility. My observations are that exactly the opposite is true. The typical government employee is not responsible. She takes actions based on arbitrary rules dictated by a handful of top-level bureaucrats and political appointees in Washington. Responsibility implies that you have the authority to use your judgment. This is atypical of government employees.[9] Few of them have any real authority. Responsibility also implies that there can be negative consequences if you take inappropriate actions. This is not true for government employees. Unless they do something that is clearly illegal, there are no negative consequences to them personally for bad decisions. As an example, most of the thrift industry failed in the late 1980s and early 1990s. The industry's regulator, the FSLIC, made many bad decisions that contributed to the industry failure. These decisions cost the taxpayers more than $300 billion. The FSLIC was merged into the FDIC, and practically all of the FSLIC employees kept their jobs. I encountered some of the old FSLIC employees 10 years later, when they had important positions with the FDIC.

Government employees have far less responsibility and are significantly less at risk than private employees. Using the responsibility argument offered by the public employees' union, public employees are more than 50 percent overpaid. Frankly, while there are some well-intended individuals who are employed by the regulators, they have a bureaucratic mindset. When we hired someone from a regulatory agency, most of the time it was to do a job dealing with a regulatory agency, not for a role based on productivity. (Of course, there are exceptions.)

Regulatory policy creates systemic risk in an even more profound manner. Regulations often provide incentives (economic "force") for financial institutions to take the same risk. In the 10-year period leading to the housing bust, the percentage of bank assets invested in residential real estate increased dramatically. This occurred for four primary reasons. First, as discussed, Fed monetary policy created a rapid appreciation in residential real estate values, which obscured the risk in this lending category.

Second, residential builders and developers did not have easy access to capital markets and were willing to pay variable interest rates when Bernanke inverted the yield curve. Third, the heavy regulatory burden imposed on the regulated banking industry (including the Privacy Act, the Patriot Act, and Sarbanes-Oxley) made banks not be cost competitive with the "shadow" banking system.

Finally, and extremely critically, the capital standards created by the regulators (under the Basel Accords, which we will discuss) created a very significant economic incentive for banks to hold home mortgages to meet regulatory capital requirements. A financial institution had to have 8 percent of the loan value as capital for a traditional business loan, but needed only 4 percent capital for a home mortgage loan and 1.6 percent capital for a highly rated home-mortgage-backed security. These lower capital requirements for home-mortgage-related assets created such a powerful economic incentive that banks rapidly increased their investment in residential real estate loans as the home price bubble accelerated. Banks had to hold less capital for a subprime mortgage loan than for a loan to Exxon.

This example is overwhelming evidence that regulatory policies increase instead of reduce risk. In a private banking system, some banks will be making fatal mistakes. However, it is extremely unlikely that the vast majority of banks will be making the same mistake. Government regulatory policy creates incentives that encourage almost all the financial institutions in the market to make the same mistake.

The same phenomena have occurred in Europe. Under banking regulatory standards (Basel), banks do not have to hold any capital to support sovereign risk (such as the debt of a euro country). In the United States, banks do not have to hold any capital to support U.S. Treasury bonds. The theory is that if the government goes broke, the banks will inevitably fail (which is certainly true in the United States, where we have fiat currency).

In Europe, this regulatory capital standard encouraged banks to purchase large qualities of sovereign debt from Greece, Spain, Italy, Portugal, and other countries that were running large deficits.

Of course, in the European system, the strong countries (such as Germany) were not directly guaranteeing the debt of the weak countries. However, the banks in the strong countries could fail (and collapse the economy of the strong country) if Italy, Spain, Greece, or some other country were to default.

The only way to control systemic risk is by having independent decision makers make different decisions based on their analysis. Some will always be wrong, but it is extraordinarily unlikely that most of them will be wrong. A private banking system is fundamentally less risky than a centrally managed banking system. The evidence is overwhelming.

5

Government Housing Policy: The Proximate Cause

FOR MANY YEARS, DATING BACK TO THE 1930S NEW DEAL, A WIDE variety of government policies have been enacted to artificially encourage homeownership. The goal has been to drive the rate of homeownership (the percentage of families that own a home) above the natural market rate. There have been more subsidies for housing than for any other economic activity. Tax policy (the tax deductibility of interest on your permanent residence) has long subsidized housing. In the last 40 years, many other financial incentives have been added to subsidize housing.[1]

Being a longtime homeowner, I understand why people want to own houses. Of course, many of us associate our home with our family. In the back of our minds, it is sometimes hard to disconnect the two. However, there have been a number of studies that suggest that homeownership per se does not change human behavior. The simplest example is when a person who has been in a rental apartment wins the lottery and buys a large house. However, he remains basically undisciplined and wastes his wealth. It appears more likely that the characteristics that cause people to be able to purchase a home, such as the self-discipline of savings, are the same positive characteristics that we observe in many responsible homeowners.

It is certainly clear that home ownership is not necessarily economically efficient for everyone. For example, for young people who anticipate moving often, the transaction cost (which is material) of buying and selling houses may overwhelm the economic benefits of owning. Also, the risk of having to carry the cost of a house that one cannot sell for what one paid for it is significant for many young people. As all homeowners know, maintaining a home is expensive and time-consuming. Young people, in particular, have a tendency to compare rent payments for apartments (which typically include maintenance) to their mortgage payments (which do not include maintenance). In addition, the current economic environment clearly proved that encouraging people to purchase houses that were too big, to speculate on housing based on government incentives, or to buy houses that they could not afford is not good either for the individuals or for society.

There are a number of other significant ethical and economic issues raised by the decision to subsidize homeownership. Homeowners tend to have higher incomes than renters. Most of the financial subsidies for housing benefit individuals with incomes far above the poverty level. Should the government subsidize high-income families? In addition, subsidizing homeownership is subsidizing lifestyle choices. As I mentioned earlier, I personally like the homeownership lifestyle. I have moved a number of times in my life, but we have now settled down and have lived in the same house for 15 years. However, this is my personal lifestyle choice. It is not necessarily the right choice for everyone. Some people like to move often. They like new locations. Some individuals would rather live in an apartment because they like the camaraderie of having other people in similar situations around them, they like the view from the apartment, they are closer to work, or for some other reason. Concluding that owning a home is better than choosing to live in an apartment is a lifestyle bias that government has no legitimate role supporting.

There is a major economic cost to subsidizing housing, which was highlighted earlier. Housing is consumption. If government policy supports consumption at the expense of investment, we have less capital goods (including technology) to enhance the productivity of our labor force. The better the machines, tools, equipment, computers, software, and other such things that a worker has at his disposal, other things being equal, the more he can produce. In the long term, and in total contrast to the popular press's glorification of the consumer, we cannot consume more than we produce. The real issue in the long term is the productivity of our economic system. Going back to the farming example, if you eat your seed corn, you cannot plant next year's corn crop. Even before the current bubble, government policy subsidized a significant overinvestment in residential real estate, which has reduced our ability to compete in a global economy and misdirected the skills development of our workforce.

While there has been a long-term trend of government subsidies for homeownership, the amount of subsidization and government interference in the housing market has accelerated in recent years, under both Democratic and Republican administrations. Lyndon Johnson's Great Society laid the foundation for increased government subsidies focused on lower-income families and minorities. Most of the original (pre-Johnson) government subsidies were targeted at middle-income home buyers. The Great Society laid the foundation for the affordable-housing/subprime bubble, which then took years and additional incentives to become an exponential problem. The same factors are also true for Medicare/Medicaid some years down the road, except that they are bigger and the result will be worse.

The Fair Housing Act (1968) and the Equal Credit Opportunity Act (1979) were theoretically designed to eliminate racial discrimination. In practice, the laws were used to give banks incentives to make loans to low-income members of minority groups—in other words, to reverse-discriminate. A milestone event was the passage of the Community Reinvestment Act (CRA) in 1977. The theoretical purpose of the CRA was to encourage banks to invest in their communities and to eliminate so-called redlining. Of course, banks have to invest in their communities to stay in business. The law was also designed to encourage small business lending, which banks did anyway. The real purpose was to force banks to make loans to low-income borrowers, especially minorities and particularly African Americans, with a focus on home loans. While there are no formal quotas, there are implied quotas for low-income minority loans (especially for African Americans).

In order to make acquisitions, open branches, and generally grow its business, a bank must have a satisfactory CRA rating. Community groups often blackmail acquiring banks, pressing them to establish very aggressive low-income loan growth goals in order for the bank's proposed merger to be approved by the Federal Reserve. Of course, in addition to the high-risk loan commitments, the bank has to provide operating funds to the politically connected community organizations. In other words, the banks pay the salaries of their blackmailers.

The CRA has not been all bad. It has encouraged some creative efforts to improve homeownership by minorities. However, net/net, it has been a disaster. The default rates on these low-income loans are extraordinarily high. Many individuals have been given incentives to buy homes they could not afford, particularly when their income was unstable or when they did not have the self-discipline to save for maintenance costs. Seeing the real-world effect on many low-income individuals is depressing.

The CRA was even more destructive in terms of its impact of its incentives on the behavior of banks. It was explicitly clear that under the act, banks had a legal duty to make high-risk home loans to low-income borrowers. It is no excuse to claim that such loans represent only a small fraction of a bank's total loans and thus can't possibly undermine its safety and soundness or that of the financial system. The CRA has been used to leverage the impact of other destabilizing regulations, and if a bank fails to obtain a good CRA rating, it can find its broader strategy in terms of lending, branching, or merging blocked or destroyed, often to large financial effect.

Consistent with the fluctuating regulatory environment described previously, under Bill Clinton, making high-risk home loans to low-income borrowers was given priority over safety and soundness from a regulatory perspective. After all, times were good. For many, this focus on low-income borrowers moved from a legal responsibility to an ethical responsibility. It was viewed as an appropriate way to redistribute wealth. Initially the loss ratios in CRA (subprime) lending were acceptable. This was because of a combination of good economic times and the fact that it takes time for a loan portfolio to mature, particularly when it is growing rapidly. Once a high-risk loan portfolio starts to experience slower growth, its loss ratios rise rapidly. The early positive losses that were experienced, partly made possible by Greenspan's constantly printing money to keep the economy from correcting, led many bankers to believe that low-income (subprime) lending was far less risky that it is. This early loan loss experience also distorted some of the models used by rating agencies to rate bonds, as will be discussed later.

While the dollar amount of loans made under the CRA was not enough to cause the real estate misinvestment, the impact on human action was critically important. It was now a legal and ethical duty of the banks to participate in making high-risk housing loans to low-income buyers who would not meet traditional bank lending standards. In the end, the ethical justification was more important than the legal. Most people today view subprime lenders as taking advantage of poorly informed low-income borrowers. By the end of the process, this was certainly true in some cases. But it is important to remember that subprime lending was primarily driven by government policy based on a goal of wealth redistribution. Early subprime lending efforts were driven more by ethics than by economics. As previously outlined, the incorrect Fed study on racial discrimination in bank lending turned subprime lending to minorities into a moral crusade for justice. Incentives matter. Ethical incentives are more powerful than economic incentives. Of course, the effects of these government-driven "ethical" crusades on the supposed beneficiaries are often disastrous, as in this case.

When I first went to work for BB&T in 1971, it was a small farm bank. I was making $600 per month. I ran into the president of the bank, Jack Satchwell, a couple of days after I started work. He offered me some advice that I will never forget. He told me that working for a small bank like BB&T, I would never make a lot of money, but he would help me learn to live on what I made. I took his advice to heart and committed to save $100 per month out of the $600 I earned. Later I did make a lot of money, but I had learned long before to live on what I made.

One of the basic rules of finance is that you cannot make yourself wealthy by borrowing for consumption. You may want to consume, and there is absolutely no reason not to enjoy your life within your means, but you cannot borrow and consume to create economic security. You must produce, save, and invest. This is an economic fact of life. Encouraging individuals through government subsidies and legal incentives (force) to overspend (that is, buy houses they cannot afford) is certain to lower their and society's standard of living. Politically correct "do-gooders" cannot wish away the laws of economics.

In 1993, under Andrew Cuomo (currently governor of New York), the Department of Housing and Urban Development (HUD) announced that it would "encourage" Freddie Mac and Fannie Mae to have half their loan portfolios in affordable-housing (subprime) loans. Freddie and Fannie did not take the announcement very seriously at the time. The "big event" that drove the monetary bubble being created by the Fed into the housing market was a decision made by the Clinton administration in September of 1999. Bill Clinton put teeth into and his political power behind the goal of Freddie Mac and Fannie Mae having at least 50 percent of their loan portfolios in affordable housing (subprime) loans.

This was a stunning announcement. I remember it well. There was an article published in the September 30, 1999, New York Times (of all places) that raised fundamental questions about the wisdom of this strategy.[2] Several economists pointed out that the legitimate affordable-housing market was not big enough to equal 50 percent of the giant loan portfolios of Freddie Mac and Fannie Mae. In order to meet this political goal of the Clinton administration, Freddie and Fannie would have to consistently lower their lending standards. In fact, one economist noted that this high level of risk taking could jeopardize the financial viability of Freddie and Fannie, and that these institutions were so big that if they failed, it could have a dramatic impact of the U.S. economy, and it could happen in ten years. Nine years later, it happened.

Many people have heard of Freddie and Fannie, but do not know what these organizations do. If you go to a bank and get a home loan, there is a 90 percent probability that the bank will sell that loan to Freddie or Fannie (or their sister organization, the Federal Housing Administration). Even if you are making your payments to the bank, your loan has probably been sold to Freddie or Fannie, and the bank is collecting your payments on their behalf. Because they dominated the housing financing market, for reasons I will describe later, they effectively set the standards for home lending in the United States.

Freddie and Fannie are giant government-sponsored enterprises (GSEs) that never would have existed in a free market. They are hybrid organizations, which is the worst of all worlds. Theoretically, they are owned by their shareholders and are responsible for maximizing shareholder returns. On the other hand, their liabilities/ debts are guaranteed by the U.S. government, that is, the taxpayers. Because of the U.S. government guarantee, they were highly motivated to maximize their leverage. They were able to operate with a much higher level of debt than private banks. Freddie and Fannie came to dominate the home mortgage finance businesses because of their government subsidies. They were receiving massive government subsidies in the form of debt guarantees worth billions of dollars annually. If you own a business, wouldn't it be nice to have the federal government guarantee all your debts for high-risk investments and also pay you big salaries and bonuses? Sounds good!

Unfortunately, for Freddie and Fannie's shareholders, there was a high price to pay in the long term for making a deal with the devil, or politicians. Fannie and Freddie's leadership was very political. For example, Frank Raines, the CEO who set up Fannie for disaster, was a "Friend of Bill's" (Clinton). He knew much more about politics than about business, which can be a problem when you run a very large, complex business.

Freddie and Fannie had a challenge in keeping the politicians satisfied and earning a satisfactory return for their shareholders (and paying big bonuses to Frank Raines). Their mission was to make homeownership affordable. However, for Freddie and Fannie, that also meant making a profit, with the help of massive government subsidies. They knew that it was risky to try to make money in the low-income housing finance market, so they focused on the middle- to high-income market. Before Freddie and Fannie got involved in the subprime market, they dominated the prime housing finance market. To the degree that the government subsidies were passed on to borrowers, the benefit went to middle- and higher-income homeowners. Banks had been pushed into the low-income high-risk housing market by the Community Reinvestment Act, but Freddie and Fannie largely avoided the low-income market for years. They did this through powerful political connections. They were big contributors to both political parties, and they enlisted the support of the politically powerful Home Builders Association, which viewed Freddie and Fannie as vital to the residential construction industry.

Their balancing act of avoiding as much of the low-income market as they could started coming apart with Clinton's 1999 goal for them to have half their loan portfolio in affordable-housing/subprime loans. However, they really lost control over an unrelated issue. In 2002, because of the accounting failures at WorldCom and Enron, the accountants at Freddie and Fannie took a far deeper look at the institutions' accounting systems. Based on this examination, both organizations ultimately had to execute major accounting restatements of their earnings. Issues of fraud by the executive management to maximize their bonuses were raised. It was a very visible "scandal."

In defense of Freddie and Fannie, the accounting rules for derivatives, especially those relating to fair-value accounting, are extraordinarily complex, confusing, and subjective. (We have a failed accounting system in the United States thanks to the SEC, which we will discuss later.) Most of the adjustments involved timing, that is, moving revenue and expenses from one year to the next. An annual accounting cycle is arbitrary for most businesses, especially businesses making loans that run for 20 years and trying to hedge the interest-rate risk in a market that they are big enough to unintentionally have an impact on.

Whether or not Fannie and/or Freddie were guilty of anything more than honest misinterpretations of complex accounting rules, the impact of the accounting problems was very significant for both organizations. Their political cover was blown. The balancing act was undone. If Freddie and Fannie wanted to keep the U.S. government guarantee of their debt, they had to focus on what Congress wanted, and Congress wanted Freddie and Fannie to become very serious about achieving Clinton's (and now Bush's) affordable-housing goals. This is when they cranked up their low-income lending business and ultimately became the primary driver of the subprime lending markets. The irony is that the internal staff at Freddie and Fannie did not want to go after this market. They knew that with their organizations' very high financial leverage, this subprime strategy was incredibly risky. Both companies had survived by making only lower-risk loans and had low loan loss ratios. Their operating formula was not designed for high-risk affordable-housing lending.

However, Congress was not going to continue to guarantee their debts unless they met the subprime goals, and if it did not do so, they would be out of business. They had no choice but to cooperate.

Freddie and Fannie traditionally operated with a leverage ratio of 75 to 1. Banks have a leverage ratio on loans of 10 to 1. Even before they experienced severe financial problems, Fannie and Freddie were operating with a leverage ratio of about 1,000 to 1. That is, for every $1 of equity, they had $1,000 of debt. How would you feel about your financial position if you had a net worth of $10,000 and owed $10,000,000? It might make you uncomfortable. Freddie and Fannie could operate with this much leverage only because the government had effectively guaranteed their debts. (Of course, when they failed, their leverage was infinite, since they owed more than their assets were worth.) Freddie and Fannie's total liabilities, including loan guarantees, were approximately $5.5 trillion (including $2 trillion in subprime mortgages).[3] Remember, a trillion is a million million. Freddie and Fannie are the "big kahunas" in the home mortgage market. It is absurd to argue that they were not a primary cause of the misinvestment in housing. Just look at the size of their portfolios.

This is the one case where the U.S. Treasury (that is, the taxpayers) did have to bail out the bondholders. Freddie and Fannie had sold debt to financial intermediaries all over the world with an implied guarantee from Uncle Sam. If Freddie and Fannie had been allowed to default, the global financial system would have collapsed. Also, there would have been a run on U.S. government debt because foreign investors would no longer have trusted us to pay our debts.

Freddie and Fannie should not exist. Congress never should have created an implied guarantee of their debts. Freddie and Fannie should not have been allowed to dominate the housing market. However, after all these bad decisions, the U.S. Treasury did have to protect the bondholders of the GSEs or there would have been economic disaster. This is the only case where there was a clear pre-financial-crisis implied guarantee by the U.S. government, and a bailout was necessary. By the way, congratulations; as a U.S. taxpayer, you now owe $5.5 trillion more in debt. Thank you, Congress (especially Barney Frank and Chris Dodd)!

In fact, politics played the primary role in the failure of Freddie and Fannie. The Financial Services Roundtable (FSR) is an organization representing the 100 largest financial institutions in the United States. I was on an FSR committee that tried for years to do something about Freddie and Fannie. It was an interesting experience that reflects the unavoidable corruptive process of government intervention in markets. Many of the banks represented on the committee had been in the direct home lending business years ago and had held the loans on their own books. However, they had been driven out of prime home mortgage lending by Freddie and Fannie. You cannot compete against the government.

All the firms represented on the committee originated loans and sold them to Freddie and/or Fannie, along with portfolioing[4] or securitizing jumbo mortgages. (Jumbo mortgages are loans that are too large for Freddie and Fannie's lending limits, but are mostly prime loans.) The effect of crony capitalism and pragmatism was clearly obvious to this group. For some of the lenders, the main goal was to not make Freddie and Fannie unhappy. After all, these banks made healthy profits selling to the GSEs. They wanted to argue about small issues.

A few of the smarter thinkers (still pragmatic) realized that Freddie and Fannie could push us all out of the origination business and therefore posed a threat to future earnings. The GSEs had traditionally bought loan packages originated by other financial intermediaries, such as banks and mortgage companies. Some of the bigger banks made additional profits by consolidating the production of smaller lenders and selling the loan packages to the GSEs. However, Freddie and Fannie were developing underwriting models that would allow them to bypass the consolidators. Ultimately, these models might allow the GSEs to totally control the underwriting business. This would allow them to drive banks out of the mortgage origination business as they had driven us out of the mortgage portfolio lending business. The bankers who understood this risk wanted Congress or the regulators to ensure that the GSEs did not violate the limits of their mission, which prohibited them from taking over the banks' role.

A few of us saw the issues in far deeper terms. We knew not only that Freddie and Fannie, left unchecked, would ultimately drive us out of the home mortgage lending business, but that they were an economic disaster waiting to happen. We observed their leverage ratios and their move into subprime lending. Early on, members of the Bush administration, to their credit, realized the risk of Freddie and Fannie and began to solicit our support for getting Congress to require more capital and place other significant constraints on the GSEs. They shared their analysis of the financial condition of the GSEs, and it was scary.

By 2005, it was self-evident that Freddie and Fannie were extraordinarily risky to the U.S. taxpayers. I had the opportunity to meet with members of Congress on this issue on several occasions. An educated layman could easily have looked at the numbers and realized that Freddie and Fannie would ultimately fail unless they raised much more capital. At this point in time, Freddie and Fannie could still have raised capital and issued subordinated debt, which would have greatly reduced the risk to the taxpayers. This was possible because the market perception was that somehow, despite the numbers, Congress would bail the GSEs out. Also, Congress could have reduced the affordable housing goals, which were where the risk was being created.

However, Congress refused to take action when it could have for two reasons. First, there was an almost religious belief in affordable housing. Doing anything to slow lending to the low-income market would be ethically unacceptable. Second, Freddie and Fannie were huge contributors to both political parties. Between 1998 and 2008, Freddie Mac spent $94.9 million and Fannie Mae spent $79.5 million to lobby Congress.[5] They also provided many intangible benefits to various members of Congress.

The individuals who are most responsible for the collapse of Freddie and Fannie and the related housing crisis are Congressman Barney Frank and Senator Chris Dodd. They both had the information to know that something needed to be done and refused to do it. I particularly blame Barney Frank. Most of the members of Congress involved simply were not intellectual enough to understand the fundamental issue. However, Barney is smart. He could see the issues, and he still refused to act—a classic example of evasion. It is truly ironic that the two primary architects of the financial reform bill are two of the people most responsible for our financial disaster.

The Dodd-Frank Wall Street Reform and Consumer Protection Act, originally proposed by the duo in December 2009, was signed into law by President Obama on July 21, 2010. The act imposes a massive array of new mandates on the reeling financial sector, yet it does nothing to (1) reduce banks' FDIC coverage, (2) curb the "too-big-to-fail" bailout doctrine, or (3) restrain the power, size, or scope of the mortgage GSEs. Senator Dodd retired in 2010. Representative Frank, who chaired the House Financial Services Committee from 2007 to 2011, was reelected to a fifteenth consecutive term by his Massachusetts constituents in November 2010 (he was first elected in 1981), but recently announced that he will not run for reelection in 2012.

By the way, one of the arguments heard from a few economists is that Freddie and Fannie cannot be the cause of the subprime problems because they were not major subprime lenders. This argument is based on false information. Freddie and Fannie never reported large subprime portfolios before they failed. However, they had very large portfolios that they classified as Alt-A. This is a class of loans that is supposed to be somewhat more risky than prime, but less risky than subprime. Unfortunately, it turns out that their Alt-A portfolios were in fact largely subprime portfolios. A careful examination of the actual credit characteristics of these supposed Alt-As indicates that they had the same risk profiles as subprime loans. This should not be surprising, given the political mandate to serve the low-income market that the GSEs were under.

Economists at the American Enterprise Institute (AEI) have estimated that Freddie and Fannie's subprime portfolio was in excess of $2 trillion.[6] This is huge. The reporting error itself materially distorted the market. If you are buying subprime mortgage bonds, or if you are a rating agency trying to rate these bonds, the size of the market is extremely important in your decision process. It is possible to make an estimate of how large the legitimate subprime market is in terms of outstanding loans. If the analysis indicates that the total debt outstanding is within this limit, it might imply that the risk in the market is acceptable. However, if the total outstanding loans are above the limit, new loans should not be made. Freddie and Fannie's failure to report $2 trillion in subprime loans misled all the market participants, including the rating agencies. This is an interesting example of government-sponsored enterprises, which would never have existed in a free market, doing double damage. They funded a major percentage of the misinvestment in residential real estate (including their prime lending) and provided materially misleading information that contributed to errors by other market participants.

It is important to note that Freddie and Fannie are the dominant players in the mortgage market. As they systematically lowered their lending standards, other market participants were forced to follow or be driven out of business.

The taxpayers will probably suffer $300 to $500 billion in direct losses from Freddie and Fannie. The indirect losses are much, much larger.

The financial crisis and the ensuing Great Recession were primarily caused by the Federal Reserve and by Freddie Mac and Fannie Mae. The Federal Reserve created a massive misinvestment (bubble) in our economy by overexpanding the money supply to try to keep us from experiencing the normal short-term downside corrections that occur in a free market.

The bubble (misinvestment) primarily affected the housing market because of Freddie Mac and Fannie Mae's affordable-housing lending, which was driven by a political goal to raise homeownership above the natural market rate.

Hearing this explanation, you might conclude that in both cases, the policy makers were acting with good intentions. It is certainly true that good intentions do not necessarily produce good outcomes. However, it might also be appropriate to reflect on what a good intention, properly understood, really requires. We will discuss this issue in the chapter on the philosophical causes of the financial crisis.

6

The Essential Role of Banks in a Complex Economy: The Liquidity Challenge

BANKS PLAY A UNIQUE AND IMPORTANT ROLE IN THE ABILITY OF modern economic systems to extend the investment cycle, take more risk, and accelerate economic growth. Through their ability to pool and diversify risk—including credit risk, interest-rate risk and liquidity risk—they fund important economic investments that otherwise would not be made.

As an example of how this process works, suppose a real estate developer has plans to build a subdivision that will cost $6,000,000 and result in 100 building lots that can be sold over time at a current price of $80,000 per lot, or a total of $8,000,000 (100 lots × $80,000). He has saved $1,000,000 and therefore needs $5,000,000 more to develop the subdivision. Based on the expected development period and sales period, it will take a total of five years for this $5,000,000 to be repaid.

Because of the relatively small size of this project, the transaction cost in the capital markets would be so high as to make the project unfeasible. In addition, it would be extremely difficult for capital market participants to underwrite the project without intimate knowledge of the local real estate market. While, in theory, the builder/developer could ask local individuals to finance the project, it could be very difficult to find "friends" who would want their savings locked into one investment for so long. The risk of having all their eggs in one basket would be too great.

A bank, however, can make this type of investment because of its ability to diversity the various risks. It can invest in multiple projects, so that if this one real estate project has problems, the loss on the specific loan will be manageable. The bank can also make other types of loans, such as car loans, credit card loans, and loans to manufacturers. It can diversify its risk in ways that small savers cannot. The bank can also have intimate knowledge of the local market, and therefore can underwrite (understand and manage) the risk better.

In addition, because the bank is funded by many individual savers, it can make longer-term investments. It knows that some individuals will be increasing their savings when other individuals are using their savings, so the bank can also pool the liquidity risk.

For a small saver, there are multiple advantages. By putting his money in the bank in a certificate of deposit, he can "have his cake and eat it too." He can earn interest on his savings and have access to the money at the same time. This probably encourages small savers to save more. Banks are able to borrow short, that is, fund their business with deposits and other short-term investments, and lend long. This intermediary process significantly extends the investment cycle and improves the economy's productivity.

All healthy economic systems have healthy banking systems. Healthy banks are a sign of a healthy economy. However, the nature of the system creates a fundamental risk. Strong banks are solvent. Being solvent means that the bank has more assets than it has liabilities. Over time, it can sell its assets and pay all its debts. However, even strong banks are not liquid. In other words, if every depositor wants to withdraw his or her money at the same time, even a healthy bank cannot meet the outflow because much of the money has been invested in loans that are to be paid back over time. In the current environment, the Federal Reserve acts as a short-term backup to the banking system. It can provide liquidity to healthy banks in the event of unanticipated deposit outflows.

The banking system improves the efficiency of small savings and allows smaller investments to be made. It is vital for small businesses and especially for smaller builders/developers in the real estate market, where local knowledge is essential to risk underwriting. Local knowledge is also of great value in most forms of consumer lending.

Economists call the system we have just described *fractional reserve banking*. This terminology is appropriate because the banks have only a fraction of the depositors' money in reserve, or "on hand." The rest is invested in loans or bonds. The system obviously has an intrinsic risk that leads to economic volatility. The depositors expect to be able to get their money whenever they want it, and yet the bank does not have everyone's money on hand. This fact does not matter until some form of panic occurs, and suddenly everyone wants his money. In addition to the risk of the bank's failing, there is another negative effect: under liquidity pressure, banks can no longer make loans, and this often puts businesses that need to borrow into financial distress, with the result that the whole economic system starts to malfunction.

Some Austrian economists have argued against fractional reserve banking (specifically for demand deposits, or checking accounts). They have identified the existence of central banks (like the Federal Reserve) as the primary cause of business cycles and fractional reserve banking as a related factor.[1] They have a valid and useful insight. In Chapter 18, on solutions to the financial crisis, I will share with you some ideas for dealing with this issue without losing the benefits of magnifying the economic efficiency of intermediate-size investments and small savings that banks provide.

The Federal Reserve and FDIC insurance were both created to deal with the issues associated with the nature of fractional reserve banking. In the short term, these "solutions" help; in the long term, they make the problem far, far worse.

FDIC insurance primarily reduces the short-term risk of bank runs because depositors perceive their deposits to be insured by the federal government. However, I previously described the fact that FDIC insurance substantially increases the credit and liquidity risk that banks take by eliminating market discipline. Based on my long-term observation of the behavior of bank executives (human nature), the existence of FDIC insurance changes the risk/return trade-offs so significantly that in the good times (when bad loans are made), bankers take risks that they would never take in a free market. FDIC insurance is pro-cyclical; that is, it increases both the size of the bubble (the misinvestment) and the magnitude of the bust.

In the short term, the Federal Reserve can be important in controlling liquidity risk. Healthy banks can borrow cash from the Federal Reserve, using their sound assets (typically government bonds) as collateral. This cash inflow can be used to meet depositors' demands. In the long term, however, the existence of the Fed magnifies risk. The Fed has the dual goals of price stability and low unemployment. As previously described, the Fed often overexpands the money supply to eliminate natural market corrections, and this effectively provides a major incentive for banks to take more risk. The Fed reduces short-term liquidity risk at the expense of increasing credit risk.

There is an interesting contrast between the early years of the Great Depression and the recent financial crisis. The evidence is clear that the early phase of the Great Depression was primarily a liquidity crisis, brought about by the Fed's arbitrary reduction in the money supply. While the recent financial crisis had a liquidity component, there was a far larger solvency issue. In other words, in a number of cases, failing institutions were not just illiquid, they were insolvent (a much more significant problem). Bernanke, being an expert on the Great Depression, treated the recent crisis as if it were a liquidity issue instead of a solvency problem. For example, the Fed saved Bear Stearns under the theory that Bear was solvent, but illiquid. However, it now appears that Bear was in fact not just illiquid, but also insolvent. The Fed's handling of Bear Stearns provided an extremely misleading message to the market, which we will discuss later.

The protection that is provided to the creditors of banks (including depositors) is the shareholders' capital investment in the bank. The more capital, other things being equal, the less risk there is to creditors and depositors. Leverage is the ratio of debt to capital. The higher the leverage, the greater the risk. To make the discussion simpler, we will use rough approximations of leverage position. Commercial banks are leveraged about 10 to 1, that is, they have about $10 of debt for each $1 of capital. The banking regulators have also allowed large banks to use "hybrid" capital. This is a form of long-term debt that the regulators let Citigroup and other such banks define as capital. Smaller banks followed with this hybrid capital because they to produce satisfactory returns on shareholders' equity (capital) to keep from being bought by the bigger banks. This hybrid capital effectively allowed for increased leverage in the financial system.

At the beginning of the financial crisis, investment banks were leveraged about 30 to 1. Given their leverage, it is not surprising that the large investment banks and highly leveraged large commercial banks were some of the first financial institutions to have problems during the financial crisis (Bear Stearns, Lehman Brothers, Goldman Sachs, Morgan Stanley, and Citigroup). The leverage of investment banks has risen significantly in recent years for a variety of reasons.

One important reason is the settlement that the investment banks reached with Eliot Spitzer, the attorney general of New York State. Spitzer attacked the traditional business model that investment banks had used for many years. Under this traditional model, these banks had relied on their financial research to generate investment banking business. According to Spitzer, the investment analysts could not be independent if they helped the investment bankers to develop clients who would issue stocks, sell bonds, and so on. Of course, all market participants knew that the analysts were influenced by their client relationships. Spitzer "discovered" this lack of independence (which everybody else had known for at least 50 years).[2]

The change that Spitzer imposed significantly reduced the profitability of the investment banking analysts model. To replace these lost profits, investment banks began to trade more and more for their own account (instead of trading other people's money), raising their leverage and therefore their risk position. It also potentially created conflicts of interest, as the investment bank's own positions in various investment instruments were more likely to be counter to their clients' and because the investment banks' investments were so large that they could potentially affect market prices.

This shift from trading clients' money to trading their own capital was facilitated by the SEC. The SEC allowed the investment banks to use mathematical modeling under the international capital guidelines (Basel Accords) to set capital ratios. Under these guidelines, the investment banks were able to significantly increase their leverage and maintain much higher leverage positions than comparable commercial banks.

Before there was the Federal Reserve, private banks typically had leverage ratios of 2 to 1 or 1 to 1. In adverse times, the more capital you have as a cushion, the better the protection for creditors and depositors. If banks had had capital ratios at this level in 2007, there would not have been a financial crisis in 2008–2009. Many defenders of the Federal Reserve drop the context; that is, they see the Fed's ability to provide liquidity as reducing risk. They ignore the fact that the very existence of the Fed creates extremely powerful incentives (human nature) for bank managements to increase risk in good times. Instead of being countercyclical, as its proponents argue, the Fed is pro-cyclical because of its effect on human behavior through the financial and psychological incentives that it creates.

7

The Residential Real-Estate-Market Bubble and Financial-Market Stress

As we have discussed, the "bursting" of the bubble (misinvestment) in the residential real estate markets led to the deterioration of the capital markets and to the Great Recession. In reality, it was the actions that led to the misinvestment (bubble) in the first place that were destructive. The bursting of the bubble was both inevitable and healthy for the economy in the long term. The bursting stopped the misinvestment process. It was the misinvestment, not the correction, that reduced our future standard of living.

Let's examine the economics of the residential real estate market. In the long term, the prices of residential real estate are driven by the cost of building a new home, the cost to rent a home, and the affordability of housing. Also, psychology (human actions based on incentives) can play a major role. If individuals misclassify housing as investment instead of consumption, they will spend more on housing than they would otherwise. The change in psychology that has occurred since the residential real estate bubble broke, with many individuals realizing that housing is consumption, will reduce the amount of money spent on housing for many years. A similar phenomenon occurred after the U.S. stock-price crash of 1929–1933; the average citizen avoided stocks for decades, and the Dow Jones Index didn't regain its precrash level for another quarter century (in 1954).[1]

Excluding these complicating factors, it is easy to see that the primary driver of residential real estate values is affordability. Individuals and families have to buy other things (food, clothes, energy, autos, and so on) in addition to shelter. If house prices go too high, families cannot afford to buy a house. At the peak of the residential real estate bubble in the spring of 2007, house prices nationally were approximately 30 percent too high based on affordability.[2] The extent to which house values were excessive varied significantly by market. In southern California, prices were 50 to 60 percent too high. In Winston-Salem, North Carolina, where I live, they were 15 percent too high. Not coincidentally, when the bubble burst, house prices (national median) declined about 30 percent from the peak (2006) through 2011. (However, the psychological change in the view of houses from investment to consumption could cause prices to fall further as consumers reassess their relative consumption desires.)

As the bubble started to deflate, housing values in the United States started to fall. The initial fall was 15 to 20 percent. Banks and other financial intermediaries finance houses. As the value of houses fell, banks, investment banks, mortgage companies, and other lenders had to significantly increase their loan loss reserves. In addition, they had to take major write-downs on their bond portfolio for mortgage-backed bonds. (Unfortunately, these write-downs were significantly and inappropriately magnified by fair-value accounting, as we will discuss.) These increased loan losses and bond portfolio write-downs destroyed almost $500 billion in capital in the financial services industry.

Remember, commercial banks are leveraged about 10 to 1. Investment banks are leveraged 30 to 1. Let's use the commercial bank leverage ratio for simplicity. If $500 billion in capital is lost in the banking industry, liquidity is reduced by $5 trillion ($500 billion × 10 = $5 trillion). This is a very big number. The reduction in liquidity had a significant impact on the ability of banks, investment banks, and other such entities to lend to each other. This started a chain of liquidity problems in the capital markets.

Banks reacted to this loss of capital by trying to raise additional capital. They were somewhat successful initially and raised about $200 billion in additional capital. This reduced the capital shortfall from $500 billion to $300 billion, which reduced the liquidity (lending capacity) loss from $5 trillion to $3 trillion. However, $3 trillion is still a very big number.

At this point, the market began to realize that there was more damage to come. House prices had fallen 15 to 20 percent, but they needed to decline a total of 30 percent to be affordable again. This decline would destroy another $100 to $200 billion or more in bank capital. This destruction of capital would reduce liquidity (lending) by $1 to $2 trillion or more. Also, there was a risk that real estate markets would drop even lower than the affordability level as a result of fear and that more capital would be lost, reducing liquidity even more. The markets became extremely nervous. However, the capital markets remained open for healthy banks.

A very significant and far underdiscussed event then occurred. The FDIC, the Fed, and the U.S. Treasury made an extremely destructive decision in handling the failure of Washington Mutual. ("WaMu" was the sixth largest bank in the United States and the largest savings and loan, with $300 billion in assets.) By September 2008, WaMu was deeply insolvent, and the FDIC took it over and sold it to JPMorgan Chase.[3] In the process, the regulators decided to pay the uninsured depositors in full. Traditionally, when a bank fails, the FDIC pays the insured depositors in full, but makes only a partial payment to uninsured depositors, such as 50 to 80 percent of the amount of their deposits that is uninsured. The unpaid deposit balance becomes a debt in the bankruptcy proceedings. Uninsured depositors do get paid in full on the portion of their deposits that is insured (theoretically, $100,000 is insured, but often much more is insured, as discussed previously). Until the WaMu failure, the idea had been that uninsured depositors would impose discipline on a reckless bank, knowing in advance that they could lose money in the event of a bankruptcy.

The reason the FDIC and the other regulators decided to pay uninsured depositors was to avoid creating a bank run. When IndyMac had failed, the FDIC had not paid uninsured depositors in full. This created lines of depositors waiting to get their money, which were broadcast endlessly by the media. The regulators were concerned that a similar display might cause the general public to panic and demand their money out of healthy banks (remember the fractional reserve issue we discussed before).

While the regulators had a legitimate concern, the manner in which they chose to handle WaMu was even more destructive. They decided to take the extra losses created by covering the uninsured depositors from WaMu's bondholders. The bondholders had expected significant losses on their bonds, but the losses were more than they had expected because the FDIC had taken part of the money that should have been available to pay bondholders and given it to uninsured depositors. This was in complete contradiction to past practice. The bondholders suddenly realized that there is no rule of law when government regulators are involved. In other words, the regulators can make up the law as they go along because of the extreme flexibility of the regulatory structure.

The decision to treat WaMu bondholders this way closed the capital markets for banks. BB&T had issued bonds a few weeks before the WaMu decision. It was a choppy market, but we had been able to raise capital funding. However, after the WaMu debtholders were crushed, the capital markets closed for all banks. I believe this was an even more significant event than Lehman Brothers' failure. I think one of the main reasons that Bernanke and Paulson were so panicky when they went to Congress for $700 billion for the Troubled Asset Relief Program (TARP)—the so-called bank bailout—was that they realized that they had closed the capital markets for banks.

Unquestionably, the handling of WaMu forced the failure of Wachovia. Wachovia had been struggling, but its fate had not been completely determined. However, once the bond market saw how WaMu's creditors had been treated, the market closed for Wachovia. Wachovia did not have a run by individual depositors, but rather a run in the capital markets. Wachovia probably would have ultimately failed, but not necessarily. By the way, Wachovia did fail. Even though it was sold to Wells Fargo (with the shareholders getting a small amount) and the FDIC did not suffer a loss, its sale was mandated by the FDIC and the Fed. If the government forces the sale of a company, that company has failed (fairly or not).

The interesting aspect of this situation is that the negative consequences for the bond market could have been avoided and the risk of retail bank runs controlled. The FDIC could have simply absorbed the extra losses paid to the uninsured depositors. The FDIC's mission is to protect the safety and soundness of the banking system. If covering uninsured depositors is necessary, it can do so, but it should let the losses fall on the insurance fund, not on innocent bondholders. Violating the rule of law has consequences.

The bursting of the real estate–market bubble turned into an international financial crisis for several reasons. First, foreign financial institutions had invested heavily in the U.S. housing market. They suffered capital losses and the resulting reductions in liquidity (lending capacity), as previously described for U.S. institutions, and these reductions were then transmitted to their home economies. Second, there were housing bubbles created by the central banks in a number of other countries (such as Ireland and Spain), and these bubbles also burst.

Finally, and most important, the U.S. dollar is the world's reserve currency. If the Fed makes a mistake, its error will be transmitted to the global economy. The Fed increased the world's monetary reserves, creating a global financial bubble. It is surprising to me, given the Fed's string of errors, that international players have not abandoned the dollar and moved to a different standard. Of course, the Chinese have threatened to do just this. (Also, it can be argued that gold is rapidly becoming the world's reserve currency.)

It was previously outlined how subdivision zoning laws played an important role in driving up residential land site values and contributed to the housing bubble. There is another set of state laws that has played an important role in keeping the housing market from correcting rapidly and has increased the losses and the destruction of wealth in the housing correction, the state home foreclosure laws. There are price corrections in all types of markets; stock markets and commodity markets are clear examples of markets in which price corrections are rapid and sometimes dramatic. Even though the price corrections may be challenging if you are on the wrong side of the bet, markets clear and everyone can get on with his business based on the new prices that more properly value the commodity or stock.

For example, I started my career as a farm lender. Every spring, some of our farm clients would plant a soybean crop. Some of them would hedge the price they were to receive in the fall; some would not. Nobody would attempt to hedge the total expected production because too many factors could affect the actual crop size.

Suppose the farmer has a good year. It rains just the right amount (which happens once every 10 or so years). He grows a lot of soybeans. Interestingly, so do his neighbors. There is a large soybean crop, and, based on the law of supply and demand, soybean prices fall. (One of the tough factors about being a farmer is that when you have a good year, it is likely that others will also, and you will face lower prices for your crop. You really need to enjoy farming to be a farmer.) The farmer has a clear set of choices. He can sell the soybeans at the low market price, or he can store them and sell them later, when, he hopes, the price will be higher. Either way, the soybean market clears. Farmers can then make informed decisions about what to plant next year based on the price information available. The inefficient farmer who had a poor crop (under good farming conditions) and loses money because of the low soybean prices gets to go out of business and do something else that he is better suited for.

Why did residential real estate prices not correct reasonably rapidly? Why have home prices declined for five consecutive years now, from 2007 to 2011 inclusive, and not for just a year or two?[4] One reason, of course, is the endless self-defeating programs that Bush and Obama have offered homeowners. Another reason is the state foreclosure laws and their enforcement by state attorneys general. In numerous states, it is many months after a borrower stops paying her mortgage before the lender can regain title to the property and sell it to someone else.

Since banks are the "big bad guys," to help make this concept more concrete, let us use a personal example to help you understand the effect of these laws. You make a $190,000 loan to Jerry and his family to purchase a $200,000 home in Florida. Jerry is your spouse's first cousin. You know it is a safe loan because house prices never decline. After all, the government will always step in to protect home values should prices start to decline. Unfortunately, Jerry develops an alcohol abuse problem and loses his job. In addition, house prices in

Florida do decline by 20 percent, so the current value of the house is $160,000 and Jerry still owes you $190,000.

The game has changed. Jerry has already lost his $10,000 and has nothing to lose. You have $160,000 to lose. Jerry will not pay and forces you to foreclose on the house. It takes 18 months to 2 years to execute on a foreclosure in Florida. Jerry and his family can live in your house for 2 years rent-free. Also, Jerry does not cure his alcohol abuse problem, and he and his family are not motivated to take care of your house. Of course, you incur significant legal costs to execute the foreclosure, and the value of the house is declining because of the market and the lack of maintenance. When you finally get the home, you sell it for a net of $135,000 after the cost of repair. The foreclosure process has increased your loss from $30,000 to $55,000. In addition, you incur $5,000 in attorney's fees for a total loss of $60,000, which is $30,000 more than the original expected loss. The foreclosure process has doubled your loss. This cost increase happens to banks all the time. The proposed moratoriums on foreclosures that are created by various state and federal regulations have increased this totally economically unproductive cost.

I do not know the total cost of this inefficient foreclosure process. However, just using BB&T as a proxy, I am certain that in this current correction, the unnecessary foreclosure cost to the banking industry in the form of loan collection salaries, legal cost, maintenance expense, and so on is $150 billion at the least and probably much more. This is a $150 billion unnecessary loss of bank capital, which turns into a $1.5 trillion loss of lending capacity ($150 billion × 10). The process also has a very significant psychological effect on the willingness of banks to lend.

The argument for this process is that it helps distressed homeowners. This argument is typically not true. Once the foreclosure process starts, it usually ends in foreclosure. In the story, Jerry enjoyed getting free rent. For many people, however, waiting to be thrown out of their home based on false hope is miserable. Better to get on with life, just like that inefficient farmer.

Also, what about the effect on others? What if the homeowner has brought it on himself—like your friend Jerry becoming an alcoholic? Should the other clients, employees, and shareholders of the bank, who will pay for the loss, be punished because Jerry is an alcoholic?

If you could have gotten "your" home back from Jerry, you possibly could have rented it at a satisfactory price to the hardworking, honest Thompsons. The Thompsons cannot afford to buy a house, but they could afford to rent yours. Since your house is not available, they have to stay in their mobile home, which unfortunately is hit by a tornado and their dog dies. Is this overdramatizing? Maybe. However, there are all types of good and bad stories and unintended secondary consequences that make the plans of the social policy "do-gooders" destructive, both economically and in terms of the effect on real human beings. Visit a mortgage collection center some time and listen to the stories.

In fact, let me tell you a story to help you grasp the moral hazard risk. In the fall of 2008, I was visiting BB&T's mortgage collection center to try to boost the morale of our employees. One of our collectors whom I had known for a long time handed me a phone call from a client. This client had moved from the Northeast to Florida about 18 months before. He had purchased a $1,000,000 house, and BB&T had made him a $600,000 loan.

According to this individual, the house was now worth $500,000. He wanted us to reduce his interest rate from $5\frac{1}{2}$ percent to 3 percent and forgive $100,000 of his debt. Interestingly, he had $800,000 on deposit with the bank. I asked him whether, if the house had appreciated to $2,000,000, he would have given us the $1,000,000 gain. I don't think so. Moral hazard is a real risk.

There is also a significant job-destroying effect of not letting the housing market correct. Individuals who do want to buy a house will not do so until they believe the market has bottomed. As long as there is a massive inventory of unsold homes in the foreclosure process, new homes will not be built because potential buyers are concerned about future home-price declines. Who wants to purchase a home for $200,000 and have it worth $175,000 six months later? The housing market must be allowed to clear for new home construction to begin and employment to return to the residential construction industry.

8

Failure of the Rating Agencies: The Subprime Mortgage Market and Its Impact on Capital Markets

ONE OF THE FIRST WARNING SIGNALS LEADING TO THE FINANCIAL crisis of 2008 was turmoil in the subprime mortgage market. Prices of residential mortgage-backed securities (RMBS) had already begun dropping sharply in 2006 along with home prices. A substantial volume of subprime mortgages had been securitized by investment banks and sold into the investment portfolios of pension plans, bond funds, and banks all over the world. Some of the highly rated subprime mortgage bonds started to default as the real estate markets began to deflate. It quickly became clear that the default rates on these subprime mortgages were going to be much higher (worse) than was implied by the credit rating on the bonds. This realization was the beginning of turmoil in the bond markets.

These subprime-backed mortgage bonds had been rated by Standard & Poor's (S&P), Moody's, and/or Fitch. These three rating agencies have the equivalent of a government-sanctioned oligopoly.

They are the only rating firms that the Securities and Exchange Commission (SEC) allows to provide credit ratings on bonds to meet ERISA requirements for public pension plans. (ERISA, or the Employee Retirement Income Security Act, is a law designed to protect pension plan participants.) Starting in 1975, the SEC designated S&P, Moody's, and Fitch as "nationally recognized statistical rating organizations" (NRSROs) and decreed that their ratings were to be relied on by institutional investors and investment banks for meeting regulatory and capital requirements.

Because of this special approval from the SEC, these three rating agencies have an apparent certification of quality from a U.S. government agency. There is a presumption in the capital markets that the government-sanctioned rating agencies know how to grade the risk of financial instruments. In addition, regulators establish capital requirements for financial institutions partially based on the rating of the bonds they hold. A bank is required to hold much less capital for highly rated bonds. Unfortunately, the rating agencies did a terrible job of rating subprime-backed mortgage bonds. The ratings were in error not by one grade, but by multiple grades—similar to a student receiving an A in a course when he actually earned an F.

There are a number of reasons why S&P, Moody's, and Fitch did such a poor job of rating subprime mortgage bonds. For one thing, their mathematical rating models failed. This occurred for a variety of reasons. First of all, the subprime market was growing so rapidly that the loan loss ratios were understated. As discussed earlier, only when a portfolio matures can losses be properly estimated. Since subprime lending on this scale was new, there was no long-term history that could be used to evaluate the amount of losses likely to be incurred during a period of stress.[1] The last real estate correction had been more than 10 years earlier (in the early 1990s) and had been milder.

In addition, this early 1990s correction was primarily in the commercial real estate market instead of residential real estate markets, and there was not a large subprime home-lending business in the 1990s that could be used for comparison. Also, the rating agencies' models were weighted heavily toward recent years (2003–2005), when losses had been very low because of rapid real estate appreciation. Furthermore, as discussed earlier, the rating agencies were misled by the early "good" results in bank Community Reinvestment Act loan portfolios.

Furthermore, to a certain degree, the rating agencies were misled by the Federal Reserve and Freddie Mac and Fannie Mae, like everyone else. By keeping natural market corrections from occurring, the Federal Reserve policies misled the rating agencies about the risk in the economy. In addition, the Fed was projecting good economic times ahead. The massive understatement of their subprime portfolios by Freddie Mac and Fannie Mae also created a major distortion of the size and intrinsic risk in the overall subprime mortgage market. It is almost certain that had the Fed let natural market corrections occur during the late 1990s and early 2000s and had S&P, Moody's, and Fitch known the size of Freddie and Fannie's portfolios, the ratings on subprime mortgage bonds would have been materially lower. In fact, the rating agencies might have refused to rate a substantial portion of the proposed subprime-backed mortgage bonds, slowing or stopping the housing bubble much earlier and materially reducing the damage from this misinvestment.

The low-income/subprime housing market was driving up prices in the overall residential real estate market. As demand for entry-level houses from subprime buyers increased, the price of entry-level houses rose. The family that already owned an entry-level house could sell the house for a gain and move up to a larger house, raising prices in the next higher tier of the housing market, and so on. The subprime-market demand was raising house prices across the total spectrum of the residential real estate market.

One factor that undoubtedly influenced the rating agencies was the way they were compensated. For years, the agencies had charged the buyers of the bonds for rating the bonds, a system encouraged by S&P, Moody's, and Fitch and that led them to be more conservative because their clients were the bond buyers. When John Moody founded his now-famous firm in 1909, he charged bond investors for the research and ratings. Tragically, in the early 1970s, the SEC, seeking to expand market access to ratings, forced Moody's and the other rating firms to fundamentally change their compensation model in a way that created serious conflicts of interest. Under the new method, the agencies were paid by issuers—bond sellers, not bond buyers. The SEC was influenced by union and government pension plans that did not want to pay the cost of the ratings. Of course, the cost of the ratings was always embedded in relative bond yields, but it was less visible than the direct cost to bond buyers. Under government-mandated "issuer pays" rules, the rating firms were motivated to lower their standards, fearing that issuers who were displeased with their ratings would yank their business and move it to a competitor rating firm.

The change in the compensation system created very different incentives for the rating agencies. Their client was now the seller (issuer) instead of the buyer (investor). This change obviously endangered investors. Of course, the sellers always want the highest rating possible, as a higher rating allows them to borrow at a lower rate. In addition, if the bond instrument is not satisfactorily rated, the seller (financial intermediary) might choose to hold the mortgages in its portfolio and not securitize or sell the bonds at all. If this happened, the rating agency would not earn any revenue. Thus, under the government-mandated "issuer pays" system, the rating agencies had a strong economic incentive to assign the highest possible ratings to bonds. It's equivalent to "grade inflation" in public (government) schools: lower-quality student (and teacher) performance is masked by an artificial cheapening of the grading standard.

How much this principle influenced the performance and objectivity of the Wall Street rating firms would be a speculative guess, but that some impact on ratings was felt seems obvious, given the power of incentives. Critics of the rating agencies who deride free markets and greed have a false focus: the change in the compensation method (from "investor pays" to "issuer pays"), which so eroded the objectivity of the rating firms, was mandated by the SEC and motivated by its favoritism toward union and government pension plans.

As damaging as the incorrect ratings were, this was a problem that investors could have avoided. One reason that BB&T did relatively well during this crisis is that we purchased a much smaller portfolio of S&P/Moody's/Fitch-rated mortgage bonds than many of our competitors. The reason for this decision was that we chose to analyze the bonds ourselves. Our executive team had been managing BB&T during the early 1990s real estate–market shakeout. We remembered how large the losses incurred were during this real estate cycle. When we examined the loan loss expectations and the subordinations that S&P, Moody's, and Fitch were using to justify the high bond ratings, we knew that loan losses in the early 1990s, even in standard mortgage portfolios, had been greater than these estimates. So we chose not to buy these bonds.

One interesting question is how this dislocation in the subprime mortgage bond market created a crisis in the overall capital markets. The private subprime mortgage market, while substantial, represented a small percentage of the total capital markets. (Freddie and Fannie's subprime portfolios were not known at this time and were implicitly guaranteed by the U.S. government.) The fundamental effect on the overall capital markets was the loss of confidence in the rating agencies. The rating agencies had misrated the subprime mortgage bonds so materially that investors in capital markets started to wonder whether the rating agencies had made the same type of mistake in rating other bonds, especially real estate–related bonds, including bonds backed by prime mortgages. The rating system created by S&P, Moody's, and Fitch is the information system used by many investors globally to evaluate risk, especially international firms investing in U.S. markets. If the rating system cannot be relied on, how can market participants estimate risk and either price or value bonds? The lack of confidence in the rating system created major liquidity problems. Even mortgage bonds that were performing could not be sold at almost any price. The only bonds that were trading were U.S. government–backed obligations.

An example of this lack of liquidity was the shutdown of the auction-rate municipal bond market. Auction-rate municipal bonds have interest rates that vary based on daily, weekly, or monthly "auctions" to potential purchasers of the bonds by investment banks that make a market in these bonds. This process creates a variable interest rate that over many periods of time was lower than the interest rate the municipal entity might have had to pay on a fixed-rate basis. The purchaser of the bonds would accept the lower rate because the bonds were perceived to be liquid, as there were other purchasers, including investment banks, that would make a market in the bonds.

The auction-rate municipal bonds were often issued by tax-exempt entities that did not have taxing authority, such as hospitals, universities, airport authorities, bridge authorities, and the like. Usually the bonds were financing long-term projects, such as an addition to a hospital. In retrospect, it would have been less risky for these projects to be financed on a long-term fixed-rate basis, but the auction-rate market was enticing to borrowers who potentially could lower their interest cost and to investors who wanted the apparent liquidity of being able to resell the bonds any time they decided to do so.

Unfortunately, the auction-rate municipal bond market practically stopped functioning as a result of the disruption in the capital market initiated by the subprime mortgage crisis. When the market quit functioning, many investors were not able to sell their bonds back into the market. Investments that they had thought were liquid were no longer liquid. For example, an individual might have purchased a $500,000 bond, expecting to resell it in 60 days to pay his taxes. When the market locked, he could not sell his bond. The actual maturity of the bond could be 10 years. Even though the interest and principal on the bond were not in default and were not expected to default, the individual had a personal liquidity issue.

Other bonds of the same general category created problems for the issuers. In these cases, the issuers were required to refund the bonds and expected to be able to remarket them immediately. However, when the market locked, the issuers (local hospitals, universities, and the like) could not refund the bonds, or if they could do so, they had to pay extremely high interest rates. The high rates threatened the economic viability of municipal entities (hospitals and universities) that were otherwise in a sound financial position.

There are two primary reasons that the auction-rate municipal bond market failed. The first reasons was the lack of confidence in the S&P, Moody's, and Fitch rating system. Some of the bonds had been sold directly based on these agencies' ratings. The second reason was related to bond insurance. Many bonds had been sold based on insurance policies (guarantees) issued primarily by two large municipal bond insurers, Ambac and MBIA. Both Ambac and MBIA had AAA ratings from the rating agencies. However, both companies had insured a huge volume of mortgage-backed bonds. The market quickly understood that the insurance companies were at risk of failure and that their AAA ratings were meaningless.

If you are an investor in Hong Kong who has been relying on S&P, Moody's, or Fitch ratings and/or on Ambac or MBIA insurance, you are suddenly fearful that your bond from the local hospital in "Acme," Virginia, will default. In fact, the hospital may be in excellent financial condition, but it is impossible for you to underwrite this risk with the information available to you. You had purchased the bond based on the ratings and the insurance, and now you are panicky. The only potential bond buyers are deep discounters, so you can sell the bond only at a substantial loss. However, because of the level of uncertainty and fear gripping the market, you choose to sell the bonds at a significant loss, which helps perpetuate the downward cycle.

Liquidity crises are odd because the money has to go somewhere. There is a flight to quality. BB&T was a beneficiary of this process. We were able to attract excess funding at a very low cost because BB&T was perceived to be strong. Because we had plenty of money and because we were able to underwrite the credit risk of the hospital in "Acme," Virginia, without relying on S&P, Moody's, or Fitch or on Ambac or MBIA insurance, BB&T was able to provide $6 billion in loans and letters of credit to help our clients deal with the turmoil in the auction-rate municipal bond market.

The failure of the rating agencies played a major role in the disruption of the financial markets. The fact that S&P, Moody's, and Fitch have an apparent sanction from the SEC (a government agency) contributed to the excessive reliance on these institutions, who themselves were misled by other government agencies, that is, the Fed and Freddie and Fannie. It should be clear by now that at the macro level, the government, through its many agencies, controls the financial markets. *It is impossible to have a systemic failure of the financial markets without mistakes by government policy makers being the primary cause.*

9

Pick-a-Payment Mortgages: A Toxic Product of FDIC Insurance Coverage

ONE OF THE MOST DESTRUCTIVE PRODUCTS IN THE FINANCIAL meltdown was pick-a-payment or negative-amortization mortgages. Pick-a-payment mortgages allow a borrower to pay less than the interest due each month, so the amount owed can increase over the life of the mortgage. This is obviously in contrast with a traditional mortgage product, where the borrower pays some principal each month so that the balance due on the mortgage is systematically paid off.

As an example of a pick-a-payment mortgage, suppose that when a young couple purchases a house, the interest on the loan is $1,000 a month, but the couple is required to pay only $750 a per month. If they make only the minimum payment, after five years, they will owe more on the mortgage than they did when they bought the house (great product!). Pick-a-payment mortgages were popular in high-growth markets, such as southern California, southern Florida, Nevada, and metropolitan Washington, D.C. The theory was to leverage yourself to the maximum—that is, to buy as big a house as possible—and to refinance after five years under the assumption that house prices would continue to grow at more than 10 percent compounded in perpetuity. This was not typically a subprime product; instead, it was often targeted at young home purchasers who were likely to become middle-income or above and who could qualify for traditional mortgage products.

Because of the long history of rising house prices (especially in the lifetime of a young person) caused by the Fed's expansive monetary policy and government housing subsidies, it was easy for people to believe that home prices would rise forever. Conceptually, these home buyers were misled into the belief that housing was an investment instead of consumption.[1]

The most significant cause of problems from the pick-a-payment mortgage was that borrowers were allowed to qualify at the minimum payment amount (in this example, $750 per month) instead of at least at the projected interest cost ($1,000 per month). This strongly encouraged individuals to purchase houses that were too large. This is a double burden in that the maintenance cost, utilities, and other expenses are greater with larger houses. Therefore, these people's housing cost as a percentage of income was set too high.

In addition, most of the mortgages had provisions that the borrower's payment would increase to at least the interest cost ($1,000) if the amount of the loan relative to the value of the house rose above a certain percentage, such as 95 percent. Of course, in a falling house-price environment, this provision magnified the problems. In southern California, for example, as house prices started to fall, the pick-a-payment mortgage borrowers were faced with significant percentage increases in their mortgage payments at the same time that their home values were collapsing. In addition, most of these borrowers had negative equity in their houses, that is, they owed more on the mortgage than the house was worth. They were already overleveraged relative to their income, so they had a double problem.

Default rates for these borrowers (who typically were not subprime borrowers) have turned out to be extremely high. One of the reasons is the economic double leverage just described. The other reason, which may be more significant, is the psychology of the borrowers. Remember, in general, these house purchasers were not primarily buying a home to live in, but rather making a real estate investment. When the investment went bad—that is, when their payments went up and the value of their investment plummeted—they simply walked away. If you buy a house that you can afford and that you want to live in, the value of the house does not change your outlook. You may be somewhat disappointed, but the home is a natural living cost for your family. If you can pay, you will continue to pay because you want to live in the house. Default rates were much higher on pick-a-payment mortgages than would be anticipated based on traditional borrower behavior.

The primary players in the pick-a-payment mortgage market were Golden West (purchased by Wachovia), Washington Mutual, and Countrywide, all of which effectively failed. In order to finance this high-risk lending business, these financial institutions built large bank branching franchises. They paid above-market interest rates on certificates of deposit and used these relatively high-cost CDs to fund this high-risk lending business.

As previously discussed, without FDIC insurance, these high-roller banks could not have funded their operations. The typical depositor did not care how much risk Washington Mutual was taking, because her deposits were insured by the FDIC. Even depositors who were above the technical insurance limit often assumed that their deposits were insured (as they turned out to be in the case of Washington Mutual).

Bondholders were also misled. After all, the FDIC and other government regulators were examining these large financial institutions. Surely, with all their regulatory authority, the government agencies would ensure that these large financial institutions were managed "safely and soundly." In fact, the core mission of the FDIC is to ensure a safe and sound banking system. Government actions, such as FDIC insurance and SEC disclosures, consistently mislead market participants. After all, these government agencies have complete inside information, have tremendous power, and are objective—dream on.

BB&T chose not to offer pick-a-payment mortgages for ethical, not economic, reasons. One of the fundamental commitments in our mission is to help our clients achieve economic success and financial security. One of my mantras with our employees is to never do anything that you believe will be bad for your client, even if you can make a profit on it in the short term, because it will always come back to haunt you in the long term. If you do your best to help your clients, they will be more successful and more loyal, and you will make more profit in the long term. We operate using the "trader principle," that is, we believe in trading value for value—getting better together. Our goal is to create win-win relationships. Treat your clients well and most of them will treat you well. (Avoid those individuals who want to create win-lose or lose-lose relationships.)

We did not see a collapse of the real estate market on the scale of what has occurred. However, we did know that residential real estate could not possibly continue to appreciate at 10 percent per year, particularly given the rapid rise that had already occurred. We knew that encouraging borrowers, especially young people, to buy houses that they could not afford was setting them up for financial disaster five years down the road. We knew that this action was inconsistent with our mission and would not be defensible to ourselves given our beliefs.

At the time, we could have made a substantial profit by offering these mortgages and either holding them or selling them in the secondary market. Of course, the irony is that those institutions (Golden West, Countrywide, WaMu, and others) that held these mortgages ultimately suffered massive economic losses. Even the banks that sold most of their production to others were caught with big inventories in process when the market closed and suffered major losses. One of the powerful aspects of free-market economics is that the vast majority of the time (not always), when you treat your customers poorly, you will be punished. Free markets tend to be just, over the long run.

There were short-term negative economic consequences to BB&T from choosing not to offer pick-a-payment mortgages. Obviously, our quarterly earnings were less than they would have been had we offered these mortgages. There were financial analysts and institutional investors who wanted to know why we were not in this apparently lucrative market segment. When we explained our ethical decision, they looked at us as if we were crazy. There were mortgage originators who were employees of BB&T who left to work for Countrywide over the decision not to offer the pick-a-payment product. After all, this is the easiest mortgage to sell because the potential borrower can qualify for a larger home. This allows the mortgage originator to receive a bigger bonus.

There were clients who asked us for this product. When we explained that this product was not in their long-term self-interest, some clients accepted our advice and bought a smaller house financed with a traditional mortgage. They are pleased now. Some clients did not take our advice. They left us and went to Countrywide and bought a bigger house. Most of these ex-clients are not so pleased. By the way, how sorry should you feel for these individuals who consciously took this leverage risk? How good do you feel about the government programs, which you are paying for, to bail out these home speculators? Do you think they would have sent you a check if the speculation had worked out?

By the way, I learned an interesting lesson about the fundamental difference between institutional shareholders and high-net-worth individual shareholders through this process. Unfortunately, many institutional shareholders are short-term-oriented and care little about principles. Their incentive systems drive them toward short-term investment. The worst institutional shareholders are state pension plans (especially CalPERS), which confuse the political correct notion of the day with meaningful principled action. The best shareholders are older high-net-worth individuals who have earned their money by running an operating business. They have a longer-term perspective, appreciate the role of principles, and have business wisdom. If you manage a business, attract all the self-made, high-net-worth individual shareholders you can.

How Freddie and Fannie Grew to Dominate the Home Mortgage Lending Business

AN INTERESTING QUESTION IS, HOW DID FREDDIE AND FANNIE come to dominate the home mortgage lending business? This government control of house finance is relatively recent and highly unusual. The U. S. home lending market is one of the most statist markets in the world, far more so than markets in western European semi-socialist economies. This is an important story about the long-term and often unintended consequences of government policy decisions. There are some important lessons for today.

When we bought our first home in 1975, my wife and I went to the local savings and loan association to finance the purchase. We put 20 percent down (an 80 percent loan/value mortgage) and got an 8 percent, 30-year fixed-rate mortgage. At that time, the vast majority of home mortgages were financed by local savings and loans (S&Ls). The S&L industry had been the primary source of financing for housing for almost 50 years (1925–1975). The industry had experienced low loan loss ratios over that period. One of the primary reasons is that they held the loans they made on their own books;

therefore, when they made a mortgage, its quality was important to them. Also, they were local institutions and understood the local real estate market.

The S&L industry was systematically destroyed by government policy over the next quarter century. By 1999, there were virtually no S&Ls left in the United States. Indeed, most had failed by 1989 to 1991. The destruction of the industry started with President Lyndon Baines Johnson in the 1960s. Johnson wanted to conduct the Vietnam War and simultaneously create the Great Society. He did not want to tax people because taxes were unpopular. So the Federal Reserve agreed to print money (that is, expand the money supply) to accommodate this program (does this sound like Bush and Obama?). His successor presidents followed with a similar lack of self-discipline, creating an increasingly inflationary economic environment in the 1970s that was clearly economically destructive. (Nixon decoupled the dollar from gold in 1971, making this money-printing spree possible.) Finally, in the early 1980s, the Fed realized that inflation was out of control and dramatically raised interest rates, with the prime rate peaking at 21 percent in 1981.

The S&Ls had been making home mortgages at fixed interest rates for many years. Suddenly their cost of funding rose dramatically. Remember, S&Ls borrow short with certificates of deposit and make long-term loans. They were paying 15 percent or more on certificates of deposit and earning 8 percent on their outstanding loans. At the same time, the economy entered a brutal economic correction, raising loan default rates. Many S&Ls failed.

Unfortunately, the industry survivors then got some help from their regulator, the Federal Savings and Loan Insurance Corporation, or FSLIC (now part of the Federal Deposit Insurance Corporation [FDIC]). Their regulator required them to hedge their home mortgage portfolio against rising interest rates at the peak of the interest-rate cycle. Unfortunately, at the time, it was not practical to hedge home mortgages because the mortgages had no prepayment penalties. When interest rates started to fall, borrowers refinanced their mortgages (without paying penalties), and the S&Ls took massive losses on their hedge positions.

The regulators also encouraged S&Ls to merge, with stronger companies taking over weaker thrifts. Unfortunately, these weaker institutions were often so weak (including having massive unanticipated hedge losses) that they ultimately undermined the financial position of the stronger companies.

In addition, the regulators encouraged the S&Ls to enter the commercial real estate lending business, making shopping center, office building, hotel, and similar loans.[1] The theory was that it was not possible to make a satisfactory return in the home mortgage business. Unfortunately, the thrifts had no lending expertise in commercial real estate finance, which is a much more sophisticated lending business than home mortgages. Their lending activity contributed to a massive overinvestment in commercial real estate, which led to an economic correction in the early 1990s, resulting in the failure of many more thrifts. The taxpayers lost several hundred billion dollars to cover the S&L failures. Part of the losses was passed on to the banking industry through higher FDIC insurance premiums for banks that had acquired S&Ls.

While Fannie Mae (launched in 1938) and Freddie Mac (launched in 1970) had been around for years, they played a secondary role in the home mortgage business until the failure of the thrift industry. As the thrifts failed, Fannie and Freddie filled the gap and became the dominant players in the prime (low-risk) home mortgage market. An interesting issue is why other non-S&L private banks did not take over the prime mortgage business as the S&Ls exited. For example, BB&T had been in the home mortgage business, including both issuing variable-rate mortgages and originating mortgages for sale to life insurance companies, for many years. Because of our variable-interest-rate loans to businesses, we could have managed the interest-rate risk effectively and filled the gap left by the S&Ls.

However, we could not compete with the federal government. Fannie and Freddie had a government guarantee on their debt. For this reason, they could effectively leverage 50 to 1 (and ultimately 1,000 to 1) without being forced to pay a higher bond yield to creditors. Fannie and Freddie had the lowest cost of capital in the financial industry. Therefore, they drove all other financial intermediaries (BB&T, other banks, and life insurance companies) out of the prime home mortgage market.

BB&T's story is typical. Over time, our life insurance mortgage financing outlets closed, as they could not compete with the government. We started sending a bigger and bigger percentage of our home originations to Freddie and Fannie and kept the servicing (that is, the client relationship). Almost all our "qualified" mortgages went to Freddie and Fannie. (Qualified loans are prime mortgages in a size range that is acceptable to the government-sponsored enterprises [GSEs]). We did portfolio (hold on our books) adjustable-rate mortgages and large mortgages that did not meet Freddie and Fannie's guidelines.

I do not have any empathy for Golden West, but it is interesting to ask why Golden West chose to enter the pick-a-payment (negative-amortization) home mortgage business. The answer is that it could not compete with Freddie and Fannie in the prime mortgage business. It had to design a unique product that would allow it to stay in business. Without Freddie and Fannie, the pick-a-payment mortgage might never have been invented. Pick-a-payment mortgages are practically nonexistent outside the United States.

In fact, four of the largest "failures" in the financial crisis were companies with a thrift history—Countrywide, Washington Mutual, IndyMac, and Golden West (Wachovia). These companies originated a large percentage of high-risk mortgages, which they either portfolioed (pick-a-payment), sold to Freddie and Fannie (Alt-A/subprime), or securitized and sold in the secondary market (subprime). In every case, their high-risk lending activity was at least partially driven by their inability to compete directly with Freddie and Fannie. I am certain that without this secondary consequence of the government's dominance of the prime home lending market, the private high-risk mortgage market would have been dramatically smaller.

While BB&T was far more conservative than most banks, we made more higher-risk mortgages than we would have made had we been able to profitably portfolio the prime mortgages that were being sold to Freddie and Fannie. This was a much bigger issue for Washington Mutual, Golden West, and the others because they did not have the commercial and industrial lending expertise that BB&T had and were effectively forced to focus much of their lending activity on the home mortgage business. Freddie and Fannie, both directly and indirectly, were the primary drivers in the high-risk home mortgage lending business.

The managements of Freddie and Fannie were happy to dominate the prime home mortgage business, generating excellent financial returns for their shareholders and outstanding compensation for the executives, largely driven by the massive subsidy from the taxpayers based on the implied U.S. government guarantee of their multi-trillion-dollar obligations.

Unfortunately for them (and the economy), Freddie and Fannie got caught up in Sarbanes-Oxley accounting issues over derivatives, as described earlier. Their extraordinarily friendly relationship with Congress deteriorated, and they were put under severe pressure to meet Bill Clinton's affordable-housing/subprime lending goals by congressmen and senators like Barney Frank and Chris Dodd. They then plunged full tilt into the subprime lending business.

Many of their traditional originators, like BB&T, were not interested in or prepared to produce large volumes of high-risk mortgages. Freddie and Fannie chose to expand their relationships with those originators that were already at least partially in the subprime business, such as Countrywide and Washington Mutual, and encourage their traditional originators to develop subprime expertise.

They also made it significantly easier for nontraditional mortgage brokers to bypass the mortgage consolidators and sell loans directly to the GSEs. This was an earnings-driven strategy by Freddie and Fannie, as they wanted to capture the consolidators' profit. It was a completely off-mission concept, as Freddie and Fannie had originally been created to support the mortgage industry's loan origination business (primarily S&Ls), not to bypass the industry. This decision turned into a significant quality control problem for Freddie and Fannie, as the bank industry consolidators had played an important role in managing quality, especially in reducing fraud.

To meet the affordable-housing loan goals established by Congress, the GSEs opened the floodgates by constantly lowering standards and working with their friends at Countrywide, Washington Mutual, and the others to drive greater subprime volume by constantly taking more and more risk.

This largely completed the change from the "originate and hold" model to the "originate and sell" model. Under the originate and hold model, a financial institution, such as a traditional savings and loan, would make a loan to finance a house and hold the loan on its own books. If the loan went bad at some point during its 30-year life, the S&L would take the loss. Under this model, the financial institution making the loan cares a great deal about the credit risk. The lender will demand a reasonable down payment (typically 20 percent) and will carefully examine the borrower's ability to repay. Also, the bank will try to be certain that the borrower's debt service as a percentage of income is manageable.

In the originate and sell model, once an originator sells a mortgage to a third party, it no longer cares about the risk. While the originate and sell model can work, it creates a risky incentive system. The originator is not concerned about the long-term risk of the loan's defaulting. All it wants to do is to get the loan sold. This substantially increases the probability of "fudging" and then fraud.

For example, a couple approaches a mortgage broker about buying a house. The borrowers claim to have earned $70,000 last year when they actually earned $60,000. The mortgage loan originator encourages the borrowers to claim that they made $75,000. This declared higher income will allow the borrowers to purchase a larger home. After all, house prices always appreciate—housing is a great investment. You want to buy as big a home as possible and leverage yourself as much as possible. Of course, the originator will receive more personal compensation from the larger loan.

At the peak of the boom, many originators dropped verification of borrowers' income, and a number of mortgage purchasers (including the GSEs) allowed the lack of verification.

Freddie and Fannie, with their debt guaranteed, effectively created the originate and sell model, although there were many private mortgage market participants. The model worked reasonably well when most of the originators were from established firms such as commercial banks. As Freddie and Fannie moved up the risk scale, however, they loosened their underwriting standards to meet the affordable-housing (that is, subprime) goals established by Congress. The whole origination market relaxed its standards to compete with Freddie and Fannie. Driven by Freddie and Fannie, the private originators created a competitive race to the bottom as the bubble continued (funded by the Federal Reserve) and it appeared that no matter how low the standards, home loans would not default.

Of course, Standard & Poor's (S&P), Moody's, and Fitch played a major role in this process. They dramatically overrated bonds backed by high-risk mortgages. Their special government sanction (via the SEC) gave them credibility. They were also misled by the artificial economic environment created by the Federal Reserve. In addition, as discussed earlier, they had a significant economic incentive to rate the bonds as highly as possible to increase their revenues.

This is where the investment banks (Goldman Sachs, Morgan Stanley, Bear Stearns, Merrill Lynch, and Lehman Brothers) magnified the misallocation of credit to the housing market. They created a series of financial "innovations" (collateralized debt obligations [CDOs], derivatives, swaps, and others, which I discuss later) that leveraged an already overleveraged product.

The explanation typically given for these ultimately very bad decisions by investment bankers is greed. However, there was plenty of greed on Wall Street before the bubble. In fact, in my almost 40-year career in banking, there has always been greed on Wall Street. There was no more or less greed on Wall Street during the bubble. Greed is a constant in capital markets, as is fear. If greed created the financial crisis, it also created the good times. Sometimes greed results in positive outcomes. Sometimes it results in negative outcomes.

In fact, there are two conflicting definitions of greed. The modern liberal definition, which is used by the media, is that greed is the aggressive pursuit of something unearned (especially money), typically using devious tactics. Of course, greed has been defined as "bad" using this concept.

However, the proper definition of greed is the aggressive pursuit of anything. You can be greedy for justice or greedy for truth. When you use the proper definition, what you are greedy for matters.

When greed is defined as the energetic and ethical pursuit of wealth, it is good, because it motivates individuals to be creative and take risk. Maybe in 2012 one of the problems America is facing as it yearns to rediscover and recapture a robust, vibrant, and entrepreneurial economy is the lack of greed (and the lack of respect for it). Individuals do not want to pursue creating more wealth; they just want to protect what they already own.

Investment bankers unquestionably made irrational decisions based on pragmatic, short-term thinking. This type of thinking is often depicted as a lack of integrity, evasion, and arrogance. Those who made these mistakes should have been fired and their companies allowed to fail. Most Americans were right if they decried corporate bailouts as unjust, but not if they did so out of a hatred for corporations, capitalism, and honest moneymaking. To the degree that "crony capitalism" protected these firms and individuals and kept justice from happening, we will have a lower standard of living in the long term. It's not capitalism but cronyism that should be removed from the mix. When politics mixes with business, whether as subsidization or regulation, the inevitable by-product isn't merely economic disarray and decay, but moral corruption. The debacle of 2007–2009 suggests the potential virtue of an unmixed economy.

On the other hand, I believe that firms of all levels were significantly misled by government policy, particularly the fundamental errors of the Federal Reserve and its unwillingness to let markets correct and by the massive effect on markets created by Freddie and Fannie's gigantic affordable-housing loan program. Yes, many investment bankers "sinned" in the past decade, but the U.S. government created the context that made these errors possible and has forced the virtuous to pay for these errors.

11

Fair-Value Accounting and Wealth Destruction

THE MOST UNNECESSARY CAUSE OF THE FINANCIAL CRISIS WAS FAIR-value accounting. Fair-value accounting, as currently interpreted, had been enacted only two years before the financial crisis. There have been accounting systems for at least 5,000 years (since the Egyptians). Therefore, the overwhelming burden of proof is on those who defend fair-value accounting. The only serious previous experiment with fair-value accounting was in the 1930s. It was abandoned at that time because Roosevelt believed that it was contributing to the Great Depression.

Fair-value accounting sounds reasonable on the surface. The idea is to mark all assets and liabilities to market at the end of a reporting period, typically at the end of each quarter. In fact, fair-value accounting is the continuation of a long-term trend, started in the 1970s, of trying to deal with the impact of inflation (caused by the Federal Reserve) on a company's income statement and balance sheet.

There are a multitude of problems with fair-value accounting. Conceptually, the major issue is that adjusting a business's income statement based on random fluctuations in its balance sheet (that is, the value of its assets and liabilities) distorts operating earnings and provides misleading and confusing information about the underlying earnings power of the business. This distortion is particularly destructive when markets are not fully clearing because of external disturbances. (Clearing means achieving a specific market price based on supply and demand factors.) In a chaotic environment, fair-value accounting violates both foundational economic concepts and the fundamental principles on which accounting systems are based. As the financial crisis heightened, the ambiguity created by government policy decisions created an environment in which markets had great difficulty clearing. The Fed saved Citigroup and let Wachovia fail. The Fed saved Bear Stearns and Goldman Sachs and let Lehman fail. Markets cannot rationally integrate this kind of government-driven uncertainty.

One of the basic requirements of the law of supply and demand is that there must be a willing buyer and a willing seller. During the chaos created by the random type of government policies just described, this basic condition did not exist. As a simple example, suppose my home is on the market for $600,000. With the huge uncertainty created by government decision makers during the financial crisis, the few buyers that are out there are looking for a fantastic deal and will pay only $300,000 for my house. I will not sell my home for $300,000. I do not owe anything on the home, and I can easily afford to wait until the market calms down. However, under fair-value accounting, my house would be valued at $300,000, and if I were a bank, I would take a $300,000 loss on the house through my income statement. This outcome is inconsistent with the law of supply and demand. Under this economic law, there must be a willing buyer and a willing seller for a market price to be established. The fact that Tom Brown had to sell his house for $300,000 because he was in severe distress does not mean that I have to or will sell my house for this price.

One of the basic principles underlying accounting models is that businesses will be valued as going concerns. In other words, the assumption is that the business will continue to operate. Fair-value accounting is inconsistent with this concept, because it effectively assumes that the business's assets are being liquidated under stress.

Fair-value accounting was a major cause of the liquidity problems in capital markets. Public companies would not purchase economically valuable assets because of the accounting risk. I personally was involved in decisions where poor economic decisions were forced on us by accounting policy.

As an example, suppose that a bond with a $100 million face value is for sale in the market. This bond is backed by residential mortgages. Some of these mortgages are in default, and some more are projected to be going to default. Based on a very careful and conservative analysis of the defaulting mortgages that back the bond, the $100 million bond should be valued at $80 million. However, because of both the economic conditions and the unnecessary uncertainty created by unpredictable government policies, the potential buyers want an extremely high return and will purchase the bond only if they can get it for $50 million. At this "market price," under fair-value accounting, the bank will have to take a $50 million loss, even though it can afford to hold the bond until the market stabilizes. Remember, banks are leveraged 10 to 1. If the bank takes a $50 million loss, its capital will be reduced by $50 million and its lending capacity by $500 million ($50 million × 10 = $500 million). This impact occurs even though the bank has not sold the bond and has plenty of funding to continue to hold the bond. (Losses in value on some types of bonds do not affect the bank's income statement in the short term, but they do affect the capital accounts on the balance sheet.)

Using an economic analysis, the bank should have taken a $20 million loss ($100 million less $80 million). This would have reduced the bank's lending capacity by $200 million ($20 million × 10 = $200 million) instead of $500 million. In other words, $300 million of the destruction in lending capacity (liquidity) was created by the accounting system, not by economic reality. Fair-value accounting became a driver in the downward spiral of the capital markets. Only after the Financial Accounting Standards Board (FASB), the accounting ruling body, "reinterpreted" fair-value accounting (in April 2009) did the spiral down in the economy come to a halt.[1]

Let me share a personal experience with you. BB&T had excess liquidity as a result of the flight to quality. We were analyzing these bonds, and we knew that their economic value was $80 million. Why didn't we become a buyer of the bonds? Why didn't other public companies with excess liquidity start buying them? In fact, if we had all started buying, the bidding process would have driven the price back to at least close to the economic value of the bonds of $80 million. The reason we did not buy the bonds was because we could not take the accounting risk, even though an excellent economic transaction was available. How could we know what random and destructive policy actions government policy makers would take next? We could not know what disruptive and destructive decisions the Fed and the Treasury might execute. At the end of the next quarter, the only buyers might be demanding an even bigger discount, and we could have to take a fair-value loss that would affect our capital and our lending capacity, even though the bonds were economically worth more than we paid for them.

Accounting systems should never drive economic activity. They should reflect it. Fair-value accounting significantly contributed to the collapse of liquidity in capital markets (in 2007–2009). It is no coincidence that things got worse when it was first adopted and began to clear up when it was abandoned.

It has been argued that fair-value accounting was misinterpreted and that the set of impacts just described should not have happened. This argument implied that some accountants overreacted in their interpretation of fair value. In fact, the reinterpretation by FASB that I described earlier that helped stop the market meltdown was not presented as a change, but rather as simply clarifying the existing rules. This seems like a rationalization based on the incredible complexity of the fair-value interpretations. If these rules were subject to widespread misinterpretation, they were irrational rules by definition. Also, the situation highlights the destructive impact of Sarbanes-Oxley. Given the risk imposed on accounting firms by Sarbanes-Oxley, it is not surprising that they were overly conservative in their interpretation of the extremely complex fair-value accounting rules. Fundamentally, accountants cannot get into trouble for being too conservative, but they are at great risk if they use rational judgment. To the degree that Sarbanes-Oxley caused an overzealous interpretation of fair-value accounting, it helped destroy hundreds of billions of dollars of wealth and millions of jobs.

There are a number of other significant problems with fair-value accounting. Proper finance theory would value assets based on a rational projection of future cash flows from those assets, not liquidation value under stress. In addition, under current accounting rules, some assets and liabilities are subject to fair-value accounting and others are not. How do you interpret a balance sheet when various asset and liability categories are subject to completely different valuation techniques?

An example of the absurdity of fair-value accounting is the treatment of corporate debt. As the financial crisis unfolded, the market became concerned about the financial position of Lehman Brothers (before the company failed). Because the market was concerned about Lehman, the value of its outstanding bond indebtedness declined. For example, Lehman had a $10 million bond that it was required to pay over 10 years. The bondholders were worried about Lehman's ability to pay, so they decided to sell the bond. However, potential purchasers were also worried about Lehman's financial health and therefore were willing to pay only $5 million for the bond that had a face value of $10 million. Under the theory justifying fair-value accounting, Lehman could have purchased the bond for $5 million and simultaneously erased a $10 million debt. Fair-value accounting would have allowed Lehman to record a $5 million profit from the fact that the value of its debt had fallen from $10 million to $5 million. In fact, two quarters before it failed, Lehman recorded a major gain/profit from the declining value of its debt, even though it did not actually repurchase any of its debt.

Of course, this accounting treatment is extremely misleading. If Lehman had been in a cash position that would have allowed it to repurchase its debt, the bonds would not have been discounted so significantly. Effectively, the company's financial deterioration resulted in increased earnings. Obviously, this is misleading to investors by overstating both earnings and the company's capital position through increasing retained earnings.

Bill Isaac, chairman of the FDIC during the financial crisis of the early 1980s, has stated on numerous occasions that the U.S. financial system would have failed in the 1980s if fair-value accounting had been utilized at that time. In September 2008, a few days after Lehman failed, he wrote: "If we had followed today's approach during the 1980's, we would have nationalized all of the major banks in the country and thousands of additional banks and thrifts would have failed. I have little doubt that the country would have gone from a serious recession into a depression."[2] Isaac has vigorously opposed fair-value accounting for many years. I also believe that if fair-value accounting had been in place during the recession of the early 1990s, the U.S. financial system would have collapsed. The rapid deterioration in commercial real estate markets during this period would have resulted in massive losses "on paper" for financial institutions. Many of the fair-value losses never occurred in reality; in other words, the asset values rose rapidly after the correction.

The U.S. economy is fortunate that fair-value accounting was only partially in place during the peak of the financial crisis. If fair-value accounting had been fully implemented and applied to all businesses in the United States on December 31, 2008, at least 90 percent of all public companies would have reported substantial operating losses and massive deterioration of their capital positions. Remember, at year-end 2008, there was very limited liquidity in practically all markets. Imagine the liquidation value of manufacturing plants, trucks, equipment, software, commercial real estate, and other assets. Global stock markets would have crashed and made the 1930s look like good times. The lack of liquidity and the amount of fear would have destroyed asset values.

Many conservatives support fair-value accounting because it is supposed to be more conservative. In the first place, it is not more conservative. The leveraging down effect we have been discussing occurred because of the timing of the implementation of fair-value accounting, which was almost simultaneous with the economic correction. On the other hand, in good times, fair-value accounting could easily lead to significantly overly optimistic valuation of assets. Think about what high profits residential real estate developers would have reported in 2005 if their assets had been marked to market in a rapidly rising real estate market.

Fair-value accounting simply magnifies swings in economic activity, thereby overreporting earnings in good times and exaggerating losses in a difficult economic environment. At a more fundamental level, however, the goal of the accounting system should not be to be conservative. The goal of the accounting system should be to reflect economic reality. Understating earnings and undervaluing assets leads to as many bad decisions as overstating earnings and overvaluing assets. Market participants need objective information in order to make decisions.

The general movement to fair-value accounting has created an environment leading to both fraud and honest mistakes by management. Fair-value accounting requires numerous estimates of future economic events and leaves a great deal of room for honest errors and intentional misjudgments. The reason this has occurred is that simultaneously with trends toward fair-value accounting, there has been a conscious movement, driven by the SEC, from principles-based accounting to rules-based accounting.

In principles-based accounting, the accounting guidelines provide broad guidance about the concepts and the purposes to be achieved. Under rules-based accounting, it is the technical compliance with the rules that matters, not adherence to the underlying principles. This sets up an environment in which it is easy to "game the system" because the accountants and the regulators cannot possibly cover every conceivable set of circumstances.

While I am clear that there was fraud at Enron, technically the fraud case was weak. The "smart" finance staff at Enron had figured out the rules and played at the margin within the rules. In the end, they violated enough rules to get them in trouble, but they were violating the principles underlying the rules much earlier. Enron violated the spirit of the law well before it ever violated the letter of the law—which means that it violated principles-based accounting long before it violated rules-based accounting, but since the latter approach dominated the accounting profession, Enron's sleight of hand could persist. Since Enron's outside accounting firm, Arthur Andersen, was focused on rule checking, it was not focused on enforcing the principles. Even the internal auditors were focused on the rules, not the principles. This situation allows fraud to last longer and be harder to identify than if more fundamental questions are being asked.

This rules-based system is also a terror for honest CEOs. The issue is not whether your company's accounting system is honest and transparent in principle, but whether all the rules are being followed. Since the rules are extraordinarily complex, it is impossible for a CEO to know whether the accounting reports are technically correct. A great deal of energy is spent on technical rules compliance, often at the expense of a rational economic evaluation or full disclosure of more important considerations.

The movement toward fair-value accounting has led to far more complex financial statements that are subject to greater error and are far more difficult to understand. A clear example is the accounting for mortgage servicing rights. (This is a technical discussion; you do not need to fully follow it, but it makes concrete the nature of unnecessary accounting complexity.) For many years, when a bank made a mortgage loan, the interest income and fees would be earned as they were paid, that is, on a cash basis. There was some gaming of this system by S&Ls in the late 1980s. They would charge high front-end fees, which would increase current earnings. The mortgage would then have a lower interest rate, reducing future earnings. Instead of defining this obviously deceptive strategy as an accounting principle violation, which it was, the accounting ruling body, under the guidance of the SEC, developed a complex set of rules for allocation of fees, production expense, and other such elements. Maintaining this system created a major meaningless cost for the financial industry and created the potential for misleading data.

The next accounting decision on mortgage servicing rights was more profound. The vast majority of banks had not gamed the system and were reporting fees, interest income, and expenses on a cash basis. If a loan was repaid because a borrower refinanced his mortgage, the related cash flows were no longer affecting income or expenses, and the accounting system was simply reporting economic reality. However, in the context of "mark to market" and "fair value," the accountants, under the direction of the SEC, decided to abandon this reliable and simple system. They decided that the value of the income stream from the mortgage loan needed to be divided into two components. One component is the interest income related to the risk-adjusted yield on the loan. The other component is the mortgage servicing right. This is the value that the bank receives for collecting the interest payments, insurance, and escrow payments from the borrower. For example, on a loan with a 6.25 percent interest rate, 6 percent might be attributed to interest income and 0.25 percent valued as a servicing fee. The accountants then required that the bank value the servicing fee on the front end based on the expected life of the mortgage, that is, on the net expected cash flow over the whole duration of the loan. The value of this mortgage servicing right has to be taken into income when the loan is made. (Are you confused? Does this sound more complex than the cash basis system? Wait; it gets worse.)

In order to make this valuation, the bank has to determine the market interest rate so that it can separate the servicing fee from the interest income. It has to estimate the expenses to be incurred over the life of the loan. The most difficult task is determining the probability of early prepayment. Because home mortgage loans do not have prepayment penalties, borrowers often prepay in advance of a loan's maturity. They may move to another location or buy a bigger house. However, the primary driver of large-scale early prepayments is falling mortgage loan interest rates, which give borrowers incentives to refinance their mortgages to get lower mortgage payments. In determining this income amount, the bank must estimate (guess) all these factors. The one thing that is certain is that the estimate will be wrong. Mortgage interest rates are constantly changing. Changes in mortgage interest rates drive estimated prepayment speeds.

After the bank makes all these estimates (guesses), it records both some income and an asset called mortgage servicing rights. This asset is the theoretical value of the income the bank has earned from creating this future income stream. At the end of each accounting period (typically quarterly), the bank will have to revalue its mortgage servicing rights asset, and the changes in the value of the mortgage servicing rights become income or expense for the financial company. These swings in income and expenses can be very large. If mortgage rates fall rapidly, the prepayment speeds accelerate, as it is anticipated that more borrowers will refinance their mortgages at the lower rates. This substantially reduces the value of the mortgage servicing rights asset and can materially reduce the bank's earnings. When mortgage rates rise, the prepayment speed slows (that is, fewer borrowers refinance their mortgages), the value of the mortgage servicing rights asset increases, and the bank's earnings increase.

These wild swings in earnings may occur even though there is no change in the actual cash flow (income) from the bank's total mortgage portfolio. The valuation is based on anticipated prepayments, not actual prepayments. As an example, BB&T tends to make as many or more new loans during a refinancing period (often to the same borrowers). The borrower refinances her mortgage with BB&T. She gets a lower interest rate, but the servicing fee does not change. However, BB&T will have already taken an accounting loss on the projected servicing income on the refinanced mortgage, even though the cash flow to BB&T has not changed at all, as the value of the mortgage servicing right is based on anticipated (not actual) prepayments.

Because these fluctuations in the value of the mortgage servicing rights can have a significant impact on quarterly earnings, because investors like stable earnings, and because management needs to understand what earnings really are, banks spend hundreds of millions of dollars hedging mortgage servicing rights. Hedging mortgage servicing rights is not easy because there is no mortgage servicing rights market. Therefore, other financial instruments must be used. Since these instruments are not completely aligned with the changes in the value of mortgage servicing rights, complex computer models and very bright individuals must be employed. Remember, this is to hedge an accounting fiction. This is not hedging a real economic risk for banks that both originate and service mortgages. The very bright individuals who develop and manage this extraordinarily complex accounting system could be put to far more productive uses. In China, they would probably be figuring out how to reduce the cost and improve the quality of the next generation of electronic technology. In the United States, they are hedging an accounting risk, which is completely nonproductive activity. By the way, accounting for mortgage servicing rights is far more complex than I have described. (Can you believe it?)

The complexity of the system sets up an accounting fraud and/or accuracy risk. I have little empathy for Freddie and Fannie, as is probably clear from previous comments. However, I do empathize with their accounting issues. Given the scale and complexity of their mortgage business and the related derivative accounting, it is not surprising that their financial information was incorrect, that is, inconsistent with the accounting rules. Of course, even when their reporting is consistent with the accounting values, it does not reflect economic reality. I once had a highly ranked partner at one of the biggest accounting firms tell me that no more than 10 people understood all the interconnections among mortgage servicing rights, mortgage origination income, and derivatives valuation. I think he exaggerated. I do not think anyone understood. They had to make it up on the fly. This is why it took years for Freddie and Fannie to release "accurate" accounting information.

The existence of these complex accounting rules creates the need for complex derivative instruments and the related derivatives markets, which are enticing opportunities for speculators. Also, it tempts bank management to take additional risk. Sometimes financial company managers overhedge their mortgage servicing rights risk because they are certain about the direction of interest rates. The very existence of this need to hedge an accounting entry creates an opportunity and significant incentive to speculate.

There is also an interesting accounting anomaly. When a bank makes a mortgage loan, it fundamentally has two options. It can sell the mortgage (and keep or not keep the right to service the mortgage), typically to Freddie or Fannie. The other option is to retain the mortgage on its books and fund it with deposits. The accounting system treats these fundamentally similar economic decisions materially differently. If the bank sells the mortgage, it records a substantially larger profit on the front end. If it holds the mortgage, its front-end profit will be less.

Unfortunately, this difference in accounting affects financial decisions. Because it is extremely difficult to compete with Freddie and Fannie (as the government guarantees their liabilities), a large portion of BB&T's mortgage originations business was sold to Freddie and Fannie. We retained the servicing to ensure a high level of customer satisfaction. There were times when, from an interest-rate risk and loan demand perspective, we would have liked to hold the loans in our own portfolio. However, the front-end accounting cost was so large that we sometimes kept selling the mortgages even though we did not think it was an economic profit-maximizing strategy. You may say that we were maximizing short-term profit. However, the income from holding mortgages would be spread over seven or eight years rather than being recognized in the current quarter. It is impossible to explain this difference to even sophisticated investors because it does not make sense.

Why did an accounting system that treats such similar transactions so differently and creates a strong incentive for banks to securitize instead of portfolio (hold on its books) home mortgages get created? Was this decision based on deep arguments about the relationship of accounting to economic value? Unfortunately, while there may have been some intellectual discussion, the fundamental motivation for this accounting change was politics, not economic theory.

The primary force behind the accounting change was Countrywide (the big subprime leader that was Freddie and Fannie's close partner, and that ultimately failed). At the time, Countrywide, while it had a small deposit base, was mainly a mortgage broker. It primarily originated mortgages for sale instead of putting the mortgages on its own balance sheet. The change in the accounting system provided a very material increase in current earnings for Countrywide, especially in relation to bank competitors that were portfolioing a meaningful part of their home loan production. In fact, this change created a "permanent" improvement in Countrywide's earnings as long as production continued to increase, as the "new" accounting model constantly pulled earnings forward.

It also created a major incentive for Countrywide to always increase its mortgage production, even if it had to take more risk. If Countrywide had slowed its production, the accounting system would effectively have double-counted negatively on earnings. Countrywide was supported in its efforts by Freddie Mac and Fannie Mae, who realized that the new model would be a major incentive (human action) for banks to securitize and sell their mortgage production to the two government-sponsored enterprises (GSEs) instead of holding the mortgages on the bank's books. This shift would increase Freddie and Fannie's market share and raise their earnings.

Both Countrywide and Freddie and Fannie were very politically connected. They asked their congressional supporters to put pressure on the SEC and FASB (the accounting rule-making body) to make these accounting changes. The changes were in the context of the general movement toward fair-value accounting, so it was easy for FASB to support and/or rationalize the changes.

There is a similar politicized story with regard to expensing stock options. For many years, stock options were not expensed, for good reasons. However, when a number of CEOs started making large gains on their stock options, a "politically correct" movement to have options expensed was created. The goal of the movement was to reduce the amount of stock options awarded to executives by using the accounting system to effectively increase the accounting cost of options. This movement was driven by a politically based populist backlash against highly compensated CEOs, and was executed by union pension plans and government employee pension plans through the political process and with support from academicians with a leftist viewpoint.

Why had stock options not been expensed for so many years? The simple answer is that they should not be expensed. Stock options are the right to purchase stock in a corporation at a future date at today's price. They have an economic value because it is expected and/or hoped that the stock price will increase over time. Of course, with the decline in the stock market, many stock options have turned out to be worthless. The reason that stock options were not expensed is that there is never a cash outflow from the business. In fact, when the stock options are exercised, there is a cash inflow to the corporation. The basis of the accounting model was designed to deal with cash flows into and out of a business, as in the end, the only thing you can spend is cash. Items that represented current or future cash outflows were expensed.

There have been many adjustments over time to deal with timing issues, such as those involving capital expenditures and debt repayments. However, as a general principle, expenses have always represented current or expected cash outflows. There is never a cash outflow from stock options. The only cash flow from stock options is an inflow. Stock options are the only activity of a business that is expensed that is a cash inflow and not a cash outflow. Despite all the theoretical discussion, expensing stock options is a violation of a fundamental premise underlying the accounting system. This is why stock options were not expensed until intense political pressure was brought on the SEC and FASB.

It is certainly correct that the issuance of stock options is of material concern to shareholders. It is appropriate for shareholders to have complete and comprehensive disclosure of stock options because of the potential impact of stock options on their share of the business's future earnings. However, this is because stock options are a transfer of ownership interest, not because the options are a business expense. To understand this concept, suppose the owner of a small business decided to give 50 percent of his business to his daughter. Certainly, there would be a major change in ownership, and the business owner would now be entitled to only 50 percent of the future earnings of the business, instead of the 100 percent he was previously receiving. However, the business itself would not have incurred any expense. There would not be a cash outflow from the business now or in the future.

Stock options represent the same type of ownership transfer. If stock options are large, they can have a material impact on the future distribution of earnings, just as issuing additional stock affects the distribution of earnings. Shareholders should be concerned about stock options and need to demand that options provide incentives that improve future performance. However, options are not cash outflows for a business and should not be expensed.

It is interesting that some investors argued for expensing stock options in order to be conservative. As noted before, the purpose of an accounting system is to reflect economic reality. Understating earnings is just as misleading as overstating earnings. Being conservative in accounting is no more justified than being liberal. The goal is economic reality. The expensing of stock options is another example of the politicizing of generally accepted accounting principles (GAAP) accounting.

Even with 40 years' experience in banking, I cannot fully understand the financial statements of Bank of America. I do not believe that the CEO of Bank of America, sophisticated financial analysts, institutional investors, or regulators can fully understand the financial statements of B of A. B of A has some complex businesses, but the accounting system is far more complex than its businesses. This complexity is not B of A's fault. It is the fault of the SEC and FASB, which make the accounting rules. Also, it is partially the fault of trial lawyers and government pension funds (like CalPERS) that have demanded more and more disclosure at the expense of integration and essentials—that is, form over substance.

The most fundamental fact to understand is that in the United States today, we no longer have, as we once did, a private accounting system with dispassionate and objective professionals in charge. We now have a heavily government-influenced (corrupted) accounting system—a "hybrid" that's no more valid or less destructive than the hybrid GSEs. For a century prior to the establishment of the SEC (a government agency) in 1935, the stock exchanges and self-interested shareholders demanded and then built a system of objective financial reporting and rational accounting rules. FASB, which began (in 1973) as an independent, private body, for years has been co-opted and controlled by the SEC, which also appoints its members.[3] The FASB appointments are partially political and tend to include academics who are far removed from daily accounting issues. The SEC itself is a political body that is influenced heavily by the president and Congress.

The accounting rules created by the SEC and FASB are called generally accepted accounting principles. I do not know of a single business, large or small, that manages its operations based on GAAP. Every business I am familiar with (and there are many) has internal accounting reports that are converted to GAAP when public disclosure is required or to apply for bank loans (as the regulators require GAAP financial reports for large bank loans). This fact alone should raise major issues about the validity of GAAP as prescribed by the SEC and FASB.

I would also argue that if an even moderately complex business tried to manage solely based on GAAP, it would soon be in financial trouble because of the practical disconnect between GAAP and cash flows—in the end, the only thing you can spend is cash. Also, many poor economic decisions are made to make GAAP accounting profits instead of to create economic value. There have been numerous studies to this end, and there are consulting firms that make large profits trying to teach managements to think of true economic value instead of accounting results.[4]

It would be very interesting if the United States had a private accounting system, as it did in the century before 1935. Certainly, there would be market-based certifications like GAAP. (An analogy is Underwriters Laboratories certifications for electrical systems.) However, I think the accounting systems that would evolve would be principle-based, less complex, and focused on essentials and would have a clear connection between operating cash flows and accounting profits. The system(s) would not be based on theory detached from reality, nor would they confuse operating earnings with random fluctuations in asset and liability values on the balance sheet.

The biggest advantage is that the private accounting system would be nonpolitical. The CEOs of Countrywide and Fannie Mae could not get their friends in Congress to change the accounting system for their short-term benefit.

12

Derivatives and Shadow Banking: A Misunderstanding

THE EXPRESSION "SHADOW BANKING SYSTEM" HAS BECOME WIDE-spread in recent years, and the system has served as a demonic whipping boy for those wishing to deflect blame for the crisis away from the real culprits. Surely those nefarious actors luring in the "shadows," out of sight and beyond public scrutiny, played the major role in (nearly) collapsing the financial system. It is suggested that while sunlight and transparency characterized the safe, sound, and regulated banking system, darkness and shadows marked the side that was greedy, reckless, speculative, and unregulated. In fact, the dark side did contribute to the bubble and the subsequent crisis, but it's also precisely the side that is most promoted, subsidized, and protected by government. A number of books have been written on this subject, dramatizing the many poor decisions made by bankers in the shadow banking system, but none that I know of seem able (or willing) to pinpoint the real root of the trouble.

The shadow banking system mainly consists of nondepository banks and financial firms—like hedge funds, money market funds, investment banks, and insurers—which grew enormously in the past decade and came to play an increasingly important role in lending to businesses, distributing securities, and insuring debts. By 2008, some estimates of the size of this shadow banking system placed it on a par with the more traditional deposit-based banking system. By one account, in 2007, the system was "built on derivatives and untouched by regulation."[1]

However, because of their complexity, the role of these instruments has been both misunderstood and significantly overestimated. It should first be noted that despite its protests to the contrary, the Fed always had the practical power to control the shadow banking system. Ultimately, the shadow system depended on funding from commercial banks, like Citigroup, Bank of America, and JPMorgan Chase. Practically speaking, the Fed could have used its almost unlimited authority to control these institutions in order to control the whole interconnected system.

One of the interesting questions is, why did the shadow banking system get to be so large in the first place? Why did so much funding leave the traditional commercial banking system? The simple answer is that government rules and regulations made commercial banks less and less competitive by driving up their cost of operations. Since the early 1970s, regulated financial institutions have faced dramatically increased costs on a multitude of "politically correct" fronts. These costs have driven commercial banks to focus on areas with higher levels of profits, such as real estate lending, which can also be more risky.

Another factor has been the disintermediation of deposits caused by money market mutual funds. These funds often pay higher interest rates on deposits than banks pay. The money market funds also claimed to be as low risk as bank certificates of deposit. Of course, when the financial crisis started, many money funds were under water because in fact they had taken more risk. Unfortunately, the Federal Reserve chose to save the money funds, which created an illusion that they are not risky. Banks have been paying FDIC insurance premiums since 1933. The money funds got the benefit of a Federal Reserve bailout without having to buy insurance in advance. This is the same concept as being able to purchase health insurance after you get sick. Since they were bailed out by the Fed, looking to the future, money funds will systematically increase their risk positions, while the individual purchasers of the money funds will assume that there is no risk. After all, under duress, the Fed will bail out the money funds. This situation creates a significant long-term cost disadvantage for regulated commercial banks and drives more capital into higher-risk markets.

There are also market forces that helped drive assets and funding out of the banking system. A major factor was the entry of foreign competitors into the U.S. market. Also, unions and government pension plans (for example, CalPERS) and university investment arms wanted higher and higher returns and were willing to dramatically increase their alternative investment portfolios, driving assets from the commercial banking system. To the degree that this disintermediation process was driven by market forces, it is a rational allocation of resources. To the degree that the disintermediation was driven by regulatory policy and politically motivated public employee pension plans, it is unhealthy from an economic perspective. As an observer of the process, I believe that regulatory policy and political allocations were the primary drivers, although I cannot prove this point.

Prior to the crisis of 2007–2009, the regulatory perception was that the traditional commercial banking business was becoming less risky because of the ability of banks to sell many credit products in the secondary market. In retrospect, the industry was becoming more risky, as commercial banks were forced to concentrate more and more of their assets in a relatively few markets where securitization was not practical and/or where lending margins were high. The primary area of concentration was in residential and commercial real estate. The fact that banks became more and more dependent on real estate lending to drive their profits made it more difficult for them to be objective about the risk in the business. There were no other sources of profitability. This was especially true for community banks and for financial institutions in high-growth real estate markets.[2]

There is no question that if Freddie and Fannie had not driven banks out of the traditional prime home mortgage business, the banks would have taken less risk in residential construction and commercial real estate lending. At the same time, without drastic regulatory cost, commercial banks would have held a much larger share of the commercial and industrial lending business, and the whole shadow banking system would have been much smaller. In conjunction with many of the issues already discussed, an unintended consequence of government policy (excessive government regulation) was a large shadow banking system that contributed to the financial crisis.

Let us eliminate one major myth: that derivatives were the prime driver in the financial crisis because the market was so large. It is easy both to dramatically exaggerate the size of the derivatives market and to misunderstand its nature. In the first place, the vast majority of derivatives are entered into to reduce risk, not as speculation. For example, suppose BB&T's interest-rate risk position based on its current investment strategy is that falling interest rates would reduce our earnings. This is because of the mix of assets and liabilities that occur as a result of our normal business operations. In order to reduce this risk, BB&T enters into derivative contracts that will increase our revenue if interest rates fall and thereby stabilize our overall earnings. To accomplish this, we agree to pay a variable interest rate on a fixed dollar amount, and the counterparty that we contract with agrees to pay us a fixed rate on the same dollar amount. BB&T might initially pay the prime rate, which at the time is 6 percent, with the counterparty paying us only 5 percent fixed. Even though we are losing money to the counterparty on this trade at this time, we are willing to do this because our concern is falling interest rates, and if this happens, the cash flows will reverse. If the prime rate falls to 4 percent, the counterparty must continue to pay 5 percent, and the earnings input will be to our benefit.

Because the only economic factor driving the cash flow is the differential in interest rates, the contracts must be very large, but the actual amount of risk is relatively small. In this example, suppose we enter into a $1 billion contract. At first we are paying 6 percent × $1 billion and receiving 5 percent × $1 billion, so the actual annual difference is only $10 million (1 percent × $1 billion). This is the "at risk" amount of the contract. If the prime falls by 33 percent (from 6 percent to 4 percent), the cost to the counterparty on a $1 billion contract will also be only $10 million (and the net reduction in revenue $20 million) There is a huge difference between $1 billion and $10 million, that is, $10 million is only 1 percent of $1 billion. Because of this phenomenon, it is easy for reporters, politicians, and laypeople to grossly overestimate the size of the derivatives market in terms of economic risk, especially upon hearing that the derivatives market is "hundreds of trillions" of dollars. Yes, but the "at risk" sum is a small fraction of the face amount.

In addition, remember that, in derivatives, for every loser there is an equal winner (less transaction fees, which are trivial). In the example we just gave, the counterparty to our contract has lost $20 million because rates fell. (He was making $10 million and now is paying $10 million.) However, BB&T has made $20 million. This is a zero-sum game. Zero-sum games *cannot* possibly crash an economic system.

In addition, the better brokers have found a second counterparty with an opposite risk from BB&T's. In this case, BB&T will make less profit if rates fall, which is why we entered into the derivatives contract. There are many financial institutions that will make less profit if interest rates rise. This type of institution, while losing on the derivatives contract when interest rates are falling, will make higher profits in its core business with falling interest rates, and therefore is neutral overall in terms of the change in its derivatives position. Most derivatives are structured to benefit both parties, which is why a contract can be negotiated. However, there are some speculators in the markets, which we will discuss shortly.

Another factor is that well-run financial institutions manage their counterparty risk by setting contract limits, just the way they do for business borrowers. If the net derivative position (the amount the counterparty owes you) goes over the limit, the counterparty has to provide cash collateral to cover the risk. BB&T had counterparty risk for our derivatives with all the major derivative market makers. The limits we set for these companies was such that even if some (or all) of the firms had failed, the losses would not have had a materially impact on our financial stability. In fact, the losses would have been trivial compared to the losses in our traditional real estate lending business.

BB&T had very long term relationships with both Bear Stearns and Lehman Brothers. In both cases, we did not suffer any losses. While in the worst-case scenario we could have experienced losses, the losses would not have been material. I believe that most traditional commercial banks had managed the derivative risk similarly and that so-called contagion risk was greatly exaggerated. For the vast majority of commercial banks, real estate losses dwarfed the derivatives risk.

The real derivatives risk was in a handful of large brokers who were the primary market makers, including Goldman Sachs, Morgan Stanley, Bank of America, Citigroup, JPMorgan Chase, and, of course, Bear Stearns and Lehman Brothers. The question is how well these investment banks had managed their counterparty risk. Had they truly acted as brokers and found parties that had opposite real risk, in which case there is no economic impact? Or were they speculating?

My guess is that most of these firms had managed their risk and would not have failed as a result of counterparty risk. A few of the firms did fail. This is good riddance. If they were not managing their risk, they should fail. There is a bankruptcy process. Also, if they had prepared for bankruptcy, the counterparty issues could have been handled efficiently without crashing the financial system. The perception that firms disappear during bankruptcy is misleading. You have probably flown on bankrupt airlines many times. It is true that financial institution bankruptcies are more complex and need to be planned in advance. Unfortunately, Lehman did not plan for a bankruptcy because it expected to be bailed out.

What was the nature of some of the more interesting derivatives—that is, the "innovations" in financial products? These instruments include CDOs (collateralized debt obligations), CDO²s, SIVs (structured investment vehicles), and other such products. Because of the complexity of the subject and the risk of confusion, let's focus on a conceptually simplified example: CDOs.

CDOs have a reasonable history, as they were designed originally to reduce credit risk. A bank purchases a $500 million bond from General Electric. Even though General Electric is perceived to be a low risk, the bank does not want to have its risk this concentrated in one borrower, so it sells pieces of the bond totaling $400 million in the capital markets, which is a legitimate risk-management technique.

Fast-forward to a very active market for bonds backed by home mortgages. Merrill Lynch has a $500 million bond that is backed by mortgages and has a B grade (on a simplified A, B, C rating system). Merrill realizes that it has some clients who would like to purchase A-rated bonds (lower risk and lower return) and some who would like to purchase C-rated bonds (higher risk and higher returns), along with some who want to purchase B-rated bonds (medium risk and medium return). Merrill decides to create "tranches" out of its B-rated bond portfolio. The way this is accomplished is by subordinating some of the mortgage bonds to the other bonds. The C tranche will take the first losses. The next losses will be absorbed by the Bs, and the final losses by the A-rated bonds. Of course, in theory, the A-rated bonds will never take any losses, as the Cs and, in the worst case, the Bs will absorb the losses.

Unfortunately, while this practice worked for a while, it ultimately turned into gigantic losses for some investment banks. The primary problems were that the underlying mortgage bonds had been misrated by Standard & Poor's (S&P), Moody's, and/or Fitch. Instead of being Bs, the bonds were D, D–, and F. Therefore, even with the tranches, the bond instruments were C–, D, and F. The losses in lower tranches far exceeded the expectations created by the credit-rating agencies' risk ratings.

The investment banks made some very poor decisions. While the decisions are generally, and incorrectly, attributed to greed, I believe they were based partly on pragmatic (that is, "rage of the moment" thinking), and partly on irrational optimism. (The optimism itself was partly created by Fed policy.) In any event, when Bernanke (the Fed) inverted the yield curve, the investment banks were faced with a dilemma. They had few assets that they could hold on their books with positive spreads. Merrill Lynch apparently decided that it could continue to sell the A and B bonds, but would hold the Cs. After all, the Cs were the only bonds with a positive carry, and they were not that risky, Merrill thought; a C is not a bad grade. In fact, a year before it effectively failed, Merrill was making an outstanding profit selling A and B bonds and holding the Cs. However, when the mortgage market started to deflate, it became clear that the Cs were really Fs, and Merrill lost 100 cents on the dollar on the Cs.

Citigroup went the other way. When Bernanke inverted the yield curve, its clients wanted the Cs because they were the only bonds with acceptable yields. So Citi sold the Bs and Cs and loaded up on the As. The Federal Reserve and the Basel capital guidelines required very little capital to back up the As. Unfortunately, the As were really Ds, and Citi owned a very large portfolio. Under fair-value accounting, the losses on those bonds were massive, creating significant accounting losses and related capital funding problems for Citigroup. (It turned out that many of the accounting losses were not real economic losses, partially explaining Citi's return to profitability.)

Of course, many of the B and C bonds had been sold to other financial institutions, which also suffered large earnings and capital losses. A substantial portion of the losses early in the financial crisis occurred in these bonds, not in direct real estate loans. Also, as discussed, this capital destruction was magnified by the leverage ratios of financial intermediaries, resulting in significant liquidity problems in the capital markets.

Another important and obscure financial instrument is a credit default swap (CDS). A CDS is basically an insurance policy that is purchased to reduce the credit risk in a debt instrument. For example, Goldman Sachs has a $100 million B-rated bond backed by home mortgages. Goldman wants to hold the bond in its portfolio temporarily. However, based on the SEC capital guidelines, Goldman will need significantly less capital if the bond is A-rated. To accomplish this objective, Goldman purchases a CDS (an insurance policy against default) from AIG. AIG is the world's largest insurance company and has an AAA rating from S&P. With the "insurance policy" from AIG, Goldman's bond is now AAA-rated, and it can hold much less capital. The advantage from holding less capital exceeds the cost of the "insurance."

Unfortunately for AIG, the underlying B bond is significantly more risky than anticipated because S&P, Moody's, and/or Fitch has misrated the bond. In addition, AIG's own mathematical rating models have significantly underestimated the risk. Therefore, AIG takes far greater losses on the "insurance" policies than expected.

Interestingly, AIG's losses are also magnified by fair-value accounting. Recall the example in the fair-value accounting chapter. There is a $100 million bond backed by mortgages where some of the mortgages are defaulting and some more are expected to default. Using an economic analysis, the bonds should be valued at $80 million, and AIG should have to reserve $20 million against anticipated future losses. However, in the panicky financial market, the only buyers are deep discounters who will pay only $50 million. Based on fair-value accounting, AIG will have to reserve $50 million (instead of $20 million) for losses. Since AIG had a large portfolio of CDSs, fair-value accounting magnified the already large losses it was experiencing.[3]

Hopefully, the analogy with an insurance policy is helpful. However, CDSs were technically capital-market instruments that could be bought and sold. Unfortunately, as the financial environment deteriorated, this created an opportunity for legal but possibly economically destructive activity. In theory, the price of a CDS reflects the risk of default; that is, the higher the probability of a "fire," the higher the price of "insurance." However, as the financial crisis started to unfold, the CDS market became very thin. There were very few buyers and sellers. This problem became more acute as AIG started to experience problems. AIG had been the major factor in the CDS market.

It became possible for sophisticated traders to legally have an impact on the market and make substantial profits. For example, there were CDSs on Bear Stearns's bond obligations. Since the market was very thin, it was relatively easy for traders to drive down the value of Bear CDSs (which drives up the cost of insuring Bear's bonds). The rising insurance rate on Bear's bonds makes it appear that Bear is more risky. It is also fairly easy to reinforce the rumors about Bear's financial problems. At the same time you are purchasing the CDSs (driving up the price to insure), you short Bear Stearns stock. When the market sees Bear's CDS price moving (its insurance cost rising), it assumes that this reflects financial problems, and Bear's stock price falls. You make a significant profit on your short position.

There is important economic value to shorting stocks, as additional information about a company's financial position is being provided to the market. Shorting stock is a valuable economic activity. However, to the degree that the market is too thin, Bear may have to deal with funding problems independent of its current financial position. Also, to the degree that the bond shorts were "naked" shorts, other market participants may be misled.

The SEC requires that before you short a stock, you need to have a position where you can purchase the stock if necessary if the price rises. (Typically, a firm "borrows" the stock before it sells it short.) To the degree that the CDS/short positions were naked shorts, other market participants were misled into thinking there was more negative pressure on Bear's stock than actually existed. We can argue over whether naked shorts should be allowed or not. However, if naked shorting is prohibited, the SEC rule should be enforced or some market participants will be misled.

Let's return to the AIG situation. One of the interesting questions is, why save AIG and, in particular, why pay AIG's counterparties in full? AIG was the world's largest insurance company. BB&T operates the sixth largest insurance brokerage operation in the world and is a major distributor of AIG insurance products. Based on a reasonable analysis of the financial data, it is highly unlikely that AIG's insurance subsidiaries would have failed, as they were legally separated from the parent company's subsidiary that was holding the CDS risk. In other words, AIG's parent company could have failed without the insurance subsidiaries failing. An organized bankruptcy proceeding would have been possible without materially disrupting the insurance market. The government bailout of AIG was a bailout of the high-risk CDS operations of AIG's parent company.

The bailout of AIG was not about saving AIG but rather about protecting AIG's counterparties. These counterparties were fundamentally dependent on AIG's contracts (insurance policies). If AIG had failed, some of the counterparties could have experienced significant losses. This theoretically could have created a contagion of financial institution failures.

AIG's single largest counterparty was Goldman. Goldman claims that it had hedged the counterparty risk with AIG. If this is so, and if AIG's other major counterparties had also hedged their counterparty risk, then the whole contagion argument is illegitimate. Of course, it is practically impossible to determine today how well the various counterparties were hedged, but I suspect that many were at least partially hedged.

However, if you are Hank Paulson, secretary of the Treasury, it is difficult to assess all these positions during the heat of the crisis. In addition, Paulson had spent his whole career at Goldman. He was a large Goldman shareholder. Many members of his staff at the Treasury had worked for Goldman. With that background, it is easy for him to honestly believe that if AIG fails, Goldman will fail and the U.S. economy will crash. Objectively, this outcome was extremely unlikely. The AIG parent was not essential to the U.S.

economy, and Goldman would not have failed, assuming that it had hedged even part of its counterparty risk.

One of the other interesting questions is, why pay the counterparties (like Goldman) in full? Given that the taxpayers were taking enormous risk, why not pay the counterparties 50 percent now and let them get the rest of their money in the future if AIG survives? The other major AIG counterparties were large European banks. The U.S. taxpayers bailed out these European banks in the amount of more than $50 billion. Why?

Was "saving" Goldman and AIG about systems risk or about crony capitalism? One reason Wall Street has such a bad reputation is because of the connection between Wall Street and the U.S. government. Unfortunately, Goldman is the ultimate crony capitalist. Goldman makes huge contributions to political parties and politicians, especially Democrats. Many Goldman alumni are in various high-level policy positions in Washington. Goldman is not an advocate of free markets. It is an advocate of special deals from Washington. It is a crony socialist. In this case, as in so many others involving Wall Street, being a "capitalist" financially doesn't necessarily make one a capitalist ideologically.

This attitude is not surprising. Instead of dealing with market forces, it is easier to influence the political allocation of resources, that is, money. However, the problem is not Goldman. The problem is that the politicians and bureaucrats have this power. If the U.S. Constitution were enforced, crony capitalism would not work because the politicians and bureaucrats would not have the authority to hand out favors to their friends.

If there were a separation of economics and state as there is of church and state, crony capitalism would not be possible. Crony capitalism is really crony socialism and is caused by politicians, that is, government. There can be no moral justification for saving Goldman and letting Lehman fail. Many insiders will tell you that Paulson hated Lehman. Did his personal feeling about Lehman cause him to allow Lehman to fail? Who knows? The issue is that a government bureaucrat had the authority to make this kind of decision.

There are those who argue that because AIG may be able to pay back its debt to the U.S. government, saving AIG was a good decision. This completely ignores the secondary consequences, which are huge. First, it is important to understand that had the government not stepped in, AIG would not have disappeared. There is a carefully created process for handling bankruptcies. If AIG had failed, the bankruptcy process would have allocated resources more justly.

It is very unlikely that the insurance subsidiaries would have failed. However, market forces would have moved insurance business to other insurance companies that had better managed their risk and deserved to be rewarded. The counterparties who had not hedged their risk would have taken the losses that they had earned; probably none would have failed for this reason.

There are three other major long-term consequences. The first is the message that if you are a big company, you can take gigantic risk and the government will bail you out. If you reward children for misbehaving, they will continue to misbehave (human action).

Second, the market knows that these big firms will be bailed out in the worst-case scenario, and the Dodd-Frank bill did not change this fact. This allows these "too-big-to-fail" firms to attract more capital at lower cost that would otherwise have gone to companies that had demonstrated better long-term risk management. It creates a competitive advantage for poorly managed businesses, which often have problems in the future. It is not surprising that Chrysler and Citigroup have been bailed out multiple times.

However, the most significant damage is the belief that additional regulations are necessary. The Dodd-Frank bill, if fully implemented, will make U.S. financial firms less competitive, drive resources out of the United States, reduce job creation, and lower our standard of living. Ironically, it will also increase risk, as unregulated firms headquartered in foreign locations will have a larger market share.

If the government is going to bail out AIG, the perception is that it should have the power to control AIG. Of course, all the firms that did not fail are also subject to the destructive legislation that follows from the bailout. The reward for running a good business is to have your worst competitors bailed out by the U.S. government and then to have massive new regulations that punish your company for sins it did not commit.

Whether or not AIG pays the taxpayers back is largely irrelevant. Government bailouts have very negative long-term economic consequences because they provide incentives for the wrong behavior.

One other very important issue to understand is that the primary losers in the shadow banking system were sophisticated investors who were taking very substantial risk. These losses did not accrue to "mom and pop" conservative investors. The big losers were university endowments, government pension plans (such as CalPERS), and hedge funds (who represented wealthy individuals). Many of these investors had previously made big gains by taking the high risk that came back to burn them.

The Harvard University endowment is a typical example of this phenomenon. This endowment had been bragging about far-above-market returns on its investments for years. Of course, the university claimed that it was not taking excessive risks because all the individually high-risk cyclical investments were being offset by other high-risk countercyclical investments. Many of these high-risk investments were in the shadow banking markets.

Of course, the fundamental fact about high-risk investments is that they are risky. You cannot manage away the risk in the long term. The Harvard endowment suffered massive losses in the shadow banking market. These losses were richly deserved. The losses were economic justice based on the risk that Harvard had taken. No one complained when Harvard was getting phenomenal returns from making these high-risk investments.

The vast majority of losses taken in the shadow banking system accrued to wealthy individuals or institutions that had previously made substantial gains from taking the high risk that turned against them. These losses are actually an example of economic justice.

13

The Myth that "Deregulation" Caused the Financial Crisis

ONE OF THE FUNDAMENTAL MYTHS BEING PROMULGATED IS THAT the banking industry was deregulated during the Bush administration, and that this was a major cause of the financial crisis. Nothing could be further from the truth. The regulatory burden was increased significantly during the Bush years. In fact, regulatory cost was at an all-time high (until the current period) during the peak of the bubble (2005–2007). Banks' operating statements reflect this cost increase, as does the multithousand-page increase in various government regulatory documents. Government spending alone (excluding costs that the industry incurred and that must be paid by the companies being regulated) on financial regulations (not company bailouts) increased, in adjusted dollars, from $725 million in 1980 to $2.07 billion in 2007.[1]

The financial industry was not deregulated, it was misregulated. During the Bush administration, three major new financial regulatory acts were passed: the Privacy Act, Sarbanes-Oxley, and the Patriot Act. The primary regulatory focus was initially on Sarbanes-Oxley and then on the Patriot Act. Sarbanes-Oxley is the legislation passed by Congress as a result of the Enron and WorldCom scandals to theoretically eliminate accounting fraud. The financial industry has been operating under its own "Sarbanes-Oxley" since the thrift crisis of the early 1990s. Sarbanes-Oxley is a redundant system on top of a redundant system. In the case of BB&T, our internal auditors are audited by our external auditors, the NC State Banking Examiners, the Federal Deposit Insurance Corporation (FDIC), and the Federal Reserve. These are auditors auditing auditors auditing auditors. There is not a shred of evidence that Sarbanes-Oxley reduced fraud by one penny during the financial crisis. However, it did significantly misdirect management's attention from the real risk in the financial industry.

The other regulatory focus was on the Patriot Act. The Patriot Act was passed after 9/11, theoretically to reduce the risk of terrorism. The financial services industry has spent $5 billion on the enforcement of the Patriot Act. On several occasions, I have had the opportunity to discuss the impact of the Patriot Act with a variety of regulators. Not a single terrorist has been caught and convicted because of the Patriot Act, nor is one likely to be. Anyone who is dumb enough to be caught by the Patriot Act procedures, which are disclosed to the public, is going to be caught anyway. What do you think the odds are of our bank tellers identifying a terrorist? Also, if we did, we would call law enforcement immediately! You do not need a massive regulatory and bureaucratic structure to accomplish this objective. The Patriot Act is one of the few ideas that is less useful than taking your shoes off to fly on a commercial airliner.

Law enforcement is very supportive of the Patriot Act, even though it knows that we will not catch terrorists. The act is being used to violate your privacy rights. The primary focus is on tax evasion by small businesses and on drug law enforcement. However, Big Brother is watching you. It is not surprising that the most significant outcome of the Patriot Act is the conviction of the governor of New York for soliciting prostitution. When he was attorney general of New York, Eliot Spitzer violated the fundamental rule of law in his treatment of business leaders. The courts have almost unanimously rejected all his indictments. He should have been impeached as attorney general and never elected governor. I do not like Eliot Spitzer.

However, it is of far greater concern to me that an act designed to prevent terrorism led to the conviction of a state governor for soliciting a prostitute. This is very scary. Would the governor of New York be a reasonable terrorism suspect? Why was this issue pursued? Since Spitzer is a Democrat, you can be confident that if there had been a Democratic president at the time, you never would have heard about this issue.

Many conservatives are generally supportive of information gathering and police authorities such as the FBI and the CIA. While there is some legitimacy to this position, please recognize what minorities, poor people, and many business leaders already understand: the police sometimes abuse their power for a wide variety of reasons. The politicians also significantly influence the use of "confidential" information and police power. You should be worried about the confidential information that is being gathered under the Patriot Act. This information will be abused some day, possibly on a major scale.

One of the interesting effects of the Patriot Act has been reduced enforcement of laws aimed at real crimes. The police authorities are so inundated with data that they have become more and more selective about which laws they enforce. Unquestionably, at the same time as Eliot Spitzer's prostitution solicitation, far more significant crimes were taking place that have never been pursued by legal authorities because they are too busy sorting data and chasing merely controversial activity.

The Patriot Act presents a practically impossible regulatory environment for banks because it is in direct conflict with the Privacy Act (which was also passed during the Bush administration). The Privacy Act requires banks not to violate your privacy. The Patriot Act requires that banks violate your privacy.

One of the primary effects of the Privacy Act is that financial institutions mail hundreds of millions of Privacy Act notices each year, at a cost of hundreds of millions of dollars. Have you ever read a Privacy Act notice? I hope not. Reading the notice is a useless exercise. I talked to the CEO of a midsize bank who ran an interesting test. He sent a sample of several thousand Privacy Act notices that on the last line of the notice offered $100 if the client returned the notice to the bank within a few days after receipt. Only one client returned the notice. The Privacy Act was part of Bush's "deregulation," that is, misregulation.

The incentives under the Patriot Act are extremely distorted. A large financial institution paid a $50 million fine for failing to file a Suspicious Activity Report (SAR) for a crime that was totally unrelated to terrorism. However, there is no penalty for filing a Suspicious Activity Report when there is no need to file the report. Given the completely distorted incentives, banks naturally file many SARs that do not necessarily need to be filed—why take the chance?

Violations (even unintentional violations) of Sarbanes-Oxley and the Patriot Act can result in criminal charges against bank executives. When the government threatens to put you in jail, it affects your decision making. One of the big costs of these regulations was focusing bank managements on regulatory risk instead of credit risk. Also, banks have limited human and financial resources. If substantial resources are being expended on Sarbanes-Oxley and the Patriot Act, there are fewer resources (including thinking capacity) to invest in other aspects of risk management. Unquestionably, this irrational regulatory focus caused bank management to do less in traditional credit-risk management. The complete lack of objective definitions of how to comply with competing regulations (Patriot Act vs. Privacy Act) created an arbitrary regulatory environment.

The regulators also placed a dramatic emphasis on the use of mathematical modeling for risk management. This effort is based on the academic belief that all economic activity can be mathematically modeled. In fact, many modern economics journals look more like math textbooks than like economics dissertations.

All the mathematical models failed. The Federal Reserve did not predict a recession, much less the Great Recession. Very few private economists predicted a recession. All the rating agencies' (Standard & Poor's and the others) models failed. The large banks' risk-rating models failed.

BB&T was under intense pressure to install mathematical models like our larger competitors. Wachovia and Citigroup (which both failed) were touted by the regulators as having "best practices" in risk management based on their mathematical models.

You may remember that when the financial crisis in the United States started, many people in Europe were laughing at our problems. Then suddenly, many of the largest European banks effectively failed. The reason the European banks collapsed so rapidly was that the Basel Accords had been implemented in Europe. The Basel Accords are an international standard used to determine bank capital levels. The first version (Basel I) was launched in 1989—and banks were told then (as now) that they needn't keep any capital against government (or government-sponsored enterprise [GSE]) bonds because they were "risk-free assets." Also, Basel allowed banks not to hold any capital against "sovereign" risk in the United States and Europe (for example, Greek debt). These capital levels are based on mathematical models developed by the banks themselves, with guidance from the regulators. Using the Basel calculations, the European banks had very low levels of capital. When the global economy began to deteriorate, those banks immediately experienced problems because they had so little capital.

Mathematical modeling can be a powerful tool. A clear example of the proper use of mathematical models is physics. However, the models used in physics capture causal relationships and are properly evaluated based on the predictive power of these causal relationships. However, in economics, practically all mathematical models capture correlations, not causations. There is a difference in kind between correlation and causation. Also, the models are based on a multitude of assumptions. The danger lies in placing far too much confidence in models based on correlation rather than causation. Economists and government regulators often fall into the trap of believing that these models are objective. However, there are important economic factors, such as human behavior, that cannot be clearly mathematized. Taking these models as "gospel" is dangerous.

There is also a tendency, in developing the models, to assume normal distributions with small "tails." (The tails are the set of unlikely events.) Since models are useful only if the tails are small, there is a tendency for model builders to show small tails; otherwise, no one will use their models. In reality, the tails often turn out to be "fat," that is, to have a greater chance of occurring than the model suggests. The tails typically represent very positive and very negative outcomes. In the case of the financial crisis, the negative fat tails (improbable events) became reality. These tails were magnified by the effect of panic on human behavior under stress. All the correlations (which were not based on causation) fell apart when human beings, who make decisions, started reacting to negative news.

In addition, it is easy to underestimate the likelihood of unlikely events. For example, if you build a house in a 100-year flood plain, you will at some point experience a flood. It may be 90 years from now, or it may be next week. Eventually (or soon), a flood will affect your house.

The mathematical models used by economists today are often floating abstractions that are not attached to reality. They are sometimes based on deductions from arbitrary assumptions, not induced from the facts. When they are imposed by regulators and treated as "the truth," they are dangerous. These models need to be tempered by human judgment based on experience. That judgment should not be colored by pressure from regulators to manage to the models.

The biggest myth is that since the crisis (2008–2011), bank regulators have been encouraging banks to make more loans. In fact, bank regulators have been making it far more difficult for banks to make loans, even though the heads of the banking regulatory agencies are saying that they want banks to become more willing to make loans. The local examiners working through the "safety and soundness" supervisory channel are making it more difficult for banks to extend new loans and to work with existing business borrowers who are struggling, especially any business with debt related to real estate.

Why is this happening? If you are a local bank examiner, the only practical way you can get into trouble in your career is for a bank that you are examining to have financial problems. Since the examiners are lifetime bureaucrats who are not going to get fired unless the banks they are examining have severe problems and who have safe federal pensions, why take the risk? The best strategy for the local examiner is to tighten up on the banks to minimize the personal risk of being criticized by their superior in the safety and soundness hierarchy. The only way the head of safety and soundness can have problems is for the banks his agency is examining to have financial issues. Why not tighten credit standards and minimize your personal risk?

Of course, the head of safety and soundness must pay lip service to the politically appointed head of the regulatory agency, who is always proclaiming that the examiners are not getting in the way of extending credit. However, the head of safety and soundness is a lifetime bureaucrat who has worked his way up through the agency for 25 years. He knows that political appointees come and go. Plus, the politically appointed heads of the regulatory agencies do not understand the banking business (they are primarily politicians, which is how they got appointed). It is easy for the experienced head of safety and soundness to convince the politically appointed head of the regulatory agency that the examiners are helping banks make good lending decisions.

State bureaucrats may seek power and prestige more than they seek wealth, but they too act consistent with incentives. In bad times, they are risk minimizers. My personal experience is that government bureaucrats at the operating level are far, far less concerned with overall economic well-being than with protecting their positions and their jobs. If you believe that government bureaucrats in regulatory agencies are working for the "general welfare," I have a bridge in Brooklyn to sell you.

Of course, the way they achieve this end is to tighten enforcement of a massive set of regulations that are already in place. Probably every banker in America has been through this experience: during good economic times, the examiners will say that this regulation or that regulation is not important. However, when times get tough, they will suddenly clamp down on a standard that was not important six months before. Your reaction might be that they should simply have enforced the standard in the good times. Unfortunately, if all the regulatory standards were fully enforced to the maximum, the U.S. economic system would grind to a halt. Banks must take risk for there to be economic growth. Driving risk to zero would destroy our economy. In addition, the banking regulators are some of the least qualified people on the planet to make this type of decision. Most of these regulators choose to work as government bureaucrats because they need a fixed structure within which to operate. They are simply intellectually and psychologically unable to evaluate risk. This is why they have chosen to take a lower-paying, totally uncreative job without any real responsibility. They can always fall back on fixed regulations to justify any action.

There is no question that BB&T is not making loans that we would make were it not for the banking examiners. We are also putting companies out of business that BB&T would have been willing to work with had it not been for the involvement of the regulators. Unfortunately, this is a self-fulfilling negative prophecy. By not working with honest borrowers, the bank increases its losses. The banking examiners have materially increased the level of loan losses in the banking industry and have significantly slowed economic recovery.

Certainly, there are times when bankers are hiding their problems, and they need to deal with their credit quality issues. However, if a bank has a strong credit culture and a history of objective decision making, the bank examiners often force irrational and self-destructive decisions. Many of these examiners have never made or collected a loan. Their whole understanding of lending is based on training provided by individuals who have never made or collected a loan.

In addition, the irony is that banks that are unable to make objective decisions in tough times would probably not be in business if FDIC insurance did not exist. Their lack of objective decision making would probably have already doomed them to failure if the banking industry were operating in a free market.

There are a number of methods the examiners use to tighten credit standards. At BB&T, they effectively forced us to change our risk-grading system. For many years, BB&T has graded client risk on a scale of 1 to 10, with 1 being low risk and 10 being extremely high risk (nonaccrual). The examiners strongly encouraged BB&T to tighten the standards, so that a client who was previously given a risk grade of 4 suddenly had a risk grade of 6 without any change in the client's circumstances. The higher the risk grade, the more loan loss reserves the bank has to maintain. Also, the bank is less willing to provide more credit because an additional credit extension may lower the borrower's risk grade.

This issue is particularly important at a critical inflexion point. If the banks are forced by the regulatory process to lower a client's risk grade from 5 to 7 (which often happens), the relationship between the bank and the borrower suffers a material change. At grade 7, a client is on the "watch list" and is considered substandard. If a client is considered substandard, it is very difficult to work with that client. There are a number of regulatory capital ratios that include capital allocations for watch list/substandard credits. If substandard loan outstandings become too large, the bank must raise additional capital in a very difficult market environment.

Given this set of regulatory constraints, once a client becomes substandard, the bank must try to reduce that client's outstanding borrowings to protect its own regulatory capital position. This typically leads to short-term decisions to raise cash through debt reduction regardless of the long-term consequences.

What is particularly disturbing is the regulatory double-talk. When they force a bank to downgrade from a 5 to a 7 (substandard) a credit that the bank does not think needs downgrading, the regulators say that this should not affect the way the bank works with the client. However, out of the other side of their mouth, they point out the bank's rising substandard ratio and tell it to reduce its substandard outstandings as soon as possible or face regulatory action of some kind. Welcome to a "Brave New World."

The regulators also forced an important change in BB&T's underwriting standards. For many years, BB&T underwrote the client relationship and developed risk grades based on the totality of the client's financial position. The regulators effectively forced the bank to underwrite based on each loan transaction instead of on the totality of the client relationship. This change in process caused a significant increase in credits classified as problems.

For example, suppose a client has five projects and a reasonable net worth independent of all five projects. Four of the projects are performing, but one project is not performing. In the past, we established risk grades based on the client's overall financial position, which in this example is satisfactory. Now the regulators are forcing us to classify part of the client's outstanding loans as unsatisfactory and basically either ignoring or undervaluing the remainder of the client's financial assets and net worth.

This change increases the amount of classified (substandard) loans and makes it far more difficult to work with the client. The bank practically has to push the client to focus on the underperforming project instead of maximizing her overall economic well-being. Many clients who otherwise might have been willing to keep the underperforming project afloat simply chose to let the project fail and protect their other assets. This regulatory-driven concept is a loss-maximizing strategy. It also forces more assets (primarily real estate) into the market and drives down prices more rapidly.

It is interesting how radically different the regulatory approach toward low-income consumers, driven by the Obama administration's policy beliefs, has been from its approach to business borrowers (especially builders and developers of residential real estate). The administration's regulators have done everything possible to keep low-income homeowners who cannot afford the homes they have bought in those homes for as long as possible, often two years or more after they quit paying.

On the other hand, the banking regulators have put tremendous pressure on banks to be merciless in handling business borrowers (primarily those in the real estate industry). Given the fundamental beliefs of the current administration that businesses are greedy and bad, this treatment is not surprising. However, their strategy is both unjust and economically destructive.

Let me share some personal examples. These are stories about longtime BB&T clients who have approached me. Because I am no longer in management, I could not help them with their situations.

As a little background, one reason that problems with commercial real estate (as opposed to those with residential real estate) have not negatively affected the banking industry as much as some analysts expected is that many commercial real estate projects are owned by individuals who have substantial income from other sources. In this example, BB&T had financed the purchase of a tract of land for a high-income attorney and several other individuals who planned to develop the tract into a shopping center.

When the financial crisis started to unfold, they decided not to proceed with the shopping center project until a stronger economic recovery had begun. The original agreement was for the land acquisition loan to be paid in three years through a construction loan on the shopping center. For three years, the high-income attorney (primarily) and his partners paid the interest on this commercial real estate loan. At the end of the three-year period, the loan matured. Under longstanding BB&T policies, we would simply have renewed the loan for two more years, knowing that the attorney would continue to make the interest payments and knowing that his overall financial position would be likely to improve and the economy would probably be better at that time.

However, under the new lending policy effectively forced by the regulators, initially we were required to demand a new appraisal of the property. Of course, the value of the property had declined. The regulatory guidelines required the attorney to make a large principal payment and reset the loan on a five-year amortization. While he could make the interest payments, he did not have the cash to make a large one-time payment, nor could he repay the remaining balance over five years. If this program had been followed to its logical conclusion, the attorney would have been forced to sell this property and other real estate he owns at a deep discount, causing unnecessary losses for him and driving down commercial real estate value in the market.

In this case, we were able to work out a better, but not optimal solution. The bank agreed to accept a small principal payment and to amortize the loan over 20 years. However, the price to BB&T was that the loan had to be treated as substandard, raising BB&T's capital requirements and increasing our reported high-risk assets, which when combined with other similar transactions drives down BB&T's stock price. In addition, practically speaking, we cannot work with this borrower on additional economic investments until this loan is paid. The borrower is angry at BB&T because we cannot tell him that the regulators caused this to happen. The FDIC prohibits banks from using changes in regulatory rules as a reason to change the terms of a loan (interesting rule!).

Of course, there was a ripple effect. While the attorney had personally guaranteed BB&T's loan, he had another project with the same partners that was also struggling; it had been financed by another bank, and he was not personally guaranteeing it. He had been using his income to pay interest on the other project because he believed that the project was viable in the long term and because his partners were also personal friends. Because of the cash he had to put into the BB&T project and the psychological impact of knowing that he could not count on the bank to help him, and because he knew that the other project had a balloon payment in six months and that he would face the same issue, he decided to stop paying the interest on this project.

His partners had personally guaranteed this loan, but they did not have enough outside income or liquid assets to cover the interest payments. The loan went into default, and the other bank foreclosed. They sold the property at a deep discount (once a bank owns a piece of property, its value typically falls 20 to 25 percent). This sale set a precedent for a new lower commercial real estate valuation in this relatively small market. The three partners all filed personal bankruptcy. (I assume the Obama administration is now worried about them, as they are truly low income and will be so for years.)

If BB&T could have worked with this high-net-worth borrower under our traditional program, our loan would ultimately have been paid in full, and the secondary negative consequences would not have occurred. Frankly, the regulators do not care about this type of issue. They have their rules, some less harmful than others, but they individually and the regulatory system as a process are unable to use judgment regardless of the destructive consequences of their actions.

Let me share with you another similar example. BB&T had financed a residential development project for a longtime client. The sale of lots in the project was much slower than anticipated because of the collapse of the real estate market, but some lots were selling. The loan had a five-year balloon because it was originally expected that all the lots would have sold in five years.

At the balloon date, the regulatory requirement was to reappraise the property and require the borrower to make a large one-time payment to bring the loan-to-value ratio into line with regulatory guidelines. The borrower had limited net worth and had sold everything he had to keep the project current. He was working himself to death trying to pay the bank, borrowing from family, friends, and others. When presented with the extra payment requirement that the regulators demanded, he simply quit and gave ownership to the bank. Even though it might have been possible to work out a better solution, as described in the previous example, he did not want to try any more. In the past, BB&T would not have even made such a ridiculous proposal. If this long-term client was honest and willing to do everything possible to pay the loan, and if he could pay interest and some principal on the loan, we would have worked with him.

In this case, the bank ended up owning the property. Our loss will be 20 to 25 percent higher than it would have been had we been able to work with this client. This individual filed for bankruptcy and is clearly psychologically depressed

As another example, a longtime client of BB&T who was in the hotel business struggled during the initial phase of the Great Recession. His hotels served business travelers, and their occupancy rates declined significantly. The net cash flow from his hotel operations became negative, that is, the cash flow was less than the debt service. Even though he had not personally guaranteed the loan on the hotels, he decided to liquidate personal assets to make debt service payments.

The hotel's performance began to improve, and the cash flow margin became positive, but only slightly positive. However, the trend was definitely upward. Even though directionally all trends were positive and the client had worked through the most difficult economic environment since the Great Depression, BB&T was effectively forced by the regulators to downgrade this client to substandard credit (even after he had turned his operation around) because the cash flow margin was tight. Also, his personal assets could not be considered, even though he had used personal assets to pay the debt.

The client had the opportunity to purchase another hotel that was under foreclosure (the hotel was being foreclosed by another bank). Because of the price at which this hotel was going to be sold and because the property being foreclosed was near to and complementary to one of the client's existing hotels, it created opportunities for operating efficiencies. Even though financing this acquisition for the client would have reduced BB&T's overall risk because of the economic viability of the proposed hotel acquisition, as a practical matter, we could not make the client a loan because his existing debt was classified as substandard by the regulators. The client lost an excellent opportunity for a healthy return. Since no other purchaser had the economic advantages our client did, the hotel sold for a significantly lower price than our client could have afforded to pay.

This lower price helped bring down the appraised values for commercial real estate in the market. As the regulators use these appraised values for determining loan values, the effective availability of credit for commercial real estate financing in the market was reduced.

Under the loan policies that BB&T has operated with since the early 1980s, we would have made this loan. With the regulatory clampdown that began in 2007–2008, we did not make the loan.

Our policies had withstood the dramatic commercial real estate crisis of the early 1990s. As the regulators have been applying their "new" policies to all banks, they have driven commercial real estate values (along with residential construction and development) below the natural market correction price. At the same time, through a large series of interferences in the market to "protect" low-income consumers, they have kept housing prices from correcting to their natural level. This combination of punishing the business real estate borrowers and attempting to protect the homeowner real estate market in unnatural and opposite directions has caused many developers to fail and simultaneously delayed the real estate correction process, contributing to higher unemployment.

There is no question but that some bankers have been slow to deal with their problems. On the other hand, why is it rational to believe that regulators are better able to make these decisions? A simple control mechanism would be to prohibit banks from lending money to pay interest beyond the originally agreed-upon finance period without the client's putting up additional collateral or other guarantors or demonstrating that the project has turned around. This is longtime, proven banking practice. The regulators' arbitrary creation of new risk-grading standards and related arbitrary rules has made the economic correction (especially in real estate markets) deeper than it needed to be. Also, loan losses by the banking industry have been significantly magnified. These unnecessary losses make banks more conservative and reduce the capital available for lending.

Both politicians and the general public believe that small businesses are fundamentally good and "big" businesses are fundamentally bad. Of course, in a free market, the reason a business gets bigger is that it does a better job for its clients than its competitors can. The other irony is the failure of government leaders to understand that regulations targeted at big businesses are often more destructive to smaller firms. In a smaller firm, the key decision maker is more important than in a large firm, where the business can afford to hire more talent. When the small business owner has to spend much of her energy on complying with regulations instead of on production, her company is less successful and ends up hiring fewer employees. The massive increase in regulations and the tightening of existing regulations is one of the primary reasons that small businesses are not creating jobs. Small banks are damaged more by the regulatory onslaught than larger financial institutions.

Exemptions to regulations for small businesses are never effective. Think about the implied negatives. As soon as you grow your business successfully, you will be punished for that success with increased regulations. The business owner will spend his time trying to figure out how to avoid the future regulations.

Contrary to popular opinion, the banking industry has not been deregulated. It has been grossly misregulated, from Sarbanes-Oxley to the Patriot Act, to regulatory interference in the real estate lending process, to the Dodd-Frank legislation. The regulators were too liberal in good times and too conservative in bad times. There is absolutely no reason to believe that they will not make these same mistakes in the future. The regulators are driven by incentives like everyone else. Unfortunately, their incentives are political, not economic. Do you trust market participants risking their own money or unelected "politicians" (that is, government bureaucrats)?

The negative impact of government regulations is far more destructive than the direct cost. While all the productive employees in a business are important, the long-term success of any enterprise is fundamentally dependent on the quality of leadership at the top. If the most important and most productive minds in an organization are spending half their time trying to satisfy government bureaucrats, the whole organization will be less productive and will create fewer jobs.

Government regulations suck the energy and will of the best and the brightest. Government regulations are most destructive to honest businesspeople who know that they have done nothing wrong. However, these outstanding producers are having to carry the ball and chain of destructive regulations created to deal with dishonest crony capitalists (crony socialists). We desperately need to separate business and state so that the best businesspeople can use their creative minds to produce a better life for all of us. When you put a ball and chain on the best and the brightest, you reduce the standard of living for everyone.

14

How the SEC
Made Matters Worse

THE SECURITIES AND EXCHANGE COMMISSION (SEC) IS SUPPOSED to protect capital-market investors. What it primarily does is make a massive number of rules designed to provide investors with "transparent" financial and operating information to ensure that they can make sound investments. Based on the performance of capital markets over the last 10 years, there is prima facie evidence that the SEC has failed miserably. Without even considering the fraud and abuse that the SEC failed to detect in cases like Enron, WorldCom, Fannie Mae, Freddie Mac, and Bernie Madoff, simply consider that the S&P 500 today (August 2011) is still 11 percent below where it traded in August 2000.

Because the work of the SEC is somewhat eclectic, we will focus on its primary policy mistakes, a number of which have been previously discussed. One of the most significant errors by the SEC is the sanctioning of the rating agencies (Standard & Poor's [S&P], Moody's, and Fitch). Under an SEC rule, only debt instruments rated by S&P, Moody's, or Fitch qualify for positive consideration under Employee Retirement Income Security Act (ERISA) rules designed to protect pension accounts. The risk grades issued by the rating agencies have a significant effect on the economic value of the related bond indebtedness. The practical effect of this ruling has been to create a government-sanctioned oligopoly in the risk-rating business for these three entities. There has also been an assumption that since the SEC has, in effect, sanctioned these companies, they are competent to do their job. Yet the three firms predate the SEC's formation in 1934: S&P was founded by Henry Varnum Poor in 1860, Moody's was founded by John Moody in 1900, and Fitch Services was founded by John Knowles Fitch in 1913. Free markets filled the need for objective debt ratings and did not need or want government's help.

Yet by 1975, the SEC had felt it necessary to place its stamp of supposed legitimacy on these venerable rating firms and then to regulate and manipulate their ways, means, and incentives. This is similar to the assumption that if Underwriters Laboratories gives its seal of approval, an electrical appliance is safe. As we have discussed, the failure of the rating agencies (S&P, Moody's, and Fitch) played an extremely important role in the financial crisis. The SEC's implied sanction made this possible.

Of course, the SEC has implemented Sarbanes-Oxley (2002), with the support of the banking regulators in the financial industry. We have previously discussed both the significant cost and fundamental uselessness of Sarbanes-Oxley in the financial industry. Also, Sarbanes-Oxley has practically destroyed the initial public offering (IPO) market in the United States. Realistically, Sarbanes-Oxley is Congress's fault, but the SEC has made the law far worse than it needed to be.

In addition, the SEC has a long history of forcing more and more disclosure in the regulatory filings (such as the 10-K) and financial reporting of public companies. The theory is that more disclosure is always better. In fact, more disclosure can be destructive if it buries important considerations in a mountain of trivia.

Even though I am a financial expert by any objective standard, as previously discussed, I cannot understand the complete financial disclosures of Bank of America. Neither can the CEO of B or A nor the financial analysts on Wall Street. In reading this financial information, it is inevitable that the reader will not be able to see the forest for the trees. Financial information and the related regulatory documents (the 10-K and others) are far more complex and confusing than is necessary. This is because the SEC is dominated by attorneys, many of whom have only a superficial understanding of economics, business, and finance. They are experts on legal details.

The SEC also worked with Eliot Spitzer to destroy the traditional investment banking model. Together, they effectively made it unprofitable for investment banks to operate large-scale investment research operations. In an effort to recoup the lost profits from the investment research business and its related services, the investment banks began to trade more and more with their own capital instead of the capital of their clients. This created two phenomena. First, while investment banks had always made markets, which potentially put them in the opposite risk position from their client, this new trend significantly accelerated this factor, as investment banks more and more became direct investors with their own capital instead of market makers. The other consequence is that investment banks became more and more leveraged.

The leverage trend was magnified by the SEC's decision to apply the Basel capital standards to investment banks. As a reminder, under these standards, the investment banks determined their own capital requirements using complex mathematical models that are sanctioned by the regulators. Fortunately, Basel was never fully implemented for commercial banks.

If the SEC, the Federal Reserve, and banking regulators did not exist, would the investment banks have leveraged themselves to this level? Without government backstops, debtholders would never have extended this level of credit to these institutions. Counterparties to derivatives and other financial instruments would have demanded more collateral. The existence of all these government "supports" creates a perception of low risk that actually creates more risk.

In addition to swamping market participants with useless information and, in effect, encouraging investment banks to take more risk, the SEC did not enforce its own rules. A very interesting area that was affected is naked shorting, which we have previously discussed. The lack of enforcement of the naked short rule misled many market participants.

The greatest damage that the SEC did was through its ownership of the accounting system. We have already discussed the incredible negative impact of fair-value accounting. Fair-value accounting was imposed by the SEC. We have also discussed the destructive trend created by the attorneys at the SEC by forcing the accounting system to change from a principles-based system to a rules-based system.

One of the areas in which the SEC has been most destructive to the banking system has been the accounting for loan loss reserves. For many years, banks created loan loss reserves based on a combination of historical loss experience and their judgment. This process combined mathematical analysis of the past with informed experience. There is an old saying (and a wise one) in the banking industry that bad loans are made in good times. This is because in good times, it is easy to underestimate risk. Bankers often raised their loan loss reserves in good times, when they had strong earnings, to protect against the inevitable rainy day, knowing from experience that the economy has cycles.

The SEC condemned this process because it claimed that banks were managing earnings, that is, that they were trying to make earnings less volatile over various time periods. In fact, the SEC issued an order forcing SunTrust (a major regional bank) to lower its loan loss reserves. The chief credit officer at SunTrust was fired because the bank's loan loss reserves were too high. Obviously, this action affected the behavior of every chief credit officer in the banking industry and materially brought down loan loss reserves in the industry. (Can you believe that the SEC made this occur, given what has happened to the economy?) Of course, no one at the SEC has ever been held responsible for this decision, and the same rules are currently in effect.

The SEC forced the banking industry to remove judgment based on experience from the loan loss reserve decision and to create a process that is almost exclusively mathematically based. This change caused banks to reduce their loan loss reserves substantially.

The SEC's method is to require banks to use mathematical formulas, primarily based on historical loan loss experience combined with future economic projections, to set loan loss reserves. Before the current economic correction, the economy had experienced a long period of relative health, thanks to artificial stimulation by the Federal Reserve.[1] Therefore, looking back, loan losses were very low by longer-term standards. In addition, practically no economists (using mathematical models) were projecting a recession (the Federal Reserve was not projecting a recession), and certainly not a single mainstream economist had projected the depth of the current recession.[2] Therefore, using mathematical models based on historical loan loss experience combined with favorable consensus economic forecasts, banks had very low levels of loan loss reserves when the financial crisis began. Unquestionably, if the banks had used the historical judgmental techniques that they had employed for years, their loan loss reserves would have been much higher when the Great Recession started. Early operating losses in the industry were partially driven by banks simply restoring loan loss reserves that they would have had without the SEC rules.

The loss of capital resulting from rapidly rising loan loss reserves (which increased much faster than actual loan losses) reduced liquidity in the capital markets. Remember, banks are leveraged 10 to 1. Increasing loan loss reserves by $100 million (above actual losses) reduces lending capacity (liquidity) by $1 billion. The building of the loan loss reserves, which would not have been nearly as significant had the SEC not changed the accounting rules, was a meaningful contributor to liquidity issues. Also, these major increases in loan loss reserves substantially magnified the reported operating losses of financial institutions, adding significantly to the fear in financial markets.

It is appropriate to make it clear that the SEC process is wrong in principle. The bad loans that are being charged off today were in fact made during the good times. The only objective standard is the judgmental experience-based process. A pure mathematical process is fundamentally detached from reality. Many important factors are not mathematizable.

Also, because banks were carrying lower loan loss reserves, they were unintentionally overstating their earnings and retained earnings. This belief that earnings were better than they really were caused banks to both raise their dividends and buy back more stock. As a result, banks had both less loan loss reserves and less capital than they would have had if the SEC had not imposed its loan loss reserve rule.

I know from personal experience that this was true for BB&T. Had the SEC and our accountants not pushed us, we would have had substantially higher loan loss reserves. Our chief credit officer was a longtime banker who had seen bad times and wanted more loan loss reserves. Our dividend payout was based on a percentage of earnings (40 to 60 percent). With higher earnings because of lower loan loss provisions, we increased our dividend more than we would have done under our traditional loan loss reserving techniques. In addition, BB&T had a target for equity capital as a percentage of assets. More earnings lead to more retained earnings, that is, a higher ratio of equity capital to assets. Because we were trying to achieve industry-level returns on equity, while we could afford to maintain a somewhat stronger capital position than our peers, we could not hold so much capital that our returns on equity were not competitive, as that would have set us up to be acquired. Therefore, we bought back some of our outstanding stock (which reduced capital) to lower our capital position to a targeted level.

Ironically, the SEC rules combined with the irrational over-reaction by banking regulators (the Federal Deposit Insurance Corporation [FDIC], the Office of the Comptroller of the Currency [OCC], and the Fed) forced banks to overreserve for loan losses during the financial crisis. This has been proved beyond question, as banks are currently (in the fall of 2011) recapturing excess loan loss reserves. The flip side of that old axiom is that good loans are made in bad times, as banks are naturally more conservative.[3] The impact of the excess reserving forced by the SEC and banking regulators was to negatively mislead markets about economic activity and reduce both the willingness and the ability of banks to lend during the difficult environment. This action unquestionably made the crisis more difficult than it should have been and the recession deeper and longer than necessary.

It does not appear to me that there is a totally reliable method for establishing loan loss reserves. The traditional method is far superior to the SEC-imposed rule, but both methods add to the volatility of the economy and unnecessarily create liquidity problems. My suggestion would be to eliminate loan loss reserves altogether and have banks take loan losses when the losses occur. The real solution is for banks to have more capital to absorb losses in difficult times, preferably through a market-based process, as will be discussed in Chapter 19.

Again, the SEC regulations made the financial crisis worse than it needed to be. The argument for regulators is that they are more objective. This is factually incorrect. They are independent, but they are not objective. Being independent does not make you objective. A random person on the streets of New Delhi is independent, but he is not objective with regard to the correct accounting system of the United States. Objectivity requires knowledge and insight. Believing that because government bureaucrats are independent, they are capable of being more objective is irrational. These government bureaucrats are not experts in real-world economics, business, or banking. They are independent, but they are not objective.

By the way, believing that getting different people at the SEC will magically change this process is also irrational. What types of individuals are going to choose to work at a regulatory agency? Markets are constantly making mistakes, but they are also constantly correcting those mistakes. Government bureaucrats are constantly making mistakes, but they are also constantly magnifying those mistakes. A financial information system selected by the market would have weaknesses (as human beings are not omniscient), but it would be far superior to a financial information system created by political bureaucrats.

$$15$$

Market Corrections Are Necessary, but Panics Are Destructive and Avoidable

IN A FREE MARKET, MARKETS ARE CONSTANTLY CORRECTING. SINCE we as human beings are not omniscient, markets are not omniscient. Businesses are constantly failing, and new businesses are being created. New windows of opportunity to create a better quality of life are being produced by entrepreneurs using the advances in technology developed by scientists, and outdated methods of production are being discarded. This is a healthy process.

Some academic economists attack markets because they are not "perfect"; that is, the market does not always produce the optimal outcome as determined after the fact from the perspective of these academic experts. This is a completely irrational attack on markets that is fundamentally philosophically flawed. (This conceptual failure is far deeper than the deceptive argument of "perfect" competition vs. monopoly.)

Human beings have a specific means of knowledge, which is our ability to reason objectively from the facts of reality. We are not God, and so what? Our limitations do not make us flawed any more than an oak tree is flawed because it cannot think. An oak tree has a nature, and humans have a nature. The same philosophers who criticize markets say that perfection is impossible. If something is impossible, it is not perfect by definition. The perfect is the best possible given the facts of reality and our current knowledge. The perfect is consistently improving as humanity's knowledge and understanding advance.

To attack free markets because they do not achieve the impossible is irrational. Free markets produce the best outcomes possible given people's means of knowledge, that is, given our nature. This typical criticism of free markets by left-leaning academic economists is to determine, after the fact, that an expert (such as themselves) could have achieved a better outcome, where the better outcome is as judged by the same experts (that is, themselves). Many times they have not taken a position before the fact, and thus it is impossible to know whether they were correct. Also, with regard to other decisions, how many times would the experts have been wrong and free markets have created a better outcome?

It is irrational to establish a standard for evaluating free markets that is impossible for human beings to achieve, given our nature as thinking beings who can make mistakes. The fact that free markets do not result in perfect outcomes in the eyes of self-declared experts as judged after the fact is a meaningless criticism of market economics. The vast majority of so-called market failures are in this category. In fact, a large percentage of current economic research is based on identifying market failures. Practically all of this analysis is incorrect in principle. The research is based on a premise of market perfection that is philosophically irrational given that humans have a specific nature and are neither omniscient nor omnipotent.

As noted earlier, Thomas Edison had an important insight in this regard. There were in fact 1,000 steps in creating the lightbulb. Every one of his failed experiments was part of the learning process.

Free markets are a collective learning process. They take information from billions of people and integrate that information to produce the best outcome possible, given human nature. In one context (the wrong, that is, left-wing context), free markets are constantly failing because they are not producing the optimal outcomes as evaluated after the fact. This is exactly the same as saying that Thomas

Edison should have skipped those first 999 experiments and performed only the 1,000th experiment that resulted in the lightbulb.

In the proper context, free markets are perfect. They reflect our best knowledge today, given all the information available and also reflecting our reason and our emotions (which are part of our nature as human beings). Free markets are simultaneously conducting millions of experiments; many of these are failing, but 1 out of 1,000 is a success representing an advance for human well-being. It is, in fact, impossible to know before the fact which of the experiments will be a success. If these elitist experts in academia and government are so smart, why do they not simply raise capital and make a fortune while driving markets to their preordained conclusion? Since they will not have to waste resources on these 999 failed experiments, they will soon be tremendously wealthy, and in a short time, they will control the world's economy. I am not at all worried that this will happen. My guess is that the academic elitist experts will go broke quickly. They know this, which is why they want to use your money through the power of the government (that is, the control of force—the gun) to implement their "elitist expert" conclusions.

Returning to the recent financial crisis and the related Great Recession, the world is a better place to live in with Countrywide, Golden West, and Washington Mutual out of business. The leaders of these organizations were making decisions that destroyed billions of dollars of wealth. They were misallocating precious resources (capital) in a destructive manner. They operated failed experiments on a grand scale. Good riddance!

Before the correction, credit standards were far too loose. Many projects (especially real estate–related ones) were being financed that should not have been financed. Capital was being wasted on multiple fronts. There was excessive leverage in the economy. Lending standards needed to be tightened.

The United States had a negative real savings rate. We were effectively eating our seed corn. The only way we could plant next year's crop was to borrow from our neighbors (that is, the Chinese and Japanese). Instead of accumulating capital to invest in technology, manufacturing capacity, agriculture, and other such areas, the United States was consuming residential real estate on a grand scale. Our real savings rate needed to be increased. This is one of the reasons that the massive federal government spending programs have been so destructive. Individuals and businesses are desperately trying to raise their savings rates, while our politicians are dramatically reducing our total savings through unprecedented government spending and the related deficits.

The overinvestment in housing and commercial real estate needed to be corrected. We needed a shift from consumption to investment. In addition, our workforce needed to develop the skills required to produce the products necessary for long-term economic well-being. Thank goodness the housing bubble burst. How much more capital would we have wasted if it had lasted longer?

We absolutely needed a correction—that is, a recession. It is important to understand that the bad event that made the correction necessary was not the recession but the massive misallocation of capital and human resources (the bubble). This is analogous to going on a weeklong binge-drinking spree and then saying that the problem is your hangover. The problem is your binge drinking. By the way, this misidentification of cause and effect is what government stimulus programs reflect. This is the same as saying that after a weeklong drinking binge, you should start drinking Bloody Marys in the morning; this will make the hangover go away, and you can start binge drinking again. Obviously, at some point, there will be a day of reckoning. In fact, if you keep it up long enough, you will get cirrhosis of the liver and die. If the U.S. economy stays on Bloody Marys, followed by more binge drinking, it will also die.

While we needed an economic correction, we never should have been in a position to have so massive a misallocation that it created a need for a decline of the magnitude that the U.S. economy experienced. If markets had been allowed to correct naturally, many of the problems that caused the depth of the Great Recession would have already been cured, and we would not have experienced such a drastic depreciation of wealth. Alan Greenspan's (the Federal Reserve's) obsession with not having an economic correction on his watch so that he could be the maestro was the foundation for massive future problems.[1]

On several occasions, students have said to me that if these policies created 15 good years, the pain we are having today is worth it. This is the same as saying, I have used cocaine for 15 years and enjoyed it very much. This cocaine withdrawal I am going through is worth the pain, given all the past good times.

The problem with this type of conclusion is that using cocaine does permanent damage to the body. Even if you are successful in defeating your cocaine habit today, your life expectancy is far shorter than it would have been if you had never taken cocaine.

The same is true of the U.S. economy. Forever, our standard of living will be less than it would otherwise have been because of the misallocation of resources that resulted in the bubble in our economy. We taught our workforce how to do tasks that are not needed. We drove manufacturing jobs to China. We created a massive amount of debt that will have to be repaid. We were fooled by the Federal Reserve and the related government housing policies. We thought we were in better health than we were, and we made wrong decisions based on this misleading information.

None of this means that the U.S. economy cannot recover. In fact, our economy can and probably will get better. If you quit smoking, you can improve your future health. However, your life expectancy will still be less than it would have been had you never smoked. Unfortunately, we smoked three packs a day for 15 years. We will need to exercise hard to repair some of the damage.

While economic corrections are a necessary part of the free-market learning experience, panics are not necessary and are particularly destructive. The panic atmosphere during the recent financial crisis was totally the result of massive mishandling of the financial system by government policy makers in the Bush administration. In fact, Bush's policies were highly destructive, and Obama has made them worse. This is analogous with Herbert Hoover and FDR's handling of the Great Depression.[2]

In the early 1980's, the U.S. economic system was in worse shape than it was in 2008 because of a 15-year period of terrible governmental policies attributable to Johnson, Nixon, and Carter (1963–1976). The Federal Reserve drove the prime rate to 21 percent and severely restricted credit. Hundreds of thrifts and commercial banks failed. Bill Isaac, who was placed on the board of the FDIC in 1978 and headed the FDIC from 1981 to 1985, took a leadership position, ensuring that a panic did not occur. He is extremely critical of the manner in which the recent crisis was handled, and rightly so. He concluded that the panic environment of 2008 was unnecessary. He is correct.[3]

The financial paniclike environment of the fall of 2008 was the result of a series of major blunders by the Federal Reserve, the U.S. Treasury, and banking regulators. Of course, these mistakes were made in the context of serious long-term monetary policy errors by the Federal Reserve and government housing policy, which we have discussed, but the extremely poor execution of decisions made during 2007–2008 made all the issues much worse.

One of the most significant mistakes made by government regulators took place early in the process, when they decided to save Bear Stearns (on March 17, 2008) by negotiating a privileged sale to JPMorgan Chase while reducing Chase's downside risk. The sale could not have taken place without the support of the U.S. Treasury and the Federal Reserve, as the latter bought $30 billion in bad assets for cash. What is particularly interesting is that the shareholders of Bear Stearns actually received compensation, admittedly at a low price. Therefore, the U.S. taxpayers were protecting shareholders! In previous bailouts, at least the shareholders almost always experienced total losses.

The Bear Stearns bailout was a terrible message to the capital market. Since Bear Stearns was the smallest and least significant of the top six investment banks, the implication was that the larger investment banks had an implicit guarantee from the U.S. Treasury. Had Bear Stearns failed, Lehman would almost certainly have taken more aggressive action over the next six months to reduce risk and raise capital. With the Bear bailout (including compensation to shareholders), Lehman believed that the worst-case scenario was a government bailout at a lower stock price. Why not keep gambling, hoping that the company could stay afloat, when we knew that in the worst case, the government would save us? Of course, Lehman failed on September 15, 2008.

Despite having a large and longtime relationship with Lehman, BB&T did not suffer any losses when Lehman failed. There were two reasons for this outcome. First, we had maintained our counterparty risk with Lehman and all other financial institutions within rational limits for many years. Second, even though Bear had been saved by the Federal Reserve, we decided to tighten our counterparty risk on all fronts. Frankly, from long experience, we had learned never to trust the regulators.

Unfortunately, many other financial institutions had learned the opposite lesson. They believed that the Federal Reserve and the Treasury would save Lehman if it got into financial trouble, so they did not act to reduce their counterparty risk. In fact, in many cases, Lehman's counterparties allowed their risk to increase after Bear was saved because the implied government guarantee of Lehman via the Bear bailout was perceived to reduce risk.

We have already discussed the significant impact of the decision by the FDIC, the Fed, and the Treasury to pay the uninsured depositors of Washington Mutual (Washington Mutual was sold to JPMorgan Chase on September 25, 2008), which substantially increased the losses for WaMu's bondholders and destroyed the capital markets for banks. This damage could easily have been avoided by absorbing the extra losses related to paying unsecured depositors with funds from the FDIC insurance pool.

Immediately after the destructive handling of WaMu by the regulators, Wachovia effectively failed because of the capital-market chaos. The bank examiners forced the sale of Wachovia and totally bungled the sales process. They initially required a bid for Wachovia, and the only bidder was Citigroup. It was announced that Citigroup had won the bid and would be taking over Wachovia.[4]

Since Citigroup was in worse financial condition than Wachovia, it was bizarre that the regulators thought that Citi could save Wachovia. The morning this announcement was made, the market knew that it was a completely irrational idea and reacted accordingly. Why would the regulators even allow Citi to bid? The limited confidence that the market had in the regulators dropped to zero.

A few days later, it was announced that Wells Fargo was going to buy Wachovia without assistance from the FDIC. This was a far more rational transaction, although it was risky for Wells Fargo shareholders. However, even though the Wells Fargo deal was far more rational than the Citi transaction, how could the regulators simply tear up the agreement with Citi? The capital markets now knew, with certainty, that the FDIC, the Fed, and the Treasury were not only incompetent but untrustworthy. They could not even be relied on to execute their agreements.

The major issue for capital-market participants was that it was absolutely clear that Bernanke, Paulson, Blair, and the others had no strategy and no plan to deal with the crisis. Decisions were clearly being made ad hoc. There was no rational pattern of decision making. Every decision seemed random and disconnected. It was also clear that the rule of law no longer existed.

The failure of Lehman Brothers has been described as a definitive trigger for the crisis, but in truth this is not what rattled the capital markets so much; rather, it was the inconsistency and arbitrariness of government policy makers.[5] It didn't help that during the chaos of September 2008, Lehman Brothers refused to take the rather ordinary legal steps necessary to enter into an orderly bankruptcy proceeding, instead eagerly trying to locate a savior among sharklike rivals, so the firm's bankruptcy also was chaotic. In the end, U.K.-based Barclays Bank paid $1.75 billion for whatever value remained at Lehman (versus a market cap of $25 billion a few months prior).

As discussed earlier, the market also perceived (fairly or unfairly) that Paulson's decisions to save AIG and Goldman and to let Lehman fail were driven by personal issues, not strategy, which materially undermined market confidence. In addition, Paulson adamantly defended the economic viability of Freddie and Fannie almost until their official failures. It appears that he may have been telling some of his close friends that Freddie and Fannie were in trouble, while indicating to the public that the companies were healthy. In any event, the failure of the GSEs after Paulson defense of them reduced his credibility even further.

In any event, it was obvious to all capital-market participants that the leaders of incredibly powerful Cabinet and regulatory agencies in Washington had not developed a strategy or any kind of plan. In short, they didn't have a clue, which wouldn't have been so bad except that they had already been established as the wisest of the nation's planners, fully in charge of the entire economy and financial system and capable of guiding, shaping, and saving it. Only these commissars could see the "big picture," we were all told. Instead, we all found in 2008 that they were myopic—and that their decisions were made on the fly, often on the backs of envelopes. Worse perhaps, the regulators were perceived as being untrustworthy. There was no more rule of law, no more fixity; now it was the rule of men, and we had to guess what they'd do—and their decisions increasingly reflected personal emotions and idiosyncrasies. No wonder the capital markets panicked.

Of course, the final straw was the announcement of the need for a $700 billion government bailout—the Troubled Asset Relief Plan (TARP). When the head of the Federal Reserve, the Treasury, and the president announced that Western civilization would end unless Congress approved a $700 billion bailout, people panicked. Before this announcement, it was clear that the economy was in a recession. However, while economic activity was slowing, it had not stopped. The announcement of the need for a bailout of this magnitude and the incredible risk if the bailout were not approved by Congress dramatically increased fear. The announcement of the need for the bailout temporarily paralyzed business decision making.

As discussed in the previous chapter, even given these mistakes, the crisis could have been avoided. The first step would have been honesty and objectivity. It should be noted that throughout, Bernanke and Paulson underestimated the depth of the problems, constantly indicating that Freddie and Fannie would not fail and that other related problems would not occur. The capital-market participants knew that the economic problems were deeper and believed that Bernanke and Paulson were either incredibly naïve or not fundamentally honest, or both. This perception undermined their credibility.

Panics create liquidity risks for all financial institutions, even fundamentally sound institutions. Panics cause lending standards to become too tight, which is destructive. Panics create self-fulfilling downward spirals that unnecessarily destroy wealth. A deep recession was avoidable from a long-term policy perspective but was not avoidable in the short term, given the huge policy mistakes that government agencies had previously made; however, a true panic could easily have been avoided.

16

TARP (Troubled Asset Relief Program)

THE TROUBLED ASSET RELIEF PROGRAM (TARP), ALSO KNOWN AS the bank bailout, was one of the more dramatic events of the financial crisis. This program was presented to Congress as an absolutely mandatory emergency act to save the U.S. financial system. President Bush made a public plea for Congress to pass TARP with the emotional implication that failing to approve this bill would almost certainly cause another Great Depression. The obvious fear shown by Ben Bernanke (the Fed chairman) and Hank Paulson (secretary of the Treasury), along with President Bush's actions, significantly increased fear in the economy.

The original intent of the proposal was for the Fed to buy "troubled assets" from commercial and investment banks, creating liquidity in the financial system. This was a dysfunctional concept that was never executed. The fundamental problem with TARP as originally proposed was how to price the troubled assets. Because of the uncertainty that the regulators had created by the arbitrary nature of their previous actions (that is, save Bear, let Lehman fail, save Citi, let Wachovia fail, and so on), along with the announcement of TARP itself, buyers were willing to pay only very deeply discounted prices for troubled assets in this chaotic environment.

If the assets had been purchased at these prices, all the banks selling the troubled assets would have failed. On the other hand, if the Fed had paid an arbitrarily high, above-market price for the troubled assets, the taxpayers would have been subject to massive losses. Determining the right price for the troubled assets was simply not practical.

Also, most of the troubled assets were bonds backed by home mortgages. Was the federal government ready to orchestrate a massive foreclosure program at the same time the administration was encouraging private lenders to have forbearance? If the delinquent mortgages were not foreclosed on, would that have created a huge moral hazard effect, with many underwater homeowners simply deciding not to pay their home loans because they knew that their homes would not be foreclosed?

I was adamantly against TARP, as originally proposed, for a number of reasons. First, it was clear that it would not work. In addition, it was a blatantly obvious effort to bail out the giant money-center banks and the investment banks. The troubled assets were basically rated bonds backed by home mortgages that were held in the investment portfolios of these major financial institutions. Traditional commercial banks primarily held direct home mortgages (not rated mortgage bonds), and the commercial banks' bond portfolio was already largely government bonds. While there would have been token benefits for large regional commercial banks, the vast majority of any benefit from the program would have been to the top five financial institutions. The concept was clearly designed by Paulson, a lifetime investment banker, to assist investment banks and money-center banks. While the primary cause of the financial crisis was government policies, the secondary cause was very destructive decisions made by the very financial institutions that were to be saved.

It was also clear that a substantial amount of taxpayer funds could be used to save nonbanks, such as General Electric, auto companies, AIG, and GMAC. It is unreasonable to argue that saving these nonbanks was necessary to prevent a systems risk issue in the banking network.

Furthermore, it was obvious that the $700 billion amount was completely arbitrary. Why $700 billion? Of course, the $700 billion has never been used. Bernanke and Paulson wanted a huge "blank check" to spend any way they wanted to, with the funds coerced from Congress under duress. Since Bernanke and Paulson's arbitrary handling of the financial situation up to that point was a major contribution to the crisis, giving them a blank check did not appear to be appropriate.

Also, it is almost certain that TARP was unconstitutional, given the limitations in the Constitution designed to prevent this uncontrolled use of taxpayers' money. (However, the modern Supreme Court might not have ruled against TARP.)

The actual use of TARP funds was very different from the original proposal. The most visible use was capital investments in commercial banks and nonbanks (GM and GMAC, among others). TARP also allowed the Federal Deposit Insurance Corporation (FDIC) to directly guarantee bank debt and increase FDIC insurance coverage.

One of the primary beneficiaries was General Electric. GE operated a high-risk equipment finance business. It funded a major portion of these subprime business loans overnight in the commercial paper market, which is an extremely risky funding strategy. With the stress in the capital markets, GE was struggling to issue commercial paper. Using TARP, the Fed stepped in and effectively saved GE Capital. Even though the funding was ultimately repaid, the taxpayers were taking substantial risk relative to the return. Also, the shareholders of GE benefited dramatically without any cost. It is not surprising that GE has become more of a crony capitalist organization since it was saved by the government. Also, do not be surprised if it returns to the same high-risk financing strategy in the future. After all, there is no downside risk when you have a strong relationship with Big Brother.

Many people have declared TARP a success because most of the money will be paid back. This is a totally improper measure of performance. Even if the taxpayers get most of their money back, the risk/return trade-off was irrational at the time the government investments were made. Private investors would not have taken this risk given the relatively low returns to be earned.

More significantly, a rational assessment of TARP must consider its short-term and long-term economic consequences. This is a challenging question to answer, but there is a historical precedent that is useful for comparison. In the early 1920s, there was a severe economic correction. The government did practically nothing to fight this correction. While the correction was deep, it was over quickly and was followed by an extended period of strong economic growth.[1]

In the early 1930s, when another major correction began, the government interfered on multiple fronts, similar to today. That correction (the Great Depression) did not end until after World War II, when many of the New Deal policies designed to fix the economy were abandoned.

It is very likely that without TARP, we would have had a deeper economic correction. However, it is also very probable that the correction would have been shorter and the long-term economic growth trend more healthy. The deeper correction would have quickly destroyed irrational investments but at the same time created an economic foundation with far less ambiguity on which business leaders could make the right kind of investments for the future.

I will share a personal story with you. I was opposed to TARP (especially as a troubled asset purchase program). In fact, I lobbied Congress strongly against TARP. I tried very hard to meet with Bernanke and Paulson. Neither of them would meet with me. In fact, two other CEOs of healthy regional banks with whom I talked had also tried to talk to Bernanke and Paulson and had been denied the opportunity. Paulson and Bernanke were in almost constant conversation with the unhealthy institutions, but they would not talk to the leaders of the healthy banks.

Despite my opposition, when TARP was passed, BB&T chose to participate. This was an interesting experience. The day after TARP passed, we were contacted by our regulators. This was an informal contact over the phone. I received a very carefully stated nondocumentable message. The essence of the message was that although BB&T had substantially more capital than it needed under long-established regulatory standards, given the current economic environment, the regulators were going to create a new set of capital standards. They did not know what the standards would be. However, they were "very concerned" that we would not have enough capital under these new standards unless we took the TARP capital. They had a regulatory team in place to reexamine our capital position immediately unless we took the TARP funding. The threat was very clear. We said, "Please sign us up for TARP."

Several months later, the regulators introduced the "stress test" to ensure that banks were properly capitalized. BB&T passed the stress test with flying colors. In other words, we never needed the TARP capital. This is proved conclusively by the fact that BB&T did not suffer a single quarterly operating loss during the crisis. How could we have needed more capital?

Even without this direct regulatory pressure, it would have been difficult to refuse TARP funding in the panicky environment. Supposedly, "qualifying" for TARP meant that a financial institution was in acceptable financial condition. If BB&T had refused TARP, the market could easily have interpreted this as meaning that we were in financial trouble, and our liquidity position could have deteriorated very rapidly. There is an analogy with FDIC deposit insurance. I am opposed to FDIC insurance (we should have a private insurance pool). However, if BB&T did not have FDIC insurance, we could not compete with our banking competitors who have government insurance. The very existence of a government program forces private companies to participate. In the end, you cannot compete with the government because it has the power to tax and to regulate—that is, these are the only people with a "gun."

An interesting question is why the Federal Reserve wanted the large banks to participate in TARP. Bernanke is a student of the Depression.[2] In fact, his claim to fame is an academic paper that he wrote on the Great Depression (the assumptions in that paper were not valid for 2008). During the Depression, the government tried to save individual banks. However, as soon as the market found out that a bank was to be helped by the government, market funding for the bank was withdrawn because it was considered to be in trouble.

There were three large financial institutions that were in severe distress at the time of the TARP discussion. Bernanke believed that if he tried to save these specific companies, the market would turn on them and they would face a major liquidity problem. However, if TARP were positioned as a program to provide liquidity to banks to encourage them to lend, instead of as a bailout, and especially if healthy banks participated, the market would not see the program as a bailout of specific firms. Even if it was viewed as a bailout (which it was), it would be seen as an industry rescue, not a rescue of specific banks. Therefore, the Fed effectively forced all banks with $100 billion and over to participate.

I talked to the CEOs of several other large, healthy institutions who also had participated after very strong regulatory encouragement (that is, carefully veiled threats). For the sins of a few, we saw that all banks were being tarred with the same TARP brush—and effectively becoming trapped by it. "He who pays the piper calls the tune." Washington was paying, so it told TARP banks what to do. Understandably, public resentment rained down on all bankers (innocent and guilty alike), and as class-warfare rhetoric spread ("Wall Street versus Main Street"), so did bailout demands, and before long a "pay czar" was visiting TARP banks and dictating pay plans.

It is also appropriate to remember that Paulson was an investment banker. As an investment banker, he realized that by "encouraging" the healthy banks to participate in TARP, he would make the TARP program appear to be more successful for taxpayers. The healthy banks would certainly pay back the loans with interest and cover at least part of the losses from unhealthy banks.

In November 2008, when we signed TARP, I was a few weeks away from retiring as CEO of BB&T. This was an amazing experience. The TARP agreement laid out all the terms that BB&T had to unconditionally comply with, and then at the end of the agreement, there was a paragraph that said that the government could change any of the terms of the agreement any time it wanted to for any reason, and that it had the power to change existing management contracts and existing retirement agreements. A contract where one party can change all the terms is not a contract. In fact, the content of the contract demonstrates that it was entered into under duress.

Of course, TARP was very negative for healthy banks. We had to pay an above-market interest rate for money that we did not need. The Treasury also took warrants on our stock. When the stress test was complete, it was clear that BB&T had not needed TARP funding. The cost of TARP to BB&T was between $50 and $100 million. TARP was a subsidy to unhealthy banks at the expense of healthy banks. When we were finally allowed to, BB&T was the first bank to repay TARP (admittedly by only a few minutes, but we were first).

In a broader context, TARP was very destructive for healthy institutions. When the government bailed out unhealthy companies, the flight to quality in the market slowed and finally stopped. Irrational competitors were kept in business to continue their destructive financial practices. Potential acquisition opportunities were destroyed. Clearly, the message was to take high risk in the good times because the government will save you in the bad times. This creates a huge moral hazard. Being conservative is a losing strategy. There is no long-term reward for not taking irrational risk. This is a very destructive message.

Also, a government-sponsored oligopoly has been created in the financial services industry. This oligopoly has been created not by market forces, but by the arbitrary action of government regulators during a government-created crisis. There are at least six financial institutions that have clearly been defined as "too big to fail" (Citi, Bank of America, Wells Fargo, Goldman Sachs, JPMorgan Chase, and Morgan Stanley). The Dodd-Frank bill does not deal with the "too-big-to-fail" issue effectively, despite the comments of its proponents. In fact, the rating agencies have indicated that the credit ratings of these giant financial institutions are several grades higher than they would be without the implied government guarantee post-Dodd-Frank.

This situation creates a major competitive advantage for these giant firms in the long term. When times are good again and the regulators look away (because of political pressure created by the massive lobbying efforts of these crony capitalist/socialist firms), the companies will be back taking irrational risk, with the goal of short-term profit maximizing. A zebra does not change its stripes. In my career, Citigroup has been saved by the government three times. Each time, it has afterward become bigger and worse. This is an almost certain outcome of the distorted incentive system that keeps incompetent companies in business.

In the meantime, these government-supported companies will develop strategies that involve terribly risky investments and that will drive their remaining midsize competitors out of whole market segments. Again, this is an almost guaranteed long-term outcome.

174 • THE FINANCIAL CRISIS AND THE FREE MARKET CURE

Also, because of the negative perception of the bailout, Dodd-Frank was passed. This is incredibly economically destructive regulation. The legislation will be more detrimental to the healthy banks than to those financial institutions that should have failed. The well-run companies will be permanently damaged by the irrationality of their competitors and the related socialist/statist government reaction.

I am opposed to the antitrust laws. Also, I do not believe that these oligopoly banks are too big to fail. However, if the government regulators do believe that these companies are too big to fail (and the government regulators and the rating agencies do believe it), they should be broken up.

Unfortunately, the antitrust policy of the Federal Reserve is completely arbitrary to the point of being irrational. A short time before the financial crisis started, BB&T acquired a small bank in the Tennessee/North Carolina mountains. We were forced to divest a $25 million branch office because of antitrust rules. Wells Fargo acquired Wachovia, creating a $1.5 trillion company with dominating market shares in a number of areas, without having to make a single divestiture. The Fed uses an arbitrary mathematical formula to determine divestitures that focuses totally on the "trees" and is oblivious to the "forest." It ignores the strategies that allow mid-tier banks to be competitive in the long term against giant financial institutions. The Fed's antitrust process and formula lead to more concentration in the banking industry in the long term.

TARP has also kept many community banks in business that should have failed. These zombie banks are reducing the profitability of the remaining healthy community banks. Also, the banking market has not been able to clear (like the residential real estate market), and this has depressed the stock prices of all community banks. The depressed stock prices keep banks that could become healthy from being able to raise capital. TARP is a curse for basically healthy community banks by keeping irrational competitors in business.

The creation of the crisis that made TARP "necessary" was the result of both long-term and short-term massive mismanagement of monetary and fiscal policy by government bureaucrats, with significant support from Congress. Given the huge problems that the regulators had created, some type of intervention may have appeared necessary. However, whatever the short-term benefits may be, the long-term impact of TARP will reduce our standard of living and increase the probabilities of crises in the future. We must learn that human action is consistent with incentives and that it is crucial to understand whether incentives encourage us to act virtuously or destructively. Implied government guarantees create incentives to think short term and to take irrational risk, which inflicts costs that are invariably paid by others who are innocent.

17

What We Could Have— and Should Have—Done

ONE OF THE FUNDAMENTAL REASONS THAT FREE MARKETS ALWAYS raise the standard of living in the long term is that free markets are just. They reward firms and individuals that provide goods and services that are demanded by consumers and punish firms and individuals who waste precious resources. The punishment process is as important as the reward system. If companies that do not use our limited resources (capital, labor, and raw materials) efficiently are kept in business, they will continue to waste those precious resources in the future. Markets must be allowed to correct if a free-market economy is to perform successfully in the long term. The first thing government policy makers should have done in 2007–2008 was let markets correct. That is, they should have let falling prices reach their level, so that markets would clear—not forestall the pain with more of the same drug ("stimulus").

Even if there is an argument for protecting certain creditors of a firm, when shareholders are protected, the firm's behavior does not change in the long term. We just discussed the example of Citigroup, where multiple bailouts have led to future bigger bailouts. Even if there is a systemic risk argument for protecting certain of Citi's constituents, such as depositors and some bondholders, why were the shareholders protected?

GMAC is a classic example of a destructive bailout strategy. GMAC (now Ally Financial) was the finance arm of General Motors. It was a major contributor to problems in the automobile industry. First, in order to provide temporary incentives to increase auto sales volumes, it became a major provider of high-risk auto finance. This can be a legitimate business if it is managed properly, including requiring healthy down payments. Unfortunately, GMAC did not manage its business properly, but instead offered high-percentage financing to the subprime auto market, which ultimately created huge losses.

Also, GMAC created the seven-year, 100 percent financing car loan. Unfortunately, after three years, the typical car purchaser owed more on his car than it was worth, so he could not buy a new car. In addition, when the consumer could not pay, the loss to the lender on repossessed cars was very high. Because GMAC was a dominant player, it distorted the entire auto finance market.

Despite this very destructive behavior, the government has bailed out GMAC multiple times during the financial crisis. The argument is that GMAC is essential to providing financing for the sale of automobiles. This is not factually correct. BB&T has been in the automobile finance business for 50 years. We are very willing to provide automobile financing. However, we are not willing to make the irrational car loans that GMAC provides that have helped to create problems in the automobile industry. Of course, these loans should not be made. What the government is doing is helping GMAC provide risky financing that was destructive in the first place.

In addition, how can GMAC's failure possibly be considered a systemic risk to the financial industry? What is the Fed doing saving GMAC? Where is the justice in saving GMAC and not helping all the local builders in the housing market that have been allowed to fail? Clearly, more damage has been done to the economy by the failure of local home builders than by the lack of financing for automobiles. Where was the Fed in helping local builders? In fact, as discussed earlier, the Fed bank examiners have forced many home builders out of business while, at the same time, the agency is saving GMAC. Where is the justice? Could it be that the highly unionized automobile industry, which has powerful contacts with the Democratic Party through massive political contributions, got special treatment?

The average Joe may not know the details of what happened with TARP and all the other government bailouts, but he smells a problem. He sees Goldman Sachs being bailed out and the autoworkers being bailed out. He sees the crony capitalists (crony socialists) and unions obtaining special favors at his expense. He then loses confidence in capitalism (although crony capitalists cannot exist in a free market), and he loses confidence in government institutions, from Congress to the Fed. Not surprisingly, he then does not act the way the government regulators want him to act when they offer their solutions for his problems.

The most interesting example of the long-term destruction caused by government bailouts is Chrysler. Recall that Chrysler was first bailed out by Washington in 1979 under President Carter. The bailout was considered a success because Chrysler had a short period of healthy profitability. However, after this brief successful period, Chrysler struggled for a number of years and failed during the financial crisis. Ironically, it was effectively sold to a European company (Fiat) as part of the new rescue.

Here is the interesting question: what would have happened if Chrysler had been allowed to fail in 1979? First, note that none of Chrysler's resources (plants, equipment, and workers) would have disappeared. The resources would simply have been reallocated. Some of Chrysler's resources (plants, workers, and dealerships) might have been sold to General Motors and Ford. This realignment of resources would have made both Ford and GM more efficient.

More important, the management and labor unions of Ford and GM would have learned the right lessons: if they did not run their companies well, they would be out of business. This insight (and fear) would have created more rationality in both the management and the United Auto Workers union, probably resulting in more effective economic decisions. Unfortunately, the lesson that both the unions and management learned from the Chrysler bailout was that in the worst case, the government will save them. This was a particularly powerful lesson for the politically connected unions, making them less willing to implement work-rule changes, until too late, that could have saved GM. (Human beings act consistent with incentives.)

Also if Chrysler had been allowed to fail, it is possible that the bulk of Chrysler's resources would have ended up in a new U.S.-owned nonunion automobile company. Because this new company would not have been burdened with destructive union contracts, it could have been competitive with the Japanese manufacturers. While the Japanese automobile manufacturers have some good management practices, by far the primary cause of their success in the United States is that they are not unionized. The lack of union interference creates several thousand dollars of cost advantages per automobile for the Japanese manufacturers relative to unionized U.S. automobile firms.

It is almost certain that the U.S. automobile industry would have been far healthier entering this financial crisis had Chrysler been allowed to fail in 1979.

By the way, in both the original Chrysler bailout and the recent bailout of GM and Chrysler, the beneficiaries were the unions. Both GM's and Chrysler's shareholders were wiped out, as they should have been. The case of the GM bondholders is particularly unjust. Through government interference in the bankruptcy process, the UAW's pension obligations were protected at the expense of the GM bondholders. The bond indenture provisions were deliberately ignored; the rule of law was jettisoned. Does any of that bode well for attracting future creditors to the bonds of firms that are forced to deal with unions? In the future, will the bondholders react aggressively at the first sign of trouble? In these cases, the government was not bailing out the companies; it was bailing out the unions. Many taxpayers with lower income and fewer benefits than union members are being taxed to bail out the highly compensated autoworkers.

In addition to allowing markets to correct, the second action that should have been taken was to cut government spending, not to increase spending. *It seems bizarre to believe that spending money you do not have on things that do not need to be done will raise your standard of living in the long term.* If you lost your job, would you increase your spending?

The notion that government spending could stimulate expanded economic activity in a recession was primarily proposed by John

Maynard Keynes in his 1936 book, *The General Theory of Employment, Interest and Money*; thereafter, it became the dominant view of how to cure recessions until it was discredited during the destructive "stagflation" of the 1970s. In his book, Keynes literally argued that during economic downturns, the government should pay people to dig holes in the ground and then pay other people to fill the holes back up. Do you think this process will raise our standard of living? As hard as it is to believe, this is the core of Keynes's argument,[1] and it made a big comeback during the economic downturn of 2007–2009.

The idea is that if we pay Joe to dig a hole, he will then use the money to buy bread, so the baker will make more money; the baker will then buy shoes, so the cobbler will make more money; and so on. This is the so-called multiplier effect. The first problem with the argument is that the government must get money from somewhere to pay Joe, so it taxes Tom. Tom then has less money to spend, so he spends less and offsets the multiplier. Even worse, we now have the useless hole that Joe dug, instead of the computer that Tom would have bought.

Of course, Keynes had a cure for this issue. He simply said, don't tax Tom, just print more money. After all, nobody will notice. Of course, just printing money is a con game because if there are no more goods to buy, but there is more money to buy them with, then your money is worth less and you have been taxed; the tax is just less visible.

Today, people have figured the con game out. They know that when the government spends money it does not have, eventually taxes will be increased and the value of their money will be devalued.[2]

It is now clear that the Obama stimulus program has failed. In technical terms, the multiplier is less than 1.[3] In other words, private spending increased less than it would have done had the government not had the stimulus program in the first place. Individuals realized that one way or the other, they were going to have to pay for this useless government spending, so they decided to spend less personally.

The U.S. stimulus program did create economic growth; unfortunately, the growth took place in China. Since many of the items purchased under the stimulus program have at least some component made in China, the U.S. taxpayer has helped to create a boom in China. The Chinese are spending the stimulus funds because, unlike U.S. taxpayers, the Chinese will not have to pay higher taxes in the future to pay the stimulus back. The Chinese should be very grateful to the U.S. Congress and the Obama administration. In addition, they are smart enough to have rapidly expanded their investments in gold as an inflation hedge against the U.S. dollar.

In the fall of 2010, I heard a story about the dysfunctionality of Obama's Keynesian-inspired $817 billion "stimulus" launched in February 2009. I was talking to a commercial contractor whose primary business is building and/or repairing municipal water systems. This is just the type of firm that would be expected to benefit from the stimulus program.

However, the exact opposite occurred. A number of municipalities had had plans to expand or improve their water systems in process. However, when they learned that the stimulus program was available and realized that they might get "free" money from the federal government, they decided to wait for the stimulus money.

After months of waiting, the rules for the stimulus program were published. When the municipalities saw all the controls that came with this "free lunch," they decided to pass on the program. In some cases, they then did proceed with their original plans. In other cases, however, because of the recession, the municipalities' finances had deteriorated so much that they decided to defer the water project. The contractor has reduced his workforce from 350 to 150.

In principle, the U.S. government should run a balanced budget, not try to manipulate economic activity through so-called fiscal policy. In addition, the federal government should be involved only in activities that are *specifically* authorized by the U.S. Constitution. The purpose of these activities should be to defend individual rights. Defending individual rights requires a strong military, an effective police force, and a sound judicial system to prevent and/or punish the use of force or fraud by those who would take property from another person who has earned it. A court system is necessary to settle legitimate disputes. The Founding Fathers were also strong advocates of sound money.

Obviously, most of the activities that the federal government is involved in today are inconsistent with the principles of limited government, individual rights, and free markets as envisioned by the Founding Fathers. If government activities were consistent with these principles, government expenditures and the related taxes required to balance the budget would be a dramatically smaller part of the economy, and fiscal policy (deficit spending) would not be an issue. Also, crony capitalism (crony socialism) would not exist because government could not dole out favors to political constituents and unions could not buy special benefits through political contributions.

Total spending at all levels of American government (federal, state, and local) was only 8 percent of U.S. GDP a century ago (1911), and the United States was rapidly ascending as a global economic force. Total government spending a half-century ago (1961) was 25 percent of GDP, at the start of a prosperous decade that ended in the moon landing. Today (2011), total spending is 38 percent of U.S. GDP (and rising quickly), and our economy isn't growing half as fast as China's.

Obviously, we live in a different world from the Founding Fathers. However, the principles of limited government are still important as guides to the appropriate policy directions. In this context, if there were to be a stimulus, the proper strategy would have been to cut taxes, especially on businesses and high-income individuals. Businesses and high-income individuals are the creators of jobs and economic well-being. They are focused on productive investments (not digging holes in the ground) that raise our standard of living.

One of the main factors that has contributed to the depth and duration of this economic correction is the huge amount of ambiguity created by government policy makers on many fronts. One of the basic rules of leadership is that when a system driven by human decision making is headed in a negative direction, the worst thing you can do is introduce more ambiguity and/or uncertainty. Under duress, humans will naturally assume the worst. BB&T executed a number of mergers during my career. We learned that the most important action we could take during the merger process was to eliminate as much uncertainty as possible so that people could think clearly.

Whether or not you think the Obama healthcare bill and the Dodd-Frank bill (financial reform) are good from a long-term policy perspective, introducing multithousand-page regulations in the middle of an economic correction is a clear failure of leadership. (I think both bills are very economically destructive, and we should start over in both cases.)

In conversations with many small business owners, I have learned that they are not hiring or expanding because they do not know what the impact of the healthcare legislation will be on their business. Also, they are concerned that their banks may be affected by the financial legislation and be less willing to finance their business's growth.

The attack on business leaders has also been destructive. In conversations with many business leaders, I have seen that there is a clear perception that this is the most antibusiness administration in our lifetime—not just from a policy perspective but based on the idea that businesspeople are fundamentally unethical money-grubbers who will do anything for a buck. Businesspeople are a barely necessary evil that must be controlled on all fronts. The fact that businesses provide the goods and services that make life possible is dismissed as meaningless. This saps the energy of business leaders, who realize that they can make mistakes even when they are absolutely motivated to lead a productive business. Why take the risk when any action will be judged negatively?

The verbal attack on the wealthy from the presidential pulpit also has a destructive impact on human psychology. Not all wealthy people are productive. However, many of the most productive individuals are wealthy. The attack on the wealthy is effectively an attack on the productive. When individuals are verbally abused, they can go "on strike" in subtle ways. They can simply decide to take less risk. After all, why take risk when you will be criticized by the president, the press, academics, and the clergy if you are successful? The highly productive already have all the money they need in order to live well. They are motivated by building, by the thrill of growing their business. While money is a motivation for some businesspeople, most successful entrepreneurs are primarily motivated by the act of creation, the ability to control their destiny, and the desire to build. Liberals totally misunderstand what motivates the best business leaders.

On a general plane, the attack on free markets undermines the confidence of investors. Most businesspeople already know that government does not create wealth. If free markets are not effective, and if financial institutions are not trustworthy, individuals do not have the confidence to make investments.

Of course, we do not have a free market in the United States. We have a mixed economy. While individual financial institutions made mistakes, the financial crisis was caused by mistakes in government policy. At an even deeper level, many of the financial institutions that contributed to the problem were crony capitalists. Business leaders can have confidence in the working of free markets. It is government interference in markets that they should fear.

At the deepest level, government decision makers (in both political parties) and the majority of academic economists are completely backward in their thinking. They are victims of the Keynesian fallacy. The underlying premise of the neo-Keynesian argument that is driving government economic policy is that demand creates supply, and that the problem in a recession is lack of demand.

This is an absurd premise on its face. The families living in the houses being foreclosed have a strong "demand" for housing; however, they are not productive enough (supply) to pay the cost of the housing. The people in equatorial Africa have a strong demand for clean water, sanitary plumbing, electricity, and other such goods. Sadly, they are not productive enough to be able to afford these necessities. The reason the United States entered a recession was not a lack of demand; it was because our resources had been misallocated, so we could not continue to consume (demand) at the same level. Trillions of dollars of capital had been misallocated to housing, and millions of workers had learned the wrong skills. There was plenty of demand. However, we did not have the resources (capital and labor) to meet the demand—that is, the demand was illegitimate because of the lack of productivity of our economic system.

It should be obvious that in the long term, supply (production) creates demand. Think of the percentage of our workforce that is involved in manufacturing, distributing products, or providing services that did not exist 125 years ago—automobiles, jet planes, air conditioners, electric dryers, washing machines, dishwashers, telephones, computers, information services (Google), debit cards, credit cards, medical technologies (CRT, MRI, x-rays, antibiotics, vaccines, and so on), and on and on. The vast majority of people in the United States have jobs doing productive activities that did not exist in 1900. In every case, scientists and entrepreneurs (business-people) created these products and services and the related jobs. In the long term, supply creates demand. Who knew 25 years ago that she would need an iPad?

When government policies attack entrepreneurs (business leaders), the quality of life in our country is lowered. The fundamental question is production, not demand or distribution. Free minds are necessary to raise our standard of living and to create jobs.

18

The Cure for the Banking Industry: Systematically Move Toward Pure Capitalism

THE FUNDAMENTAL ISSUE UNDERLYING THE BOOM-AND-BUST CYCLE in the financial industry is the lack of sound money. Unfortunately, the Fed is constantly manipulating the value of the dollar. The Fed is charged with two goals, controlling the price level and maintaining full employment. In practice, the full-employment goal almost always has priority. This is because the Fed is a political institution (despite its theoretical independence), and because Congress cares more about full employment than about price levels. (Ironically, a debased dollar will ultimately undermine the Fed's full-employment policy goal.)

The most fundamental cure for this crisis and future financial crises would be to eliminate the Federal Reserve. The United States has already had two failed central banks. Between 1870 and 1913, the United States experienced the greatest economic boom in history without a central bank. While there were economic corrections during this period, none were as destructive as the Great Depression or even the current lingering Great Recession. Other countries have grown successfully without a central bank.

The transition to a private banking system would be complex, but it is achievable. The private banking system would operate on a market-selected monetary standard, which would probably be gold. There is nothing magical about gold. However, it is rare, hard to find, expensive to dig up, and therefore difficult for politicians to manipulate. As long as the federal government can print money at will, the politicians (both Democrats and Republicans) will accumulate debt until the United States experiences a financial collapse. The real issue is not the efficiency of a central bank and the inefficiency of gold or the related technical arguments. The real question is, do you expect politicians to exercise self-discipline before our economy faces major problems? Based on unquestionable historical evidence, it is irrational to trust politicians. The political forces underlying the Fed's decision making will ultimately result in economic disaster.

If the Fed cannot be closed and a private banking system created for political reasons, then the second best solution is to make the dollar convertible in a fixed exchange rate to a quantity of gold. The conversion ratio would be based on current market prices with time allowed for the market to adjust to the announcement. For example, an ounce of gold might be worth $1,600. It is enlightening to realize that when Roosevelt took the United States off the gold standard in the 1930s, an ounce of gold was worth $32. The Fed has rapidly destroyed the value of the dollar. Gold has not become more valuable; the dollar has become materially less valuable.

The United States effectively operated on a gold standard for many years. As was discussed earlier, the gold standard was falsely accused of being a major contributor to the Great Depression. The benefit of the gold standard is that it limits the ability of politicians and government bureaucrats to debase the value of the dollar.

After World War II, the U.S. dollar became the reserve currency of the world and foreign governments could ask the United States to convert dollars to gold. Under Lyndon Johnson, the Fed printed so many dollars that the U.S. Treasury did not have enough gold to make the dollar-to-gold conversion. For this reason, Richard Nixon completely decoupled the dollar from gold in 1971. For the first time in 5,000 years, there was no connection of the world's base currency to a naturally occurring standard (such as gold) that could not be manipulated by politicians. Of course, politicians had found other ways to cheat, but, at least, with a gold standard debasing the currency was harder.

We have been running a high-risk experiment since 1971 by relying on government bureaucrats to self discipline. The problems with the euro reflect the risk in this experiment. Should the U.S. dollar lose its status as the world's reserve currency, the consequences would be severe. The Fed's radical expansion of the money supply in reaction to the recent financial crisis is a form of Russian roulette. It may work but is very risky.

It is noteworthy that most liberal economists treat the advocates of the gold standard without any respect. Yet, the gold standard was fundamentally successful for long periods of time. The fact is these economists and their political cronies do not want to be disciplined by the rationality of markets. They want to wish away the laws of economics based on theories that are detached from reality.

There has been a great deal written about the gold standard. I refer you to the work of George Selgin at the University of Georgia and Larry White at George Mason University. A private banking system or a gold standard for the dollar are the best alternatives. However, if these options are not politically achievable, Milton Friedman proposed an alternative that would move us in the right direction. By law (probably a constitutional amendment), the Fed should be required to grow the money supply at a fixed rate of, for example, 3 percent. This concept would take away the Fed's ability to manipulate the money supply for short-term reasons. Since the Fed has consistently made major errors in its short-term management of the money supply, this proposal is not very risky. Friedman proposed a number of exceptions to this rule. I would not allow exceptions, because the exceptions will become the rule and because stable money is the foundation for long-term prosperity.

If none of these "radical" solutions is acceptable in today's political context, there is an achievable set of steps that would greatly reduce the risk of economic cycles and buy us time to move toward a private banking system.

1. *Require banks to have substantially more capital.* This would shift the risk from the taxpayers to the shareholders. The additional capital requirements would be phased in over 5 to 10 years. Banks should have at least 20 percent shareholders' equity in relation to risk-weighted assets.
2. *Eliminate FDIC insurance (or at least reduce it back to $100,000).* FDIC insurance destroys market discipline. As an alternative to FDIC insurance, create a private insurance pool, with private companies, not government bureaucrats, managing the risk. While this would not be optimal, the private insurance pool might be allowed to purchase, at a market price, catastrophe insurance from the federal government until confidence in the pool has been established.
3. *Make it explicitly clear that the Federal Reserve cannot save non-financial institutions.* If you buy GE or GMAC commercial paper, the risk is yours. Banks cannot operate with a strong capital position if their competitors (GE Capital, for example) are implicitly protected by the federal government.
4. *Eliminate 90 percent of the regulatory burden and related social policy burden placed on the industry.* The banking system should not be used to hide the cost of Congress's social programs. While Congress should not be allowed to subsidize housing, if it is going to do so anyway, at least the subsidy should be transparent. Many banking regulations are actually social subsidies that are unconstitutional and whose costs are hidden from taxpayers.

   A very significant part of the noninterest expense cost structure in a typical commercial bank is directly or indirectly related to some form of regulation. Banks cannot make acceptable economic returns on the increased capital with the current massive regulatory burden. Many of these regulations result in destructive economic investment (affordable housing being the prime example) and thereby reduce the long-term standard of living. Banks should make investment decisions based on rational economic analysis, not politics. If politicians want to subsidize favored groups, let them do so directly.
5. *Privatize or liquidate Freddie Mac and Fannie Mae, and close the Federal Housing Administration (FHA).* The political risk in these

organizations is tremendous, as witnessed by the affordable-housing bubble.

At a deeper level, subsidizing housing does not make economic sense. Housing is consumption. What the United States needs is a greater ability to produce. Our ability to produce determines the quantity and quality of meaningful jobs in the United States. Shifting resources from investment to consumption (housing) lowers our long-term standard of living.

Freddie, Fannie, and the FHA currently control more than 90 percent of the housing finance market in the United States. The reason that they have this large market share is that they are taking irrational risk. They are taking risks that market participants will not take. Because Freddie and Fannie have a government guarantee, these risks are passed to the taxpayers.

Freddie and Fannie are taking an extraordinary amount of interest-rate risk. The FHA is taking a significant amount of credit risk with 3 percent down payments. These are ultimately the taxpayers' risk. We might get lucky, but these are not risks that a rational investor would take.

The best strategy would be to simply announce that in one year, Freddie, Fannie, and the FHA will quit making home mortgage loans. After they wind down their origination business, they will liquidate or sell their existing mortgage portfolios. Unfortunately, the taxpayers will assume the losses (which already exist anyway), but at least this liquidation will eliminate future losses.

Market participants will quickly fill the home finance gap. Financing homes is an excellent business. The S&Ls were successful in this market for 50 years before they were destroyed by government policy.

The government should not in any way interfere in the market process, especially by subsidizing the originate-and-sell mortgage model that Freddie and Fannie created. The investment banks and mortgage bankers make substantial profits from their relationship with Freddie, Fannie, and the FHA. As typical crony capitalists, they will argue strongly for government subsidies via credit guarantees and other such supports for the originate-and-sell model. Of course, the investment banks will capture most of the value of the subsidies as profits for themselves. A purely market-based originate-and-sell model will evolve. The model will deal with the fraud issue and will underwrite to rational credit-risk standards.

Not only Freddie and Fannie but also the FHA must be eliminated. The FHA is a huge distorting factor in the low-end home finance market. If Congress wants to subsidize housing, it should do so directly, where taxpayers can clearly see the cost and where all of the benefits flow to the low-income home purchasers.

A major component of the solution will be provided by existing commercial banks that retain home mortgages in their portfolios the way the S&Ls did. One of the few major economic systems to have limited problems as a result of the financial crisis is Canada. One reason the Canadian banks did relatively well is that they portfolio home mortgages. While there are some housing subsidies in Canada, the banks do not have to compete with the government, that is, Freddie, Fannie, and the FHA. Also, since the banks were holding the mortgages on their books, they cared about the credit risk and underwrote the risk rationally.

Having commercial banks make and hold home mortgages using rational underwriting standards (that is, appropriate down payments, debt-to-income ratios, and so on) would reduce the risk in the commercial banking industry. Properly underwritten home mortgages are low-risk assets.

Life insurance companies will also reenter the market, as home mortgages are a natural fit for their long-term investment portfolios. However, it is critical that the regulators adjust capital requirements. Many life insurance companies and other investors like having government guarantees on their assets (via Freddie, Fannie, or the FHA). However, this is very destructive public policy because it pushes the risk to taxpayers and not market participants.

6. *The Fed must not have the authority to save money funds.* Money funds claim to be less risky than bank deposits. The financial crisis proved that they are more risky, but the Fed bailed out the money fund investors. Banks cannot compete pricewise with money funds that take more risk and pay higher returns, but claim not to be taking the risk.

All six components just outlined must be fully executed for this program to be viable. Piecemeal execution will not work. Banks cannot be required to raise their capital and still carry the regulatory burden.

If we do not deal with the issues raised here, there will be another incredibly destructive crisis in our financial system in the next 10 to 15 years. Without structural change, the lessons from the current financial environment will be lost. We need structural change to make freer markets, not more tinkering at the margins.

The Dodd-Frank financial reform bill is not a solution; in fact, it will make problems bigger in the long term. It is not my intention to go into details on Dodd-Frank. However, the four major deficiencies of Dodd-Frank are

1. The consumer compliance segment of the law is not about consumer compliance, it is about credit allocation. This is a fundamental move toward statism. If the government wants to control the economic system, the most effective way to do so is to control the allocation of credit and capital.
2. The legislation does not deal with "too big to fail." Instead, it identifies companies that are "too big to fail" and ensures that they will be protected by the government.
3. The Durbin amendment on debit card fees is price fixing. It will reduce the availability of banking services to low-income consumers and increase costs for middle-income consumers. This is a government-mandated redistribution of wealth from bank shareholders and consumers to large retailers, such as Walgreens.
4. The law radically expands the power of the Fed and banking regulators. It gives the institutions that created the crisis more ability to cause bigger problems in the future.

The Dodd Frank bill should be repealed and not amended. It is not fixable.

19

Some Political Cures: Government Policy

IN THE LONG TERM, WE CANNOT CONSUME MORE THAN WE PRO-
duce. Our standard of living is fundamentally driven by our ability
to produce goods and services that improve our quality of life and
the quality of life of those with whom we trade. The question is,
How can government policy contribute to the kind of environment
in which human productivity is maximized and in which individuals can pursue their personal happiness?

Obviously, this is a complex question, but there is also overwhelming evidence that a society based on the rule of law in which
individual rights, including property rights, are protected and in
which government interference in markets is extremely limited produces the highest standard of living in the long term. In this context,
the following are government policy structures that lead to a better
quality of life. These recommendations are based on a 40-year career
in business and a careful and educated observation of the impact of
government policies and of psychological and philosophical incentives on human action, especially on the behavior of business leaders.
In the end, it is only human action that matters. The Soviet Union
failed because of its incentive system, that is, from each according to

his ability, to each according to his need. This is an incentive system designed to create many needy people. We need a government policy incentive system that is designed to maximize the productivity of the human mind, especially business leaders.

1. *Low or neutral tax rates increase productivity and raise the standard of living for everyone, including the poor.* High tax rates discourage investment and encourage high-income individuals to spend a great deal of their intellect and their capital trying to avoid taxes.

When I started my career, I was paid $600 per month. My last year as CEO, I made more than $5.0 million. People believe that because I made so much money, I could easily afford to pay a lot of taxes (which I did). However, this is not the issue. During my tenure as CEO, BB&T grew from $4.5 billion to $152 billion in assets, and we weathered the financial crisis better than almost any other large bank. I think I earned the $5.0 million just as much as I earned the $600 per month. Actually, because I was inexperienced, the $600 per month was based on the future, not on what I was contributing at the time.

My family lives well today, but not extravagantly. The issue for me about taxes is justice. I do not receive any more services from the government now than I did when I was making $600 per month, and yet today I pay a huge amount of taxes. I am certain that a large percentage of the money that I spend on taxes is wasted and, in many cases, worse than wasted—that is, it is wealth destroying. I would rather give out money to random people on the street than pay taxes to a destructive government. It is not the money. It is the principle.

I know many successful people who feel the same way I do. My wife and I do not intend to leave a large amount of money to our children. In the banking business, I have seen many situations in which the children of financially successful people have not been able to create a sense of purpose and are less happy than they would have been with less money. We plan to give most of our wealth to education, because we enjoy the energizing impact that proper knowledge creation can provide. But we want to give our money to those whom we want to give it to and not have it taken from us by force, that is, by the threat of the gun. This psychological effect often causes high producers to obsess on how to avoid taxes to the point of making noneconomic investments and deciding not to work. On the other hand, low marginal tax rates typically result in increased tax revenues because high producers work harder and invest more wisely when tax rates are lower. The perception of injustice is based on both the percentage of your income that goes to the federal, state, and local tax collectors and the absolute amount of taxes that you pay.

High-income individuals save more of their income, which provides the capital to increase human productivity. The better the machines, equipment, and technology that a worker has, the more productive that worker is likely to be. Education requires capital, as an individual's productivity is delayed (and she must live while she is being educated).

Neutral taxes means that the tax code is not providing incentives for specific economic activities. Examples of the failure of nonneutral tax codes are the homeownership deduction, ethanol subsidies, farm subsidies, and the like. All of these special tax rules prevent a rational allocation of capital and resources to the most economically productive projects.

Steve Forbes's flat tax[1] and the equally compelling case for the fair tax[2] are clearly examples of tax structures that create more tax revenues in the long term by helping to create an environment of greater growth and less focus on avoiding taxes by high-income individuals. By the way, some conservatives argue against the flat tax because they claim that it would be easier to raise the tax in the future. This is ridiculous. A properly designed flat tax would be harder for Congress to increase because the increase would have a negative impact on all voters.

2. Government spending as a percentage of GDP needs to be materially reduced. It is amazing to me how politicians from both parties talk about how difficult it would be to cut government spending. I wish they would give me an opportunity.

For example, federal employees are paid about 25 to 50 percent more for the same level of job than workers in private industry.[3] The public employees' unions argue that this is because government employees have more responsibility. Are you kidding? As noted earlier, my experience in dealing with many government employees is that few of them have any authority, nor are many of them capable of making independent decisions. The adjustment for responsibilities for federal government employees would go in the opposite direction from what the union implies. If government employees are paid 25 percent more at each job level, including compensation for having independent authority and decision making, they are paid 50 percent too much. The reason public employees are overpaid is because of the tremendous political clout of the public employees' unions.

I recently talked to a top-level manager of a large governmental unit who proudly told me that turnover in his unit was less than 1 percent. He said it was because his employees were dedicated to their work. I told him it was because they were grossly overcompensated (including their pensions and other benefits) and that private employers would not hire them anyway because of their inability to use judgment. As bureaucrats, they have been trained to think mechanically.

One of the most important areas where costs can be reduced is military spending. The United States spends almost 50 percent of the world's military budget. Unfortunately, the vast majority of our military spending is not designed to defend the United States.

The Founding Fathers did not see the purpose of the U.S. military as being to eliminate injustice on the planet, as the liberals demand. They did not expect the U.S. military to make the world safe for democracy, as the neoconservatives demand. They viewed the role of our armed forces as being to protect and defend the United States. George Washington wisely advised us to avoid foreign entanglements. The Founding Fathers were familiar with the economic waste of European military adventures.

Do Iraq and Afghanistan pose a military threat to the United States? No. Do China and Russia pose military threats to the United States? No. If they do, why are we trading with them, including providing technology that can be used for military purposes?

On the other hand, we should be concerned about Islamic terrorism and the states that sponsor terrorism (beginning with Iran). Should we be concerned with rogue states like North Korea? Of course. Unfortunately, a very small portion of our military budget is devoted to dealing with these real threats.

As long as the United States roams around the world getting involved in wars that are not clearly in our own self-interest, other nations will react. If it were absolutely clear to the world that the only purpose of the U.S. military is to protect the United States from a clear and present danger, other nations would almost certainly reduce their military expenditures accordingly.

The real issue for our defense spending is not our need for weapons. We have plenty of weapons. The real issue is the lack of clarity of our goals and, more important, the lack of moral certainty. If it were unquestionably clear that the role of the U.S. military was to defend the United States and that we would take any action necessary to that end, peace on the planet would be ensured. Our foes know that we have the weapons, but they also know that we lack the will. If they know that we will use our weapons without hesitation, they will leave us alone.

It is clear that the defense budget of the United States could be cut at least 25 (and probably 50) percent while making the United States better defended than it is today. This would require focusing on our true enemies and letting them know that we will act without hesitation because the United States has the moral high ground.

Congress should set a goal of reducing other nonentitlement public spending by at least 30 percent in three years. This is an achievable objective. If members of Congress were committed to curing our deficit problems and not devoted to making their political supporters vote for them, cost cutting would be easy, although not painless. This expense cutting would also be a true stimulus for economic growth, as taxpayers would know that taxes will fall in the future and that inflation can be managed. Subsidies to businesses should be cut first (such as ethanol and farm subsidies). Republicans should lead the way on cutting subsidies to businesses, especially large companies.

3. *The most important focal points for cost control are the massive entitlement programs: social security, Medicaid, and Medicare.*

As discussed earlier, social security is fundamentally designed like a pyramid scheme, even if it does not technically qualify as one. The early participants received a free ride, as they paid in very little but were paid out a great deal.

As long as America's younger population was growing rapidly, the scheme worked. However, the massive retirement of baby boomers will break the system with actuarial certainty unless the formula is changed. Fixing social security is relatively easy, but it will not be popular. It means further hiking the already high payroll tax, curbing the growth of benefits, and/or raising the eligibility (retirement) age. Note that none of those changes would enhance our standard of living. Also, these fixes fundamentally represent a default by the U.S. government. If agents of a life insurance company told you that the company would pay only $75,000 on your $100,000 life insurance policy, you would rightly be incensed. This is effectively what the U.S. government is doing when it changes the payment terms for social security. However, the fact is that the government does not have the resources to pay the claims under social security as currently structured.

While this will solve the social security deficit problem, it will not cure a very destructive aspect of the program. While social security is designed to increase individual savings, there are no savings at the societal level because Congress has spent all the money. There is no actual social security trust fund containing previously accumulated payroll taxes. The money was spent and replaced with Uncle Sam's IOUs. People would have saved more had they not had payroll taxes taken all these years.

If the money had actually been saved, the United States would have more capital to invest to create jobs. We would owe the Chinese and Japanese far less than we do. Stock prices in the United States would be higher, and unemployment would be lower. Our standard of living would be better. In other words, the problem with social security is not just the deficits, but that the savings of individuals have been squandered by the government. Instead of creating real capital (that is, more seed corn) social security has provided incentives for excessive consumption and destroyed real savings.

The cure for this problem is to privatize social security, at least for individuals under a certain age, such as 40. Being an advocate of individual rights, I would simply let all individuals opt out of social security completely if they chose to do so. Of course, they would have to accept the consequences if they did not save enough for retirement. In other words, the long-term best solution is to eliminate social security altogether.

If a pure opt-out is not politically acceptable, privatization could result in individuals having a fixed saving rate, but being able to make free choices regarding their investments. The economic benefit would be a massive increase in real savings and investment over time that would accelerate economic growth. I believe many (possibly most) people would opt out of social security if they were given the choice. Interestingly, so do the opponents of privatizing social security. The opponents believe that given a voluntary choice, most people would opt out of social security, and they do not want this to happen. Obviously, these opponents do not believe in individual rights. They are the "wise ones" who will protect us from ourselves. Given what they have done with social security, I will take my chances.

Unfortunately, even if social security is privatized for young people and individuals are allowed to opt out, we will all still have to be taxed at some level to pay for the existing deficits. Unfortunately, your grandmother has (unintentionally) been participating in a quasi-pyramid scheme, and you are the victim. However, in 20 to 30 years, the increased productivity created by real savings from allowing individuals to invest privately will cover a substantial portion of the existing social security shortfall.[4] The real capital from private savings will increase the productivity of American workers and raise our standard of living.

Medicare and Medicaid are much bigger problems than social security. Unless there are changes, the cost of Medicare and Medicaid will consume our total GNP by 2050. The system will have to be fixed. The new healthcare program (Obamacare) only aggravates the problems in the system by promoting more healthcare demand and spending while curbing incentives for the providers of healthcare. I will not offer a diagnosis of Obamacare except to state that, as designed, it is mathematically certain to fail.[5] It creates massive incentives for private employers to push their employees onto the government program. It will increase, not decrease, cost. We need a new answer.

Offering a solution to the Medicare problem is beyond the scope of this book. I do recommend several studies from the Cato Institute.[6] However, a discussion of the fundamental nature of the Medicare issue is appropriate.

The first problem with health insurance in the United States is that it is not insurance. Insurance is for protection against unanticipated major events: a car wreck, a house fire, or a robbery. You cannot insure against normal expenses. Most healthcare costs are expected. Because there is a third-party payer for expected expenses, the administrative overhead is huge and totally wasteful. Imagine if you had food insurance: every time you went to the grocery store, you would file a claim for your food purchases, and your insurance company would negotiate with the grocery store over the prices and maybe ask you to take back something that it did not think was good for you.

One of the fundamental laws of economics is that if a good or service is priced at less than it is worth, it will be overused—that is, wasted—because the pricing mechanism has been destroyed. The typical consumer of health services in today's government-enforced hybrid system never negotiates with his doctor over price. In addition, the doctor has a major incentive to overprescribe because the more she does, the more she gets paid and the more she reduces the risk of being sued. I have had numerous doctors confidentially admit that they request far too many procedures because these procedures are "free" to the patient, and why take the liability risk? For many individuals, more than one-third of their lifetime healthcare costs are incurred in the last few months of their life. We torture old people to death to reduce liability risk and because it is "free" to the family, whose members are already feeling guilty about not taking care of grandmother.

BB&T was able to substantially reduce both its and its employees' healthcare cost and, even more important, enable employees to have longer, healthier lives through a wellness program. The program included reduced insurance cost to the employee as an incentive to participate.

The employee typically was required to have biannual physicals performed by a nurse, including annual blood work. One of the major goals was to reduce smoking. You could not get the insurance discount if you smoked.

Employees were rated at different health levels, and exercise, diet, and weight goals were established. One of the benefits of the blood work was the early identification of chronic health problems such as diabetes.

The long-term effect of the wellness program was to reduce BB&T's healthcare cost to 15 to 20 percent less than our competitors' and to reduce health-related absences materially. There were many stories of individuals (who would not otherwise have had a physical) having had a problem identified during their health exam and their lives having been saved. Incentives made the program work.

Directionally, the solution to the healthcare cost problem is clear. We need to move toward less government, not more. We need to create incentives for patients and doctors to control cost. We need to create incentives for individuals to take better care of themselves. Socialized medicine has failed or is failing all over the world. We do not need to replicate a failed system. The proper long-term solution is a purely private medical system in which charity would help individuals who need it without any form of government involvement.

It is important to understand that the United States had a far more cost-efficient and equally just healthcare system before Medicare and Medicaid were created. In terms of the available technology, healthcare was available to individuals with basically the same distribution of quality care relative to personal income as exists today. About 10 percent of the population relied on charity, which was provided by doctors, nonprofit hospitals, and charitable foundations. Medicare, in particular, was not designed to deal with a social problem; it was created to buy votes for the Democratic Party. There was a massive subsidy to early participants in Medicare (as there was to early participants in social security). Obviously, these beneficiaries had an incentive to vote for the politicians who provided them with a free lunch.

Medicare has been economically destructive in a way similar to affordable housing. Because it is a massive subsidy to individuals over 65, it has reallocated resources to medical care for old people on a grand scale. Since you can spend your resources only once, if you provide incentives for overinvestment in old-age medical care, you reduce investment in other areas that might improve the quality of life more. For example, free markets might have driven a greater amount of investment in agricultural technology that would improve the quality of food and lower the cost. By having to spend less money on food, individuals might have had more time for leisure activity or more time to exercise, which would have improved their quality of life. A high percentage of medical cost has been the result of artificial incentives, through government policy, to invest in short-term life extension. If you ask me whether I would rather live better now and until I am 85 or live an extra 6 months, I will take

204 • THE FINANCIAL CRISIS AND THE FREE MARKET CURE

now. Furthermore, government bureaucrats do not have the right to make that choice for me.

4. *Government regulations must be radically reduced.* According to an annual study, the total cost of U.S. federal government regulations in 2008 was $1.75 trillion, which was 12 percent of GDP, 46 percent of total federal spending, and 120 percent of pretax corporate profits, and the cost has been rising by 10 to 15 percent per year in the past decade.[7]

One way to control the indirect cost of government is to require every government agency to reduce its regulatory rules by 50 percent in 18 months. Obviously, this would give each agency an opportunity to reduce its staff accordingly.

In my career, the amount of regulation of our industry has increased exponentially. As a simple example, in 1971, when I made my first loan, it required two sheets of paper. Today, a small "book" is required, much of it created by the massive expansion of financial regulations and litigiousness. Also, I believe the borrower had a better understanding of the terms of the loan in 1971 than she does today, because the fundamental conditions were clear. The complexity of the documentation makes it harder for the typical borrowers to comprehend the agreement.

In addition to the economic cost, think of the massive amount of brainpower that is wasted. If the millions of people involved in dealing with our extraordinarily complex tax laws and other regulations could be using their minds to create new products, services, or technologies, our standard of living would be much higher.

Reducing the massive cost of regulations is obvious and easy from an economic perspective. The issue is political will.

5. *Free trade is essential for economic well-being. People trade because they are better off. The Founding Fathers understood this concept. So should we.* One of the primary reasons for creating the United States was to provide a free-trade zone. Individuals in North Carolina trade with individuals in California because California is better at producing raisins and North Carolina is better at growing sweet potatoes. We mutually benefit.

The same principle is true when we trade with China. Both parties must benefit or the trade will not take place. It is true that there are complexities created by different currencies, different environmental standards, and other such factors. However, our problems are not caused by the Chinese. We have caused our own problems. Free trade, not protectionism, provides a cure.

One of the events that precipitated the Great Depression was the Smoot-Hawley Tariff Act (1930), which raised the equivalent of tax rates on more than 20,000 categories of goods imported by Americans to record levels. With this one act, the U.S. government effectively triggered a global trade war. Other nations retaliated by imposing high tariffs on their own imports (that is, U.S. exports). Between 1930 and 1934, the volume of international trade plunged by 60 percent. President Hoover and a GOP-led Congress placed a high tax on imported goods initially to help farmers, then to protect manufacturers. The tariff war played an important role first in triggering and then in deepening the Great Depression.

6. *Immigration of productive and hardworking individuals must be encouraged.*

The United States is a society built by immigrants. People chose to come here in order to have the opportunity to work.

In addition, with the retirement of the baby boom generation, we have a significant demographic problem. There will be too few young people to feed too many old people. This demographic problem is the primary source of Japan's economic woes. Western Europe will soon follow.

Japan's boom was based on a rapid decline in the number of babies. Babies are expensive (as are old people). However, babies are a future investment. In Japan, the young people that those babies would have become do not exist and therefore cannot produce the goods and services that the old people need. China's current boom is partly based on less investment in expensive babies. In 30 years, there will be a major demographic problem in China. The lack of babies is why the Chinese have such a high savings rate and why they will expect the United States to pay them back in 20 to 25 years.

It is particularly important that we encourage smart people to come to the United States. Smart people create jobs. If we keep the smart people in India, they will create jobs in India. Current U.S. policy in this regard is self-defeating. Students from all over the world come to American universities to earn degrees in architecture, engineering, mathematics, the physical sciences, biotechnology, medicine, and business, but when they graduate, most of them are forced to return home. Under current U.S. law—which has been in place for many years—only 65,000 of these foreigners in brainpower fields can work in the United States, and even then, only under a temporary "H-1B" visa.

Unfortunately, because of our social welfare systems, we cannot afford to have open immigration to the United States. Many people would immigrate not to work, but to get the "free lunch" that our welfare system provides. The answer is to eliminate the social welfare system because it also destroys the work incentive for U.S. citizens. Assuming that the welfare system will not be fixed, immigration will need to be controlled.

However, we should encourage smart people and people who want to work hard to come to the United States. We could have an extended work period required and a very comprehensive education and American values program to earn citizenship. The issue of cultural dilution is very critical. If we allow people to vote who do not share the fundamental principles that made America great and do not share the unique American view of life, our society will be in trouble.

While we should encourage the right type of immigration, failing to have a comprehensive and rational strategy to deal with the immigration issue will be a disaster.

7. *At the macro level, we must restore discipline to our political system.* Above all, we need policies that encourage savings and investment and discourage unnecessary spending, but that means a restrained political system with a government that once again is put in its proper place—a government that preserves life, liberty, and the pursuit of happiness by ensuring the rule of law, the sanctity of contract, private property, and national defense.

It is incredibly important to realize that there are no painless solutions to our problems. We have a form of cancer that will be terminal if it is not treated. The good news is that it can be treated. The bad news is that the treatment (like chemotherapy) is painful. However, failure to treat the disease will cause death.

Of course, the ultimate cure is for the government to stop doing the many things it was not designed to do. It should only be in the business of protecting individual rights by preventing the initiation of force and fraud.

20

Our Short-Term Path and How to End Unemployment

WE HAVE EXPERIENCED A SERIOUS AND LINGERING RECESSION. THIS recession was the inevitable consequence of a massive misallocation of capital and labor, primarily caused by destructive public policies. The depth of the recession has been magnified by unending mistakes by political leaders and bureaucrats and the related destruction of confidence.

Unfortunately, economics has not developed to the point where reliable economic projections can be made. The complexity of a globally integrated economy and the unpredictability of human actions make economic forecasting mostly guesswork. However, the demand for economic predictions is very strong, so let me provide one, for whatever it is worth. As of this writing (fall 2011), I believe we are in an economic recovery following the Great Recession of 2007–2009. Unfortunately, this recovery is likely to be long, subpar, and painful and could be interrupted by another recession based on the magnitude of the past errors. We have a serious hangover from our spending binge.

Over the next five years, we should experience a relatively slow pace of real growth, with unemployment above the natural market rate. The most likely outcome is for a period of "stagflation," which means slow real growth, relatively high inflation, and relatively high unemployment. The 1970s was a period of stagflation. It is not a terrible economic environment, but it is not a healthy environment. While this is my "most likely" economic prediction, a significant directional change in government policy (less regulation, more rational taxes, lower deficits, and so on) could rapidly increase the pace of economic growth. We will still have to deal with our long-term economic issues, but even stagflation is not inevitable (although it is likely). Also, it should be noted that while there may be healthy investment opportunities in a stagflation environment, making the right investments will be difficult.

It will be a major challenge for the Federal Reserve to undo the massive monetary stimulus that it has already injected into the financial system without causing a rapid rise in interest rates.[1] Unfortunately, the inflationary process for which the Fed has already laid the groundwork will be destructive to the allocation of capital and resources.

For example, when inflation begins to accelerate, commodity prices tend to rise first. This causes overinvestment in commodities. When the other factors of production start to adjust, commodity producers are less profitable than expected, and failures ensue. The prices of Midwest farmland may already be reflecting this effect. There may be a bubble in farmland and other areas of the commodities markets that will be paid for in the future.

Even if the Fed can mitigate the macro effect of printing too much money, it cannot undo the micro effect—that is, the misallocation of resources. When resources are misallocated through manipulation of the money supply, our long-term standard of living is reduced.

The irony is that all this damage is unnecessary. The main focus of the Federal Reserve's monetary policy is on attempting to lower unemployment. It believes that it can do so by printing money; however, the high unemployment rate in the United States (currently 9.1 percent) is caused directly by government policy. Politicians would like to "wish away" the laws of economics. Unfortunately, the laws of economics are laws, just like the laws of physics. Economic laws are immutable. The law of supply and demand is not negotiable, any more than the laws of thermodynamics are. This is true whether the politicians like it or not.

The law of supply and demand demonstrates that there is a market-clearing price at which supply and demand are equal. At this price, the producers of a good or service (supply) will provide exactly the amount of the good or service that the users (demand) want to purchase. The market will clear; that is, all the production will be sold to willing buyers.

If the price is forced below the market-clearing price by government policy (price controls), the users of the good or service will want to purchase more than the providers of the good or service are willing to provide at that price. Some users will not be able to purchase the quantity of the good or service that they want at this price. Typically, in this situation, a black market develops, where users pay a premium above the government-established price to purchase the good or service that they need or want.

The same phenomenon happens in reverse when the government raises the price about the market-clearing price. In this case, the suppliers are willing to provide more of the good or service than the users desire at the government-induced price. For example, suppose that tomorrow the government set the price of milk at $100 per gallon in order to protect the profitability of dairy farmers. When you went into the store, you would probably buy less milk. In fact, you might not buy any milk at all. A lot of milk would go unsold—it would be wasted.

Wage rates are simply the price of labor. The price of labor is set by the law of supply and demand, just like the price of any other good or service. In fact, to some degree, the prices of all the goods we purchase reflect the price of the labor used to produce these goods or services. The dinner you purchase in a restaurant reflects the labor of the cook, the waitress, the restaurant manager, the truck drivers who delivered the raw materials to the restaurants, the factory workers who built the truck, the farmer who grew the food, the farm workers who picked the crop, the factory workers who built the tractors, the engineers who designed the trucks and tractors, the construction workers who built the restaurant, the construction engineer and architects who designed the restaurant, the entrepreneur who created the restaurant chain, the financer who saved money or raised capital to finance the restaurant operation, the teacher who taught the engineer mathematics, the intellectual who advanced electrical design, the doctor who cures the workers so that they can continue to produce, and so on.

In a free market, wage rates are determined objectively based on the law of supply and demand, just like the prices of other goods and services. In fact, wage rates and labor costs are embedded in the prices of all goods and services. Since the law of supply and demand is as true for labor as it is for any other good or service, the lower the supply and the stronger the demand, the higher the wage rate will be (other things being equal). The term *labor* includes both physical work and mental work. Because the human mind is the only true natural resource, mental labor is much more valuable and productive than physical labor. In fact, physical labor has rapidly declined in value as technology, created by thinking (not manual labor), has rapidly advanced.

CEOs of large companies are paid very highly because there are very few people who can successfully manage a complex business in a globally competitive environment (supply is limited). Also, demand for the few people who can achieve high performance is strong because the CEO has a big impact on the productivity of many people.

On the other side, even though garbage removal is an essential service and there is strong demand for this service, there are many, many people who have the skill set to act as garbage collectors. Therefore, the wage rate for garbage collectors is relatively low, as it should be.

When government arbitrarily raises the wage rate above the market-clearing price, labor will go unsold, exactly as in the previous milk example. Minimum-wage laws raise the wage rate above the market-clearing price and thereby create unemployment. From immediately before the financial crisis until today, the minimum wage has been raised from $5.15 per hour to $7.25 per hour, or 41 percent. The prices for practically all other goods and services have either fallen or risen only a little. So in the face of a severe economic correction, the government has raised the price of labor far above the market-clearing price.

The minimum-wage laws are the primary cause of the high unemployment levels in the United States today. In a free market, labor rates (wages) for many jobs would have fallen just as prices for other goods and services have fallen. Many jobs that have left the United States for China would have stayed in the United States. Instead of laying off employees, many businesses would have cut wages and kept their employees. Unemployment would be much lower than it is today. There will always be some level of structural unemployment, because individuals change jobs and industries are always in transition. Structural unemployment is probably about 3 percent compared to 9 percent unemployment today.

To make this concept more concrete, a small business owner who is faced with a hiring decision must decide whether the additional worker will produce more than the cost of hiring that worker. If the worker will add only $6 of income per hour, and yet the minimum-wage law requires the small business owner to pay $7.25 per hour, she will not hire that worker. In fact, if she did hire workers at this level of cost to value, her business would soon be broke. Because of unemployment insurance, healthcare, and multiple regulatory costs, the $7.25 minimum wage turns into a cost of more than $9 per hour for the small business owner. Unfortunately, many entry-level and unskilled workers cannot create $9 per hour in value, so they are not employable.

Unbelievably, there are economists who argue that the minimum wage does not create unemployment. We must wonder about their motivation. The law of supply and demand is a long-proven law; in other words, it is not negotiable. Also, if the minimum wage does not create unemployment, why not set it at $100 per hour, or maybe $200 per hour? The minimum-wage laws are the primary cause of unnecessary unemployment.

The typical victims of the minimum-wage laws are the individuals that the laws are supposed to help by guaranteeing that these workers get a "living wage." Instead, these potential employees get no wage. Remember the discussion of the construction workers who must make the transition to other employment. These workers cannot get a job at the high minimum wage, so they do not have an opportunity to learn a skill set that will make them more valuable in the future.

The biggest victims of minimum-wage laws are minority teenagers. It isn't coincidental that their jobless rate perpetually hovers around 35 to 40 percent, even when the national average is 9 to 10 percent. Because of the failure of the public school system, they often do not have the skill set to join the workforce at a high wage rate. However, if they could get a job at a lower wage, they could learn the skills that would allow them to be more productive in the future. Instead, they seek employment selling or distributing illegal drugs, and we put them in jail. Great humanitarian plan.

I got my first summer job during high school, clearing brush and trash from the sides of roads for $1 an hour. Even with inflation, this wage rate is far below the current minimum wage of $7.25 per hour. While this work was not much fun, I did learn to show up, to work with others, and that I did not want to do this type of work for the rest of my life. School became more tangibly important as a means to achieve a better career.

We have an acquaintance who is from Africa. He had two jobs, one full-time and one part-time. He is saving every penny he can to bring his children from Africa to the United States. He lost his full-time job because his employer closed its local facility. He would be glad to work for $6 per hour instead of having to survive on a part-time job. No matter how good their intentions, the politicians and their supporters who have raised the minimum wage in the face of a severe economic correction are inflicting an injustice on the individuals who would be willing to work at a lower wage rate. It is both immoral and unconstitutional to deny a person the right to work on terms that are acceptable to him.

By the way, the two main forces behind the minimum-wage laws are liberal "do-gooders" who are ignorant of the laws of economics and unions that do not want low-wage competition for their members (even if, over time, their members' jobs end up in Asia).

The other factor driving excessive unemployment is unemployment insurance. Unemployment insurance was designed to help workers through the transition to a new job, which should be accomplished in 90 days, or 6 months at the maximum. The existence of long-term unemployment insurance creates a high incentive for individuals not to seek work—especially when they need to make a fundamental career transition (the problem that excess construction workers are facing) that will require a lower entry-level wage rate. Unfortunately, because these workers do not get back to work, they tend to become less valuable over time, as their background work skills fade.

Both the Republicans and the Democrats are wrong on the extension of unemployment insurance. The Democrats are wrong in failing to admit that extending unemployment insurance creates an incentive to stay unemployed and in failing to admit that many beneficiaries are taking advantage of the system. The Republicans are wrong because there are many honest workers who would like a job, but who cannot obtain employment because of the minimum-wage laws. It is unjust to deny people work and, at the same time, not provide unemployment benefits.

The correct answer is to eliminate the minimum wage, or at least reduce the minimum-wage rate back to its prerecession level of $5.15 per hour. Unemployment insurance could then be reduced to six months at the maximum. This combination would eliminate all but the natural market unemployment process where individuals are seeking new jobs and would quickly reduce unemployment from today's 9.1 percent to 4 percent or less. (A number of economists are estimating that the effective unemployment rate may be as high as 16 to 18 percent, as many individuals have simply dropped out of the workforce and are not included in government statistics.)

By the way, the Federal Reserve understands that the excessive minimum-wage rates are a primary cause of unemployment. Bernanke's drive to create inflation is designed to lower real minimum-wage rates by decreasing the value of the dollar while the minimum wage is not raised. For example, 3 percent inflation compounded over five years will reduce the real minimum-wage rate by almost 16 percent. This will encourage a higher level of employment. Unfortunately, there will be significant long-term damage to the economy because of the resource misallocation that inflation always creates.

At a deeper level, the fundamental cause of unemployment and underemployment in the United States is the failure of our educational system. Many individuals do not have the skill set necessary to be successful in a globally competitive environment. We will discuss this in Chapter 24.

The Deepest Cause
Is Philosophical

THE DEEPEST CAUSE OF THE FINANCIAL CRISIS IS NOT ECONOMIC policy. The fundamental cause is philosophical. The financial crisis is a result of the philosophical ideas that have been taught in the liberal arts departments of the most prestigious universities in America for more than 50 years.

The fundamental cause of the financial crisis is a combination of altruism and pragmatism. Altruism does not mean kindness toward others; it literally means "other-ism." Altruism is defined as selflessness, that is, believing that everyone else is more important than you are. The good of the individual is irrelevant. It is only the good of "others" that matters, and this is interpreted by liberals as being the good of "society." This assumes that society is a living entity and that the effect on actual individuals does not matter. In reality, however, there are only individuals. There is no such entity as society.[1]

The "common good" (or the "public interest") is an indefinable concept. There is no such thing as the public. The public is only a number of individual people. When the common good of a society is regarded as something apart from and superior to the individual good of its members, the good of some people takes precedence over the good of other people, with those others consigned to the status of sacrificial animals.[2]

Altruism should not be confused with benevolence. Altruism means that other people (society or the tribe) are more important than you are. Altruism is an unquestioning duty to others. It is not about being nice to people. It is about self-sacrifice.

A classic economic error made by liberals is to assume that good intentions produce good outcomes. Economic theory unquestionably demonstrates that so-called good intentions often produce very bad outcomes. This is the "law of unintended consequences" that is so relevant to policy makers and others who not only fail to achieve their aims, but also cause results that are directly opposed to their aims—as when central banks and regulators seek to ensure "safe and sound" banking, but instead make banks and the system more dangerous and precarious. However, if you are an altruist, moral good is defined by your intentions to help others, not by the actual outcome. In fact, altruism often serves as an excuse for bad behavior (and bad intentions).

Where did the idea of "affordable housing" (that is, subprime home finance) come from? Everyone has a right to a house. Provided by whom? Everyone has a right to free medical care. Provided by whom? My right to free medical care is my right to imprison a doctor to make him provide that care or to force someone else to pay for the doctor. This is exactly the opposite of the American concept of rights. America's Founding Fathers believed that each of us has the right to what we produce and what we create, not to what someone else has created.

Altruism leads to a redistribution from the productive to the nonproductive. In fact, it implies that no one has a right to her own life. Everyone is everyone else's property. This is a rejection of the concept of rights.[3]

In business, altruism is combined with pragmatism. A business cannot survive in a globally competitive economy if it is actually altruistic. While businesspeople may be altruistic in their individual lives, if they attempt to be seriously altruistic in their business, they will go out of business. Bill Gates has chosen to personally become an altruist. However, anyone who competes (or does business) with

Microsoft knows that Microsoft is a tough competitor. The company is not altruistic.

The backup philosophy for business is pragmatism. In fact, pragmatism is systematically taught in business schools. Many business leaders are proud to be called pragmatists. Pragmatists do "what works." They are "practical." However, actually being practical requires that we act on principle. Nothing is less practical than doing what works in the short term. The pragmatic philosophy is based on the concept that there is no permanent truth—that truth is what works today. The validity of a truth is based on its consequences this afternoon, not on any fundamental principles. According to pragmatists, nothing can be known with certainty in advance. Meaning and truth are determined by the short-term practical consequences.

Unfortunately, many things work very effectively in the short run but are extremely destructive in the long term. Negative-amortization mortgages (pick-a-payment mortgages) were "successful" for more than 10 years and then did tremendous economic damage. Subprime lending was "successful" for a number of years and then resulted in a massive destruction of wealth.

A pragmatist cannot be rational. Rationality requires a long-term perspective. It is a virtue that is based on fundamental truths consistent with the pursuit of long-term goals. A rational person acts in a way that is consistent with his principles and moves him toward long-term success and happiness.

A pragmatist cannot have integrity. Integrity is acting in a way that is consistent with one's principles. If you do not have clearly defined principles, you cannot act "on principle." It is not surprising that so many business leaders lack integrity. They are proud to be pragmatists. Because they are pragmatists, they do not have principles. They do what "works."

Many commentators have raised the issue of why more business leaders did not see the future economic consequences of their risky housing investments. However, if your goal in decision making is to do what works (that is, if you are a pragmatist), you will keep doing what you are doing as long as it works. Pick-a-payment mortgages appeared to be working until the market crashed and burned. Charlie Prince, the CEO of Citigroup, was famously quoted as implying that he knew Citigroup was taking huge economic risks but that the company would keep "dancing" as long as the band was playing. Of course, he was fired a few months later, and Citi subsequently collapsed.[4]

The combination of altruism and pragmatism leads to the "free lunch" mentality. Despite the huge deficits in social security and Medicare, in the current presidential election neither candidate has proposed a meaningful solution to these deficits, and if either did make a meaningful proposal that required some sacrifice, he would not be elected.

The free lunch mentality leads to a lack of personal responsibility, which is ultimately the death of democracies. The Founding Fathers were very concerned with the potential for the "tyranny of the majority." They were primarily focused on the protection of individual rights: freedom of speech, freedom of religion, property rights, and so on. However, they realized that when 51 percent of the people can vote a free lunch from 49 percent, fairly soon the party will be over. Because then 60 percent will want a free lunch from 40 percent. And then, 70 percent will want a free lunch from 30 percent. And, finally, the 30 percent will quit.

A lot of the intensity from the Tea Party movement and conservatives in general is over the issue of whether the United States has gone over the 51 percent line. Are there so many voters who receive a free lunch from the government that we are headed toward a statist or totalitarian society?

It is important not to underestimate the power of a moral code. Altruists would far prefer that everyone be equally poor rather than having everyone be wealthier, but with substantial differences in wealth. Altruists will support economic policies (such as raising taxes on high-income households in the middle of a recession) where there is overwhelming evidence that the policy will result in less economic growth if they believe that the policy will result in a more even distribution of income. Their view of justice is based on equal outcomes, not equal opportunities. The fundamental battle for a free society is over ethics and, specifically, *personal responsibility*.

22

The Cure Is
Also Philosophical

JUST AS THE CAUSE OF THE FINANCIAL CRISIS IS PHILOSOPHICAL, so is the cure. The cure is the restoration of the principles that made America great in the first place: "life, liberty, and the pursuit of happiness"; each individual's moral right to his own life; and each individual's moral right to the product of his own labor, which includes the right to earn great wealth if you produce a great deal and the right to give away as much of your wealth as you like to whomever you want for whatever reason.

As a moral code, "life, liberty, and the pursuit of happiness" demands personal responsibility because there is no free lunch. It also demands and rewards rationality, self-discipline, and justice. It is consistent with man's nature as an independent being who must use his mind to succeed in a demanding environment. It is a set of ethical principles that recognizes individual rights and implies limited government. The corollary is a free, independent, and self-reliant society.

There is a difference in kind between my choice to give away what I have produced and having someone (in this case, government) put a gun to my head and take my wealth. It is particularly infuriating when you know that your wealth will be given to individuals who have not earned it and you know that these beneficiaries will then turn around and vote for the members of Congress who took it from you.

While many individuals are aware of the incredible importance of liberty to human well-being, many underestimate the significance or implications of the pursuit of happiness.

During the Middle Ages, before Jefferson and before the thinkers of the Enlightenment, no one existed for her own good. Everyone owed her life to the king, to the state, or to the church. No one had a right to her own life. Jefferson said that your life is yours. Live it to the fullest on your own terms. Pursue what makes you happy. The context in which the term *pursue* was used in the Declaration of Independence is different from the context in which we use *pursue* today. To the founders, pursuing happiness meant *earning* happiness—the right to attempt to *earn* happiness from how you lived your life.

When each individual has the moral right to his own life and the responsibility for his own life and when each has the freedom to pursue his own personal goals, people are more productive.

When individuals have the right to the pursuit of their personal happiness, they are naturally nicer to other people. In communist and socialist societies, in the end, many people hate one another because they are slaves to one another. It is not surprising that by any measure, charitable giving is larger in the United States than anywhere else in the world. Charitable giving is far greater in the United States than in the social welfare countries of Western Europe.

The United States is the only country founded on the concept that individuals should pursue their long-term rational self-interest. The idea that we should act in our rational self-interest goes against much of what is taught in our culture today, and yet this idea is implicit in the concept of the pursuit of happiness.

In fact, a very commonly held belief in our culture today is that as human beings, we are born bad—because we are selfish, and being selfish is bad. We learn this belief at a young age.

Johnny, age three or four, is in the sandbox playing with his truck. He is not bothering anybody. He is having a good time playing with his truck. Along comes Fred. Fred would like to have Johnny's truck. Johnny does not want to give Fred his truck. A discussion and then an argument ensues. Mom, Dad, or the kindergarten teacher gets involved in the discussion. Mom says, "Johnny give that truck to Fred. You must share. Don't be selfish. Don't be bad."

Two great moral lessons are being taught right there in the sandbox. The first lesson: where did Fred get the right to Johnny's truck? This lesson from the sandbox is the moral justification for our social welfare system. Johnny has a truck. I do not have a truck. I want Johnny's truck. Why should Johnny have a truck when I do not have one? Johnny is greedy. He is selfish. He is bad. Give me his truck. I will vote for Barney Frank. He will get me a truck from that greedy Johnny.

How about the moral lesson for Johnny? (And the people who are reading this book are far more likely to be Johnny than to be Fred.) What lesson did he learn? Do not go for what you want. Other people's needs are more important than yours. You must consider others as being more important than yourself. After all, Fred "needed" that truck. Your life is secondary. Everyone else's "need" is more important than your life.

It is interesting to reflect objectively on the concept of selfishness. An immutable, nonnegotiable law of nature is: *everything that is alive must act in its own self-interest or die.* This is how Mother Nature designed the system.

A lion has to hunt or starve. A deer runs from the hunter or gets eaten. Trees shade out other trees to get sunlight. Amoebae take chemicals that other amoebae would like to have. By definition, life is self-sustaining action. Anything alive that does not act in its own self-interest will die. This is how Mother Nature designed the system—sorry.

To say that people are bad because they are selfish has the same implication as saying that people are bad because they are alive. This is analogous to saying that the sun is bad because it is hot or gravity is bad because it holds us down. The sun should be hot and gravity should hold us down; these are nonnegotiable facts of reality. These attributes are consistent with the fundamental laws of nature. As living entities, human beings should act in their own self-interest, that is, selfishly. This is a fundamental aspect of our nature—in other words, it is a nonnegotiable fact of our very survival.

It is important to understand what acting selfishly really requires. The proper goal is acting in our long-term rational self-interest, properly understood. Unfortunately, we are constantly presented with a false set of alternatives. These alternatives are to take advantage of other people or to sacrifice ourselves. Neither of these options makes sense.

Many people define being selfish as taking advantage of other people. Taking advantage of other people is not selfish; it is self-destructive for two reasons. First, if you attempt to mislead other people, soon no one will trust you. Without trust, you will not be successful. You might fool Tom and Jane, but fairly soon they will tell Dick and Harry, and no one will trust you. Without trust, your relationships with others will not be successful or generate happiness.

At a deeper level, attempting to manipulate people's minds is very self-destructive. Other people's psychology is often a complicated mess. When you let go of the truth (the facts) in an effort to distort someone else's reality, you do psychological damage to yourself.

In my role as CEO of a large public company, I have had the opportunity to meet many financially successful people. I have never met anyone who was both financially successful and happy who achieved this result primarily by taking advantage of other people. I have met a few people who were financially successful who, I believe, achieved this result based on some level of deceit. These are the unhappiest people I have ever met.

Of course, other people's consciousness exists independent of you, and you often want to influence other people's beliefs. However, when you let go of reality, when you distort the truth to convince others, you do more damage to your own mind than you do to them. Attempting to take advantage of others is not selfish. It is self-destructive.

The other false alternative is self-sacrifice. In fact, this is the moral code of our society. Let me ask you a fundamentally important question: *Do you have as much right to your life as anyone else has to their life? Of course you do!* Why would you believe anything else? Do your children and your friends have a right to their lives? Of course they do!

Self-sacrifice carried to its logical extreme is altruism, which we discussed briefly earlier. Let's take our discussion of altruism to a deeper level. Altruism is a philosophically self-defeating concept because it demands that human actions be brought down to the level of the least productive person. Therefore, if I have anything more than Beverly has, I am obligated to give it to Beverly. However, even though Beverly is poor, if she has anything more than Brandon has, she is obligated to give it to Brandon. Even though Brandon is very poor, if he has anything more than Adam has, he is obligated to give it to Adam. Even though Adam is very, very poor, if he has anything more than Molly has, he is obligated to give it to Molly. Unfortunately, there are always people who are in the process of dying, and the only way to be equal to someone who is dying is to die yourself. There are not many true altruists today. Some of the monks in the Middle Ages were good altruists. They beat themselves with whips, drank dirty water, and slept on stones so that they could be equal with the poorest people. That's not a great way to live.

While neither taking advantage of others nor self-sacrifice is a rational alternative, there is an uncompromising moral code that underlies a free society and free markets. This moral code can best be described as the "trader principle." Successful human relationships are about trading value for value—getting better together. In our business at BB&T, we are morally committed to doing our best to help our clients achieve economic success and financial security, because we expect to earn a profit while achieving this end. Of course, there are times when there are difficult trade-offs, and sometimes one of the parties does not keep his agreement. However, the goal is a mutually beneficial relationship in which both parties are better off because of the value-for-value trade. This very fundamental idea is why free markets create a better quality of life. Through voluntary trade, we all benefit. When government (or anyone with a "gun") interferes in these voluntary trades, at least one party and sometimes both parties are worse off.

In life, there are only two stable relationship conditions—win-win and lose-lose. Whenever we set up a win-lose relationship, our partner will get bitter and the relationship will ultimately become lose-lose. (Unfortunately, you sometimes observe this pattern in spousal relationships.) Whenever we become self-sacrificial and create a lose-win relationship, we will ultimately become bitter and end up in a lose-lose relationship.

In any important relationship in your life, you should ask yourself how the relationship will benefit you. This is a fair and important question. However, you should also ask what benefit your partner will receive from this relationship, because if your partner does not benefit, the relationship will not be beneficial to you in the long term. Seek out others who also believe in voluntary win-win relationships.

Of course, it is in your rational self-interest to help the people whom you have judged to be valuable to your well-being (including your psychological well-being). It is appropriate to support the people you objectively value: your family, your friends, and the people you work with. These people provide valuable human relationships that are meaningful to your life. If you love your children, taking care of them, while often hard work, is not a sacrifice.

In fact, love is the ultimate expression of selfishness. With college students, I use an example to highlight this concept. You are getting ready to get married, which is a big event in your life. Your future spouse comes up to you and says, "Honey, I am so excited about marrying you; this is the biggest self-sacrifice I have ever made." That's not exactly what you want to hear.

I believe it is in my self-interest to support the United Way. The United Way is an umbrella charitable organization that does a great deal of good in our community. I would not want to live in a community where there was not a United Way, and I would not want my children to live in that community. I believe it is in my rational self-interest to support the United Way. I also contribute to educational and other organizations that defend the ideas underlying a free society, because freedom is incredibly precious to me.

Taking advantage of other people is not selfish; it is self-destructive. Dropping the context—that is, seeing the world through tunnel vision—is not selfish. Doing things that are bad for you (drugs, crime, fraud, and the like) is not selfish. Many moral leaders attribute the world's problems to people acting selfishly. My observation is that very few people act in their long-term rational self-interest. Most people act at least partially in a self-destructive or mutually destructive manner.

To act in one's rational self-interest requires holding the context. You must ask yourself what kind of world you would like to live in and what you would enjoy doing to help create that world. You might like a world with better music. If you have the talent, you can write, sing, and/or play music. If you do not have the talent, you can earn money using your other talents and give to the opera.

Genuinely selfish people have a clear sense of purpose, take care of their bodies (exercise), take care of their minds (study, read, and think), and create meaningful, life-supporting human relationships with others who share the same values. They do not act irrationally; they do not join "tribes," cults, or ethnic groups or wage wars (except in self-defense). They seek out ways to improve their lives through voluntary trade with others. Just imagine if everyone acted selfishly in this context. The world would be a dramatically better place to live. Whim seeking, hedonism, shortsightedness, fraudulent manipulation, and narcissism, are not the acts of a person who is pursuing long-term happiness. These are the acts of a person with low self-esteem.

I had a friend who drank 24 beers a day. He developed cirrhosis of the liver and continued to drink. He died. People say he was selfish. I think he was self-destructive. Bernie Madoff is often described as selfish, which is ridiculous. By his own admission, Madoff was miserable before he was caught. He was stealing from his best friends and from his family. He was self-destructive, not selfish.

The most important lesson we can teach our children is that they should act in their long-term rational self-interest, properly understood. Acting in your rational self-interest requires a lot of thinking and a lot of work, but it has an extraordinarily high payback. Our children (and we) need a sense of purpose, a commitment to take care of their minds and their bodies, and a desire to create beneficial, nonsacrificial relationships with other people. Have you taught your children that their life is their most precious possession?

My favorite book, by far, is *Atlas Shrugged*, which was written by Ayn Rand in 1957. Rand said that one of the goals of her writing was to make her predictions not come true. She predicted that a once great and prosperous country might degenerate into chaos and stagnation if it followed the wrong code of ethics. However, she highlighted that a proper code was also possible. Unfortunately, her predictions are coming true. If you have not read *Atlas Shrugged*, you should read it. If you have not read it recently, you should reread it. The "bad guys" in the financial crisis are in the book. It gives you a deep insight into where we will go from here unless we change direction.

23

How the United States Could Go Broke

UNFORTUNATELY, IF THE UNITED STATES CONTINUES DOWN ITS
current economic path, driven by a combination of altruism, pragmatism, and the related "free lunch" mentality, we have a recipe for
economic disaster. The forces that could make such a disaster the
most likely outcome in 20 to 25 years are currently in motion.

Our government has made huge commitments that it cannot
fulfill as promised. The unfunded liabilities under social security,
Medicare, state and local public employees' pension plans, and the
new healthcare program are quickly approaching $100 trillion. The
federal government's annual operating deficit is almost $1,3 trillion,
and it is likely to remain high indefinitely into the future.[1]

America is saddled with a dysfunctional foreign policy. Iran is
developing nuclear weapons and delivery systems. North Korea has
nuclear weapons and delivery systems. The United States is engaged
in three wars that are not in our self-interest. We have made gestures
of friendship to countries that hate us and alienated our allies. It is
almost impossible to ascertain the logic in our foreign policy actions
(this lack of purpose existed long before the Obama administration).

The United States has a significant demographic problem created by the retirement of the baby boom generation. In the coming decades, we will have too many old people to be fed, clothed, and sheltered by too few young people. While the problem is mathematically worse in Europe, the dysfunctionality of our school systems, which means that we have more dependent young people, creates an extra risk for the United States. To the degree that medicine continues to advance and extend people's life expectancy, the economic impact of our demographic challenge becomes even more significant. Attracting well-educated and productive immigrants is the best cure for this problem. However, we must be able to successfully integrate these newcomers culturally or they will become a part of the problem. If immigrants also come to the United States for a free lunch, our problems will be magnified.

One profound issue facing the United States is the failure of our public school system. More than 20 percent of students do not graduate from high school. Many of those who do graduate do not have the skill set they need if they are to be satisfactorily productive in a globally competitive environment. Over the long term, we cannot consume more than we produce. There is only one true natural resource—the human mind. If we do not have a productive workforce on all levels, we will not be able to sustain (much less improve) our standard of living.

Given all the intergenerational financial commitments that have been made by Washington (and the states), many of which will be extraordinarily difficult to fulfill (social security, Medicare, pension plans, and so on; see table), there is the risk of labor strikes and unrest, potentially leading to social deterioration and a move toward statism or fascism. Greece has provided a small example of the phenomenon, and its pain to date has been minimal compared to future issues. Few global leaders are advocating meaningful restructuring of welfare states.

Given the current direction, in 20 to 25 years, the United States will go broke. This is a mathematical certainty. It reminds me very much of the calculations referred to earlier that demonstrated that Freddie and Fannie were certain to fail. However, countries do not fail the way businesses do. They typically fail to fulfill their commitments, defraud bondholders, and/or hyperinflate the currency.

The Obama Deficit Blowout
Federal Tax Receipts, Spending, and Deficits, Fiscal Years 2007–2011,
Billions of Dollars

	Receipts	Outlays	Deficit	Deficit as Share of GDP
2007	$2,568	$2,729	$161	1.2%
2008	2,524	2,983	459	3.2
2009	2,104	3,520	1,416	10
2010	2,162	3,456	1,294	8.9
2011	2,303	3,600	1,298	8.6

Source: Congressional Budget Office; *Wall Street Journal*, October 18, 2011.

Since the United States is the world's largest economy and the U.S. dollar is the world's reserve currency, a financial failure of the United States would create a global financial upheaval, possibly leading to international and/or civil war(s). Large "empires" sometimes do not go quietly. However, the more likely scenario is for the United States to slowly decline into third-world status, with our children and grandchildren having a lower and lower quality of life. In the 1920s, Argentina had as high a standard of living as the United States; however, it moved toward statism and is a third-world economy today. Unfortunately, this is our future unless we change direction.

This negative outcome is certainly not inevitable. There are practical cures for the economic challenges that face the United States, a number of which have been previously outlined. The open question at this stage is not whether we have the ability to solve our problems, but whether we have the will to do so—and our willingness will be heavily influenced by the moral code that we choose to accept. If we continue to accept and try to practice altruism (self-sacrifice), we'll get still bigger government, more redistribution, and more debt in a world of social unrest and poverty. But if, as Americans, we reject altruism and instead embrace what is in our long-term, rational self-interest—guiltlessly—we can succeed in achieving happiness, peace, and prosperity. One plan that is certain to fail is to allow the Republicans to cut taxes and the Democrats to increase spending. Our problems cannot be cured painlessly. The analogy used earlier is appropriate to reenforce. We have been identified as having a kind of cancer that is terminal if it is not treated. The good news is that it can be treated. The bad news is that chemotherapy is painful. However, without chemotherapy, the United States "dies."

The cure is fundamental. We must return to the principles that made America great: individual rights, limited government, and free markets. These are principles based on personal responsibility and self-discipline. We need less government, not more. We need less regulation and more freedom.

I am, by nature, an optimist. There are many objective reasons to be optimistic. Giant advances are being made in technology, biology, and other areas. Global trade is bringing billions of producers into the world economy, raising their standard of living and, through trade, benefiting all of us. Knowledge is advancing on many fronts. Life expectancy is rising. Malnutrition and hunger are being reduced. The world is a relatively war-free place. All this is good news.

However, ideas ultimately determine outcomes. The great ideas that are the foundation of Western civilization and especially modern market economies are under attack in our most important educational institutions. Rome fell when the principles that had made it successful were abandoned and replaced by mysticism, debased currency, authoritarianism, and the "circus." Western civilization went into decline for almost 1,000 years. The Egyptian dynasties experienced long periods (hundreds of years) of decline and then semirevival over ideas. The same pattern can be observed in Chinese history. Cultures are very intangible. Human progress is not one straight upward spiral; rather, there are many long periods of significant decline. It is clearly a two steps forward, one step back process. There is evidence that Egyptian technology was more advanced in 5000 BC than in 2000 BC. What happened to the Mayans? Progress has to be earned based on the right ideas. Even if the long, long term is positive, there could be a hundred or a thousand years of decline.

The Founding Fathers of the United States grasped, at least implicitly, the principles underlying a successful social system—a recognition of reason as a means of knowledge, rational self-interest as a motivator, and individual rights as the condition necessary for optimal human well-being.

Fortunately, the American sense of life still captures these ideas.[2] As defined by Ayn Rand, "A sense of life is an emotional, subconsciously integrated appraisal of man and of existence. It sets the nature of a man's emotional response and his basic character." The American sense of life is individualistic, self-responsible, hardworking, "can do," and benevolent. The Tea Party movement, despite its flaws, is driven by the American sense of life.

Americans are skeptical of big government and skeptical of elitists. They value freedom and common sense. These are great protectors. The American sense of life is very different from the dominant sense of life in Western Europe and most of the rest of the world. Our sense of life is my greatest source of optimism that we will ultimately face our challenges and return to the principles that made us great. However, a sense of life is subconscious and intangible, and it can be led in a destructive direction when it is not consciously held and fully integrated.

The objective reality is that the most likely outcome for the United States is a long-term and significant decline into statism. The reason for this trend is not economic policy but philosophy. As long as both liberals and religious conservatives defend altruism and attack rational self-interest, our decline is inevitable.

On the other hand, I am at heart an optimist. While the most likely scenario is negative, there is still hope. That is why I bothered to write this book. If the ideas that made America great can be rediscovered and combined with knowledge on people's productive nature gained since the Industrial Revolution (as expressed by Ayn Rand), the United States can be returned to greatness. Our children and grandchildren can have wonderful lives.

The long-term key to success is to recapture the elite universities from the Left. It is critical that we restore meaningful academic freedom in which there is honest and open debate about important ideas. In relation to this issue, there is a very interesting question regarding about how the United States moved from "life, liberty, and the pursuit of happiness" (that is, limited government, individual rights, and free markets) to the "redistributive state" (big government, statism, collectivism, and a highly regulated economy). These trends have been in motion at least since Woodrow Wilson.

The answer is that by the power of philosophical ideas, the Left took over our universities, and therefore the education of future leaders. In the late 1800s, college professors in the United States were still defenders of the Founding Fathers' principles. Twenty years later, the culture in universities had changed radically. At the time, the United States was rising as a world economic power, and our colleges wanted to become world-class universities. To become universities, they needed to have PhD programs, but since they did not have PhD faculty members, they could not educate PhDs. To solve this problem, the American colleges hired a large number of PhDs from Europe beginning in the late 1800s (and American students went to German universities to earn their PhDs).[3]

The strategy was a huge success in the hard sciences. The U.S. colleges and universities attracted world-class scientists, propelling our economic development. Unfortunately, the strategy was a disaster in the liberal arts, especially philosophy.[4] The students (who were now PhDs themselves) of the German philosophers (such as Kant and Hegel) who had laid the intellectual foundations for collectivism and statism in Europe were attracted to the United States. In Europe, these ideas ultimately led to Nazism and Communism. In the United States, the ideas were partly moderated by the American sense of life, but they led to the New Deal and the ideology of the current administration.

Of course, the universities educate the teachers. Therefore, the Left took over the K–12 educational system by indoctrinating schoolteachers. Because the professors determine which new PhD graduates will get tenure at the university, the system is closed. This is particularly true in the liberal arts, where evaluating accomplishments is highly subjective. If you are in significant disagreement with your professors over fundamental issues, you are unlikely to get a PhD, get a tenure-track job, get published in the "best" journals, or get tenure. Numerous studies have documented that the faculties at the vast majority of universities are far to the left of the American mainstream.[5]

It is a closed, self-reinforcing system that educates elitists who at a deep level believe that they are smarter than the rest of us, and that their ideas are more insightful. Of course, there are some high-quality, thoughtful, honest people in academia. But even the best often operate with subconscious premises that drive their thinking—premises that are inconsistent with a free and "messy" society that is not ordered and directed by the "best and the brightest," the elite who know what is good for you and have only your welfare as their goal. Even though history is littered with multiple failures of elitist-driven cultures, the Left always attributes these failures to poor execution—errors that will not be made in the future. Despite the fact that communism killed hundreds of millions of people,[6] there are many defenders of communism on university campuses.

BB&T has sponsored 65 programs on the moral foundations of capitalism at universities and colleges in our market area. We are trying to support those professors (who are a small minority) who have a deep understanding of why free markets and individual rights are both moral and necessary for human well-being. Our programs have been extremely well received. Students are excited by these ideas, which many of them are hearing for the first time.

Another interesting question is the continuing defense of K–12 public schools by the majority of the public from many different political persuasions. By any set of objective standards, the K–12 public school system has failed. In fact, its failure has been documented for more than 20 years. More than 20 percent of students fail to graduate from high school. U.S. students are ranked below those of most of the developed world (and some of the underdeveloped world) in academic achievement. This is a systematic destruction of precious human capital.

The answer from the public school establishment and liberal politicians is that we need to spend more on public schools. However, spending on public schools has been rising very rapidly without any material improvement in academic achievement. Catholic schools and charter schools consistently outperform public schools at dramatically lower cost. It is not surprising that teachers' unions defend the public schools because their primary concern is taking care of teachers, not students. Also, a union is mostly in the business of defending mediocre and poor teachers. After all, the best teachers do not need to be defended because they are worth more than they are paid. Many of the best teachers are driven out of the system because of bureaucratic union rules designed to protect the mediocre.

The primary justification for public education is to help students from low-income families. However, there is overwhelming evidence that the biggest victims of public schools are low-income students and especially members of minority groups. The graduation rates and educational attainment of students from low-income families are disastrous. The liberal politicians realize that the public schools have failed low-income students. However, they can get reelected by promising to fix the schools by making a greater investment in them. Also, liberal politicians see the schools as primarily involved in indoctrinating students in the ideas that the politicians think are important, that is, statism, environmentalism, and redistribution. They are not concerned with teaching students to think independently. Independent thinkers tend to vote for limited government and liberty, not for bigger government and more controls. Independent critical thinkers do not have a dependent mindset.

It is interesting that many people realize that public schools have failed, and yet they defend the school their own children attend. Maybe the school is good, or maybe the parents feel guilty because they have abdicated the responsibility for getting their child a better education in a private school. To afford a private school, the parents would have to make a financial sacrifice. Even if they could have afforded the private school, the parents may have chosen a nicer home or more comfortable car and rationalize that even though public schools in general have failed, "their" school is very effective. Of course, many people do not want to have to pay taxes for public schools and tuition for a private school. Obviously, by subsidizing public schools, we have given parents a major incentive not to explore the best choices for their children. This is an injustice to both students and parents.

The problem with public schools is fundamentally a systems design issue. Practically speaking, public school cannot fail. When a business does a poor job of meeting the needs of its customers, it ultimately goes out of business (unless it receives a crony capitalist subsidy). If a school performs poorly in educating its students, over time it typically receives more resources.

In fact, what makes a free-market economy successful is the ability to experiment constantly. Business (especially small business) is a giant series of simultaneous experiments. New businesses are constantly being created, and existing businesses are constantly failing. For every Google, there are a thousand failed Google "wannabes."

We need to privatize education initially by subsidizing the students (through tax credits or vouchers), not the schools. (The ultimate goal is truly private schools with no subsidies.) This would lead to intense competition in existing education. Many private schools would be challenged in this environment. What is needed is 100,000 educational experiments, many of which would fail. However, there would be a few breakthrough ideas that would transform the quality of education. There are some Thomas Edisons, Sam Waltons, and Bill Gateses who would change the world of education. The failed experiments are necessary to optimize the learning process. (Even the failures would probably be better than most public schools.)

The foundation for the educational solution will be to help students to learn to solve problems, make decisions, and think independently, using their ability to reason from the facts of reality. The idea that all students should go to college is false.[7] Not everyone has the type of intellectual talent that is appropriate for college education, but practically everyone does have a talent that can be productively developed in a free market. Our public school system destroys the talents of many students.

People who think independently for themselves and who have confidence that they can make the best decisions for themselves want to be free. The systematic attack on critical decision making and independent thinking that happens in public schools stifles innovation and creates a dependent society. To return America to the principles that made it great, it is essential to privatize education and restore intellectual balance in our universities. Self-confidence based on the ability to make independent decisions is the foundation for the American sense of life.

24

The Need for Principled Action

A QUESTION THAT I AM ASKED OFTEN IS, WHY DID BB&T PERFORM so well during the financial crisis? On the surface, we should have performed very poorly. Our fundamental business is residential real estate lending in the Southeast, and many of our markets had severe real estate corrections (Florida, Atlanta, and the coastal Carolinas). Our primary competitors (SunTrust, Regions, Wachovia, Fifth Third, Bank of America, South Financial, First Horizon, and so on) who are in the same basic markets as BB&T all suffered multiple quarterly losses, whereas BB&T did not have a single loss quarter. While U.S. Bancorp outperformed BB&T, it had a much smaller residential lending business, with limited exposure in the markets in which the most severe corrections occurred. Adjusting for business mix and markets, BB&T was clearly the best performing of the major banks in the United States during the financial crisis.

Many people assume that this was because we are more conservative. However, BB&T was not conservative. During my tenure as CEO, we grew from $4.5 billion to $152 billion in assets. This growth pace is not conservative. However, we are principled. We believe that competitive advantage is in the minds of our employees.

For this reason, BB&T invests substantially more in employee education than our competitors and less in marketing. We have a concept of lifelong learning that is facilitated through the BB&T University. BB&T has grown its business by word of mouth from satisfied clients who have referred their friends.

I have tried to personally exhibit the attributes necessary for lifelong learning. Every month, I read a difficult book (typically one that was not directly business-related) and referred the best books to our senior leadership team. I took the time for two weeks of education each year. Typically, one week would be related to economics and the other week would be devoted to studying philosophy. I particularly studied Austrian economics. Since most business leaders my age studied Keynesian economics from Paul Samuelson's incredibly misleading college textbook, they were far easier for the Fed to mislead. A deep understanding of the Austrian economic school is a tremendous competitive advantage in making long-term economic decisions. (You should read *Human Action* by Ludwig von Mises.)

Because we believe that the way to achieve optimal organizational performance is to allow individual employees to use their minds effectively, we operate with a highly decentralized organizational structure. One problem for the large banks that had regulator-driven risk-management systems is that a mistake in a centralized system, while less likely, is incredibly more destructive because the mistake is forced throughout the whole organization. Since we were decentralized, individual mistakes tend to offset one another. Also, our decision makers are held personally responsible for their performance. Committees do not make any credit decisions.

Unfortunately, BB&T's highly decentralized decision structure has largely been destroyed by the recent regulatory attack. This is true irony in that while BB&T's structure radically outperformed the industry, we have been forced to replicate the credit decision structure of Citigroup, Wachovia, Bank of America, and others, which fundamentally failed. However, a centralized structure gives the regulators a greater sense of control. After all, it is less messy. However, the fact that the regulators are forcing all major banks into centralized decision making and using Basel capital guidelines to herd banks into the same lending segments is a recipe for future disasters.

BB&T is also very process-oriented. We continually experiment to find and refine processes that produce better results. For example, our studies have shown that client satisfaction is driven by reliability, responsiveness, empathy, and competence. Employees can learn these attributes, and systems can be designed to achieve this goal. For example, the BB&T branch managers had the authority to approve loans. All our competitors, including community banks, used some form of centralized loan approval process. While our branch managers had access to a loan decision model, they made the final decision. Clients prefer to deal with someone who is a decision maker and can treat them as unique individuals.

BB&T had other attributes that contributed to its relative success, but by far the most important was a fundamental belief in principled action based on principled leadership.

In fact, a secondary, but important, cause of the financial crisis was failures of leadership. There were serious failures of leadership both in business and in government. These failures were based on the fact that many leaders have not internalized fundamental principles to govern their decision making in all types of environments. In fact, most failures of leadership are failures of self-leadership. We all must lead ourselves to become who we want to be.

The key strength of BB&T has been a deep commitment to making decisions based on long-term principles. These principles guide our actions in both good times and bad times. We are committed to actions that are consistent with our principles regardless of the current environment, because we know that the principles improve the probability of success in the long term. Our principles are non-negotiable and will not be compromised. Our 10 core principles are outlined in the "BB&T Philosophy" booklet.[1]

Underlying these principles are what I believe are the three great virtues: purpose, reason, and self-esteem. These virtues define the context for successful individual, organizational, and societal behavior.

The organizing principle of human action is purpose. As human beings, we are purpose-directed entities. We have to know where we are going if we are to get there. Organizations (businesses, churches, universities, civic clubs, and others) are simply groups of individuals.

For an organization to be successful, the individuals in the organization must vest in the purpose of the organization.

As a concrete example, BB&T is a purpose-driven organization. Our purpose is clearly stated in our mission:

TO MAKE THE WORLD A BETTER PLACE TO LIVE BY:

- Helping our CLIENTS achieve economic success and financial security;
- Creating a place where our EMPLOYEES can learn, grow and be fulfilled in their work;
- Making the COMMUNITIES in which we work better places to be; and thereby;
- Optimizing the long-term return to our SHAREHOLDERS, while providing a safe and sound investment.

We are not confused or conflicted. In a free market, our primary fiduciary obligation is to our shareholders. This commitment is defined by the free market, and this is as it should be. Our shareholders provide the capital that is necessary to make our business possible. They take the risk if the business is unsuccessful. They have the right to receive economic rewards for the risk that they have undertaken.

However, creating superior long-term economic rewards for our shareholders is an effect that can be accomplished only by providing excellent service to our clients, as our clients are our source of revenues.

To have excellent client relationships, we must have outstanding employees to serve our clients. To attract and retain outstanding employees, we must reward them financially and create an environment in which they can learn and grow.

Our economic results are significantly affected by the success of our communities. A community's "quality of life" affects its ability to attract industry for growth.

Therefore, we manage our business in a long-term context, as an integrated whole, with the ultimate objective of rewarding the shareholders for their investment, while realizing that the cause of this result is high-quality client service. Excellent service will be delivered by motivated employees working as an integrated team. These results will be affected by our capacity to contribute to the growth and well-being of the communities we serve.

Individuals also need a personal sense of purpose. It is discouraging to talk to many people who view their work as just work. When you think about all the time and energy you spend at work, if you view your work as just work, you are missing out on a lot that life has to offer. By the way, this is it. You are not practicing to live. You are living.

If you want to have passion and energy in your life, you must have a sense of purpose in your work. As another concrete example, the following is a series of questions that I ask the employees of BB&T. How would you answer these questions in your own context?

Are you truly making the world a better place to live through your work? Are you really helping your clients achieve economic success and financial security? Are you providing the quality of advice that ensures that they make better decisions? Have you trained yourself so that you have the skill to provide excellent advice? You cannot be responsible for your clients. They will make their own decisions. However, you should never do anything that you believe will not be in your client's best interest, even if you can make a profit in the short term. This type of behavior will always come back to haunt you. If you genuinely help your clients make better decisions, they will be more successful and more loyal. Life is about creating win-win relationships.

Are you helping your fellow employees be more successful? This is especially important if you are in a leadership role. If you help your fellow employees be more successful, they are very likely to help you. In addition, there will be less turnover and a more successful team. That's another win-win opportunity.

Can we count on you to support the United Way, the March of Dimes, and similar organizations that are important to the well-being of our community?

Are you rewarding our shareholders? They are the people for whom you work. In the banking business, this requires making good loans and providing deposit products, financial services, wealth management, and other such products. In a support function, it requires that you manage your function in a highly effective and efficient manner in the context of the organization's overall goals.

While the content of purpose will vary greatly, I believe the context is the same for everyone who is reading this book. The context has two fundamental components. First, I believe everyone who is reading this book wants to make the world a better place to live. You would not be reading this if at some level you were not interested in the quality of life on this planet. In fact, I believe that the vast majority of people want to make the world a better place to live. This desire is the typical (but not exclusive) human condition.

There are many ways to make the world a better place to live. You do not have to feed hungry children in Africa to make the world a better place to live. Successful businesses make the world a better place to live. They provide high-quality products and services that improve human well-being. In fact, the primary difference in the quality of life in the United States and the quality of life in Africa is that we have more productive businesses. *Business is noble work.*

The act of production is a noble act. Before something can be given away, it must first be produced. When business leaders forget that they are in business to make the world a better place to live, their businesses soon get in trouble.

I find it frustrating that many students believe that joining a charitable organization is more noble than working for a profit-making business. If you want to work for a charity, more power to you. However, it is the act of production (creation) that is the noble act. In my life experiences, I have found it far easier to give wealth away than to create it.

Good doctors, good truck drivers, good teachers, good attorneys, and good homemakers make the world a better place to live. There are many ways to make the world a better place to live, but you need to believe that your work is making a difference if you are to have a sense of purpose, that is, to have meaning in your life.

The second aspect of an empowering sense of purpose is equally important and far less discussed. *You need to make the world a better place to live while doing something that you want to do for you.* You should teach your children to make the world a better place while doing something that they want to do for themselves.

You (and each of your children) have a fundamental right to your own life. If you were to make the world a better place, but you did not enjoy doing it, you would have wasted the most precious thing you have—which is you. Besides, if you try to make the world better by doing something that you do not enjoy doing, the odds are very high that you will fail in your efforts.

In order to have passion in your life, you need a sense of purpose in your work—a sense of purpose in which you believe that you are making the world a better place while doing something that you enjoy doing. Principled leaders positively motivate themselves and others by focusing on the purposefulness of their lives. The purpose is not bigger than us, but it is part of who we are. It does not have to be grand, but it needs to be consistent with your abilities and talents. It cannot be too small relative to your abilities because you will be bored. Nor can it be greater than your abilities because you will fail. I have a painting of a railroad worker throwing a switch as a train approaches. He is intensely focused on his task. This is clearly not highly intellectually challenging work; however, if he does not throw the switch, the train will crash. This is important work. The railroad worker is the kind of person who "holds the earth together," that is, who gets the necessary job done under normal and also very challenging conditions. He somehow always gets the job done.

I find it amazing that some intellectuals have defined homemaking as menial work. There is no more important and no more difficult work than raising children properly. The question is not the scale of the work or its visibility to other people, but rather its importance to you and the enjoyment you get from it.

The means by which we accomplish our purpose is our ability to think; that is, we use reason to accomplish our goals and achieve our values. Every species has a method of staying alive. A lion can hunt. A deer has speed to avoid the hunter. Human beings have the capacity to think. Our capacity to think is our only means of survival, success, and happiness. There are no shortcuts and no free lunches. Our ability to reason objectively from the facts of reality is our means of survival and success.

Reason is the faculty in our mind that identifies and integrates the information about reality provided by our senses.[2] Reason, as used here, is not about being a genius or having a high IQ. In fact, there are certainly people with high IQs who are destructive, and there are people with modest IQs who are very productive. Also, after a certain age, while you might be able to raise your IQ marginally, affecting your IQ is very difficult.[3] Reason is a broad concept that for our purpose means using your intellectual talents to achieve the best outcome you can.

I tell the employees of BB&T that I do not expect them to become geniuses, but I do challenge them to have mental discipline and, therefore, to commit to being lifelong learners, which requires that they have an active mind. Individuals who are committed to being lifelong learners read more. They take advantage of educational seminars. However, they are especially effective at learning from experience. In fact, experiential learning is the foundation for our most basic knowledge. Humans can induce general principles from their concrete life experiences. This type of process is the basis for so-called common sense (which, unfortunately, is not too common).

Over the years, we have hired individuals with only high school degrees whose performance ultimately exceeded that of their college-educated peers. These individuals are superior experiential learners. They learn more rapidly and more effectively from their daily life experience.

Superior experiential learners do two simple but profound processes unusually effectively. All of us can associate with learning from mistakes. You can probably reflect on mistakes that were significant learning experiences in your life. However, many times we do not learn from our mistakes, which gives us the opportunity to essentially make the same mistake again and again. In fact, many people have built mistakes into their personality. They do something they wish they had not done and realize that they have made the same mistake multiple times in the past.

Why do we not always learn from our mistakes? Sometimes we are guilty of the ultimate psychological sin, which is evasion. Evasion occurs when you are presented with some information that at least at a subconscious level you know needs to be examined. However, you refuse to examine the information because it threatens your beliefs about the world or about yourself. You literally do not "hear" the information. When you evade, you are detached from reality, which is a dangerous disconnect.

I started my career in the banking business as a small business lender. One observation from that experience is that the single most common reason small businesses fail is that the leader of the business evades. The business is performing satisfactorily, and then something happens in the economy or at home. The business leader refuses to acknowledge what has happened and runs the business into the ground.

Citigroup, at the time the largest financial institution in the world, hired a group of "geniuses" to manage its affordable-housing/ subprime-lending business—PhDs out of Harvard, MIT, and other such schools. I guarantee that long before any of us realized the potential disaster in subprime lending, these geniuses in the backroom of Citigroup knew, at some level, that something was going wrong. What did they do? They evaded. Why did they evade? They would make less money and Citigroup would make less money if they acted. They evaded and drove Citigroup into the ground.

Unfortunately, almost everyone evades in some aspect of his life. Your parents, spouse, friends, and managers have been telling you about your evasions for a long time. The next time you hear something you have heard before and you know that you have refused to examine this information, have the courage to examine it. Being detached from reality is an unhealthy place to be. Many of the most destructive decisions made in business are acts of evasion.

Superior experiential learners also realize that life is a constant education if you choose to make it one. When I was CEO at BB&T, we operated with 33 community banks. I would visit all these banks. Part of the visitation process was to have a luncheon with our local advisory board members and our highest-performing officers. I never had a boring luncheon. These business and community leaders were always asking questions, seeking feedback, and raising issues. It was easy to understand why they were successful. They were living their lives in focus, with active minds. This constant focus allowed them to learn more rapidly. Unfortunately, many people live most of their lives out of focus. Life passes them by. They do not learn effectively because their minds are not "in gear."

Superior experiential learners evade less and stay in focus more, which is a huge competitive advantage in life. Some successful business leaders have high IQs. However, what distinguishes most business leaders who are successful in the long term is that they evade less and stay in focus more. They learn from their mistakes more rapidly and tend to make fewer big mistakes.

There are two societal pillars that support the ability of individuals to reason objectively and allow the human mind to be used most productively. The first pillar is freedom. By definition, all human progress is based on creativity (innovation). Unless someone does something better (that is, different), there can be no progress. Creativity is possible only for an independent thinker. Someone who thinks like "the crowd" cannot be innovative, cannot be creative, and cannot contribute to human progress. This is why entrepreneurs are so important.

In order to be innovative, to be creative, individuals must be able to think for themselves, to think independently. Statist (socialist) societies are ultimately doomed to failure because they stop creativity, which destroys human progress. The idea that there can be a highly successful and creative authoritarian society in the long term is not factually correct. The idea often pictured in fiction of a highly successful authoritarian society and a messy, less economically successful, but happier free society is false. The choice is between being authoritarian and poor and being free and wealthy. Compare North Korea and South Korea, East Germany and West Germany, Cuba and Florida, and so on. Statism does not even result in more equality. There are always some individuals in statist societies who are more equal (those who lust for power).

Freedom raises our standard of living because, given our nature, we must be free to think if we are to be productive, creative, and innovative. Many professors vigorously defend academic freedom (although they often do not act consistent with the concept). However, many of the same professors support intrusive regulation of businesspeople. These regulations literally keep business leaders from being creative. During my career, I had a number of opportunities to introduce new products that would have improved the lives of our clients. However, some government rule or regulation prevented the creation of these products. Typically, these destructive regulations were supported by inefficient business competitors but defended in the name of the public good. It is crucial to understand that freedom is essential for thinking. People literally cannot think if they are forced to act in ways that are inconsistent with what they believe is the right conclusion. Galileo was forced to recant to the Pope, but he could not hold an idea that was inconsistent with what he knew to be true.

The other institutional pillar that maximizes the productivity of the human mind is education. In order to produce, we must know how to do so; that is, we must have knowledge. Knowledge comes from education in the broadest context. In the previous chapter, we discussed the importance to our economic well-being of having a highly successful educational system. The ultimate cause of unemployment and underemployment is that our education system has failed to teach students to think critically within the context of their natural abilities. Only a private educational system driven by competition and innovation can achieve this end. Just as a free, unsubsidized, and unregulated economy produces more and better physical (and financial) capital, so a free, unsubsidized, and unregulated school system produces more and better human capital.

When we are clear about our purpose and when we use our ability to think (reason) to accomplish our purpose, we create the opportunity to raise our self-esteem. Over a long career, it has been my observation that the primary reason individuals at high levels in organizations fail is low self-esteem. These individuals are smart enough and well educated enough to be successful. However, they have a subconscious low self-esteem that results in self-destructive, and often organizationally destructive, behavior.

In addition, self-esteem is the foundation for happiness, and happiness is the end goal in life. Happiness is used here in the Aristotelian sense of the concept. This is not happiness in the context of having a good time on Friday night, but rather happiness in the context of a life well lived—hard-earned happiness and hard-work happiness, happiness earned by blood, sweat, and tears.

Happiness is the psychological reward for achieving one's values— the deep kind of happiness that comes from fundamental accomplishment. Happiness is earned through the successful achievement of important goals: graduate from high school or college, get a job, get married, have children, help your children through high school or college, write a great book, build a successful business, and so on. You must be free to pursue your personal goals if you are to have an opportunity to attain happiness.

Some businesspeople get confused. They believe that money is the end goal in life. In fact, honestly earned money is a proper value. However, money (wealth) is not an end in itself. Money can be a means to an end, but it is not an end. Happiness, in the Aristotelian sense of the concept, is the end goal. Happiness has to be earned. Self-esteem is the foundation for happiness.

Self-esteem is a complex subject. However, let me offer a few basic insights. Self-esteem is fundamentally self-confidence in your ability to live and be successful, given the facts of reality. You earn self-esteem by how you live your life. No one can give you self-esteem. You cannot give anyone self-esteem. You cannot give your children self-esteem. Promoting children who have not mastered their school grade lowers their self-esteem.

When you live your life with integrity, you raise your self-esteem. This is one of the reasons it is so important that you have an integrated value system that is consistent with life on this earth. If you hold fundamental beliefs that are inconsistent with one another and/ or are not consistent with living in the real world, you cannot have a high level of self-esteem.

In addition, for practically everyone reading this book, the single biggest driver of your self-esteem is your work, because you spend a disproportionate amount of your time, energy, and mental focus at work. I am defining work in its broadest context. Raising children well is very hard, very productive work.

For many years, I have expressed the following concept to the employees of BB&T. It is very important to BB&T that you do your work well. However, it is far more important to you. You might fool me about how well you do your work, and you might fool your boss about how well you do your work, but you will never fool yourself. If you do not perform your work the best you can possibly do it, you will lower your self-esteem. The best you can possibly do it depends on your level of knowledge and your skill; you cannot do the impossible. However, if you do not do your work the best *you* can possibly do it, you will lower your self-esteem.

The good news is that the flip side is also true. If you perform your work the best you can possibly do it given your level of skill and knowledge, you will raise your self-esteem. Raising your self-esteem is more important than whether you receive a promotion or earn more money. Raising your self-esteem is a foundational aspect of building your character. A stronger sense of self-esteem will give you more self-confidence to pursue your values, leading to a more successful, more self-fulfilling, and fundamentally happier life.

I apply the same lesson when talking to college students. For students, their education is their work. If they do not perform their schoolwork the best they can possibly do it, they will lower their self-esteem, even if they receive a good grade. If they perform their schoolwork the best they possibly can, especially in the context of improving their ability to think critically, they will raise their self-esteem, which is far more important than their grades.

There is a very significant societal concept related to this issue that can be seen from an example. An entry-level construction worker, a bricklayer, has a tough life in many ways. He works hard in all kinds of weather. His income varies with the availability of construction projects. He reminds me of my grandfather. However, he and his wife raise their children. Maybe his granddaughter becomes CEO of a large public company, maybe not. Even though his life is hard by many measures, he earns something very important from his work. He gets to be proud of what he has accomplished. He earns self-esteem.

Take that same construction worker and give him welfare. He may be better off materially, but he loses something that is incredibly important. He loses his pride. He loses his self-esteem.

There has been a great deal of discussion in the public policy debate about security. Americans care about security. However, this is not the land of security. People did not get on a boat and travel to Jamestown to be secure. America is the land of opportunity—the opportunity to be great, and the opportunity to fail and try again. But, most important, that bricklayer's opportunity to pursue life on his own terms, to be free to pursue his own happiness consistent with his beliefs, his values, and his capabilities. This powerful motivator was essential to making America great. This idea is why immigrants have flocked to the United States. This is the unique American sense of life, and that sense of life is what is so, so precious to protect.

25

Conclusion

GOVERNMENT POLICIES ARE THE PRIMARY CAUSE OF THE RECENT Great Recession and the related slow economic recovery. The Federal Reserve overexpanded the monetary base to avoid the pain of short-term corrections and thereby pushed the problems into the future, creating a bigger misinvestment of human and financial resources.

The misinvestment was focused in the housing market primarily because of the actions of the two giant government-sponsored enterprises (which could not have existed in a free market), Freddie Mac and Fannie Mae. They dominated the affordable-housing/subprime-lending business as a result of mandates forced on them by Congress.

A number of large (and small) financial institutions made serious mistakes and should have been allowed to fail. However, their mistakes were secondary and took place within the context of government policy.

Unfortunately, many people have learned the wrong lessons from the crisis because of both a lack of understanding of a complex issue and serious bias in the media. Most of the policy decisions made since the crisis started, even those that may help in the short term, will be destructive in the long term.

The Federal Reserve, the primary perpetrator of the misinvestment/overinvestment, now has more power, not less. Freddie and Fannie (along with their clone the Federal Housing Administration [FHA]) still dominate the housing finance market and are still politically controlled. Regulations have been increased. Government spending and government debt have expanded rapidly. The Federal Reserve is "printing" money (through quantitative easing, or QE2), laying the foundation for the next bubble (misinvestment/overinvestment).

Unless the United States changes direction, we face severe financial problems in 20 to 25 years. The deficits in social security and Medicare, unfunded government pension liabilities, annual operating deficits, demographic issues, and a failed K–12 educational system will lead to a much lower real standard of living. While dealing with our economic problems is extremely difficult, the negative direction can be changed. It will be interesting to see if we have the courage to deal with our major issues.

Unfortunately, most people do not realize that the real challenges are philosophical, not economic. It is the combination of altruism and pragmatism that threatens our long-term well-being.

In fact, many people absolutely refuse to face the proven fact that an altruistic government policy, affordable housing, was the root cause of the financial crisis. They need to believe that greed (which is "bad"), not altruism (which is "good"), caused the crisis.

In the Declaration of Independence, the Founding Fathers proclaimed that all men are created equal. However, they meant equal before the law. Just because your father had been an earl gave you no special privileges. But they did not believe that human beings were equal in every respect, nor were they advocates of equal outcomes. They were afraid of the tyranny of the majority and of the propensity of large groups to use the power of government to take what other individuals produced.

Life, liberty, and the pursuit of happiness was a revolutionary moral premise defending each individual's right to his own life, including the right to the product of his own labor. This moral premise is what makes the United States a special place.

Despite the unending failures of statist economies from the Soviet Union to Eastern Europe, to North Korea, to Cuba, and so on, liberals hold on to the belief that intellectual elites with good intentions can direct human activities better than the experimental process of human interface and competitiveness in free markets. Whenever the liberals' theories fail, as they always do, they blame the failure on markets and greed. The disaster in affordable housing/subprime lending was a predictable outcome of liberal "do-gooders'" policies to increase homeownership.

Many independents and moderates who are skeptical of big government believe that we do need many regulations. They fail to recognize the incredible march of the regulatory state. They also do not understand that, as public choice theory has proven, government bureaucrats are often motivated by destructive incentives. In my career, since 1971, I cannot think of a single additional regulation placed on the financial services industry that did not reduce the efficiency of the industry and lower the country's overall standard of living. The only success stories have been deregulations (such as interstate branching).

There is an important role for government in preventing fraud and the use of force. This is why we need a strong military to protect us from foreign tyrants, an effective police force to protect us from villains, and a principle-driven court system to allow us to settle legitimate disputes without the use of force. When government starts doing more than performing those basic roles, it is in the business of taking something that someone has produced and giving it to someone who has not earned it. It also destroys innovation and creativity by misallocating resources and limiting experimentation. Crony capitalists can exist only when the government has the power to dole out favors.

Mother Nature does not automatically provide us with the goods we need in order to survive and be happy. We have to produce and mold nature to our needs. We have a special means of producing, which is our ability to think, to reason. While our ability to reason is our means of survival, we are not infallible. This is a complex, constantly changing world. We must try to live by principles (values such as honesty and integrity) that improve our chances of success and happiness. We are in a constant process of trying to improve our productivity, using these principles as basic guides to action.

Capitalism is the only economic/political system that allows individuals the freedom to think for themselves and rewards those who create the most productive ideas, products, or services as determined by the actions of other productive people in purchasing these ideas, products, or services.

People cannot think unless they are free to think. Government rules and regulations literally prevent thought and prevent experimentation. A free market is a massive experiment in competing ideas, the most productive of which win out. Most of the experiments fail, but even failed experiments lead to better understanding. When the intellectual elitists stop the experiments because they are smarter than the rest of us and know what is in the "public good," the learning stops—witness the Soviet Union. By now, the elitists should know better. Often, they use the public good as an excuse for their own lust for power. Those of us who have had to face government bureaucrats often see the lust for power as the true motivation and the "public good" as the bureaucrat's rationalization.

Capitalism is good because it is consistent with human nature. Capitalism "works" (that is, results in a higher standard of living) because it is good. Proper governments support individual rights and economic freedom while preventing the use of force and fraud.

At a fundamental level, freedom is necessary for the pursuit of happiness, in the deepest sense of that term. Happiness is the end goal of the game of life. The advocates of a free society based on individual rights and limited government have the moral high ground. We are the defenders of the pursuit of happiness.

Notes

Chapter 1

1. It is tragic that the leaders of technology companies try to use government power to attack their competitors. The antitrust attack on Microsoft was led by Microsoft's competitors. These companies are then surprised when the government attacks them. Unfortunately, many business leaders are crony capitalists. They do not want a level playing field. They want some special favor from the government.
2. I started to title the book *How Greenspan, Bernanke, Paulson, Frank, Dodd, Geithner, Johnson, Clinton, and Bush Caused the Financial Crisis*, but it seemed a bit long.
3. I also thought about titling the book *How the Critique of Pure Reason by Immanuel Kant (1783) Caused the Financial Crisis*, but that was too obscure for most people, although it was more accurate, since Kant was the major philosophical opponent of reason who put an end to the Enlightenment century (1700s) that indelibly shaped the founding of the United States.

Chapter 2

1. House prices are ultimately determined by construction cost, rental rates, and affordability. At the peak of the housing bubble, house prices nationally were 30 percent too high based on affordability, which is the primary long-term driver of home values.
2. In the 1960s and 1970s, the personal savings rate in America averaged a healthy 9 percent, but it declined thereafter and averaged only 2 percent in the years before the peak of the house-price boom (2005–2006); since then, it has averaged 5 percent.
3. Of course houses may increase in value, but this does not mean that they are not still consumer goods. An antique car or a painting can also appreciate in value. The fact that a consumer good can appreciate in value does not make it a capital good. Some people use the term *investment* for goods that can increase in value, but the proper distinction is between goods that are used to produce

more or other goods (capital goods) and goods that are consumed (consumer goods).

Chapter 3

1. It is worth noting that the so-called Misery Index, defined by economists as the sum of the U.S. inflation rate and jobless rate, has been substantially higher since 1913, under the Fed, than it was during the prior century (1813–1912).
2. During and after the U.S. Civil War, government controls on money and banking increased, and were largely responsible for the occasional money panics and bank runs in the late 1800s; however, the half-century prior to the Fed's founding in 1913—the "Gilded Age"—saw tremendous gains in U.S. economic prosperity and living standards, along with very low rates of inflation and joblessness.
3. See Richard M. Salsman, *Breaking the Banks: Central Banking Problems and Free Banking Solutions* (Great Barrington, MA: American Institute for Economic Research, 1990).
4. See Christina D. Romer, "Is the Stabilization of the Postwar Economy a Figment of the Data?" *American Economic Review* (June 1986), pp. 314–334.
5. See Ben S. Bernanke, "Remarks on the Occasion of Milton Friedman's 90th Birthday," Federal Reserve Conference at the University of Chicago, November 8, 2002, http://www.federalreserve.gov/BOARDDOCS/SPEECHES/2002/20021108/default.htm.
6. See Milton Friedman and Anna J. Schwartz, *A Monetary History of the United States, 1867–1960* (Princeton, NJ: Princeton University Press, 1963), especially Chapter 7, "The Great Contraction, 1929–1933," pp. 299–407.
7. Numerous other government policies, such as the Smoot-Hawley Tariff Act of 1930, the tripling of the top U.S. income tax rate to 63 percent in 1932, and FDR's New Deal policies (1933–1940) also contributed to the Great Depression and made it longer and deeper than necessary. See Amity Shlaes, *The Forgotten Man: A New History of the Great Depression* (New York: Harper, 2008), and Burton W. Folsom, Jr., *New Deal or Raw Deal? How FDR's Legacy Has Damaged America* (New York: Threshold Editions, 2009).
8. See Charles Goodhart, *The Evolution of Central Banks* (Cambridge, MA: MIT Press, 1988).
9. In the three years through summer 2011, the Fed caused a 41 percent boom in the U.S. money supply (currency plus checking deposits, or M-1), a growth rate not seen since World War II and World War I, when the U.S. inflation rate was in double digits. More ominous still has been the Fed's three-year 1,675 percent increase in U.S. bank reserves since the summer of 2008, more than 11 times faster than the previous record rate of growth (149 percent from 1937 to 1940).
10. Thomas Sargent was recently awarded the Nobel Prize in Economics for his work on rational expectations. My actual experience in banking and working

with business decision makers supports his technical conclusions. Human actions drive economic activity.

11. See Peronet Despeignes, "'Greenspan Put' May Be Encouraging Complacency: Moral Hazard May Be Created by the Interventions of the Fed," *Financial Times* (London), December 8, 2000, p. 20. See also "When Markets Are Too Big to Fail," editorial, *New York Times*, September 22, 2007.

12. See George Selgin, "Less than Zero: The Case for a Falling Price Level in a Growing Economy," occasional paper, Institute of Economic Affairs, London, 1997.

13. One widely cited alternative to the current CPI that extends the discontinued (pre-1983) series using house prices instead of rental rates estimates that official government reported CPI rates since 1990 have been roughly 3 to 7 percentage points below actual CPI rates. See www.shadowstats.com/alternate_data.

14. See "The Yield Curve as a Leading Indicator," Federal Reserve Bank of New York, http://www.newyorkfed.org/research/capital_markets/ycfaq.html, and "The Yield Curve as a Predictor of U.S. Recessions." Federal Reserve Bank of New York, http://www.newyorkfed.org/research/current_issues/ci2-7.html.

15. See Nell Henderson, "Bernanke: There's No Housing Bubble to Go Bust," *Washington Post*, October 27, 2005.

16. In November 2007, a month before the recession began, Bernanke told Congress that "we have not calculated the probability of a recession" and "our assessment is for slower growth, but positive." See "Fed Chairman Says Economy Likely to Slow," *New York Times*, November 8, 2007, http://www.nytimes.com/2007/11/08/business/09fed-web.html?pagewanted=print. See also "Bernanke Sees No Recession, but Big Challenge," National Public Radio, February 27, 2008, http://www.npr.org/templates/story/story.php?story Id=74992288.

17. See Friedrich A. Hayek, *The Fatal Conceit: The Errors of Socialism* (Chicago: University of Chicago Press, 1989).

18. See George A. Selgin and Lawrence H. White, "How Would the Invisible Hand Handle Money?" *Journal of Economic Literature* (December 1994), pp. 1718–1749.

19. Deflation can be bad if it simply reflects a change in the long-term length of the monetary yardstick. The problem with a paper money system (fiat money) coupled with fractional reserve banking is that the velocity (turnover) of money becomes a major factor in the amount of usable money in circulation. Paper money systems with central banks (like the U.S. Federal Reserve) encourage banks and other financial intermediaries to increase their leverage, and this creates a greater risk of bank failure, together with a currency multiplier effect that is much larger. If there is not a government agency to rescue private-market banks in difficult times, they will be less leveraged and less vulnerable to failure, so the multiplier effect will be less significant. What this means is that in good times, individuals and businesses tend to spend their money faster because they feel safer. In bad times, individuals and businesses

tend to spend their money more slowly because they are less secure. The effect of these changes in spending patterns is multiplied, in both directions, by the leverage in the banking system. Private banking systems with less leverage not only are less likely to fail, but also exert less of a multiplier effect and thus are less volatile. In a paper money system, the central bank, theoretically at least, can offset those multiplier effects by increasing or reducing the base level of money, but in practice central banks are driven by politics and thus tend to overexpand money in good times until they have created misallocations of resources that cannot be overcome by printing more money. At some point, the ability of an economic system to produce real goods and services will decline and reduce the standard of living. If money printing would cure real economic problems, Zimbabwe would be fantastically wealthy (at the end of 2009, $1,000,000,000,000,000 Zimbabwe = $0.01 U.S. dollar).

Chapter 4

1. Only a few days after his first inaugural in March 1933, FDR said, "The general underlying thought behind the use of the word 'guarantee' with respect to bank deposits is that you guarantee bad banks as well as good banks. The minute the government starts to do that, the government runs into a probable loss. . . . We do not wish to make the U.S. government liable for the mistakes and errors of individual banks, and put a premium on unsound banking in the future." Cited in Warren C. Gibson, "Federal Deposit Insurance: A Banking System Building on Sand," *The Freeman*, June 2010, http://www.thefreeman online.org/featured/banking-system-built-on-sand/.
2. Technically the FDIC fund is not guaranteed by the U.S. Government. The FDIC has the equivalent of a line of credit with the Treasury. Practically, the fund is guaranteed because if the FDIC failed the U.S. financial system would collapse. This is a perfect analogy with Freddie and Fannie. The GSE's debts were not technically guaranteed by the tax payers, but if they had been allowed to default the U.S. financial system would have collapsed due to the implied guarantee.
3. See Alicia H. Munnell, Lynn E. Browne, Geoffrey M. B. Tootell, and James McEncaney, "Mortgage Lending in Boston: Interpreting HMDA Data," Working Paper 92-7, Federal Reserve Bank of Boston, October 1992, and "Mortgage Lending in Boston: Interpreting HMDA Data," *American Economic Review* (March 1996). For critiques at the time, see Nobel economist Gary S. Becker, "The Evidence Against Banks Doesn't Prove Bias," *BusinessWeek*, April 19, 1993, p. 18, http://www.businesswekk.com/archives/1993/b331513arc.htm, and Stanley Liebowitz, "A Study That Deserves No Credit," *Wall Street Journal*, September 1, 1993, p. A14.
4. See *The State of the Nation's Housing 2009*, Joint Center for Housing Studies, Harvard University, http://www.jchs.harvard.edu/publications/markets/ son2009/index.htm.
5. In October 2010, as an ex-CEO, Mozilo settled out of court on civil fraud charges for misleading investors on risky mortgages, but Countrywide's buyer

(Bank of America) ended up paying most of the $67 million to the SEC. Bank of America also paid $600 million to settle a class-action lawsuit filed by Countrywide's robbed shareholders.

6. See Bert Ely, "Financial Innovation and Deposit Insurance: The 100% Cross-Guarantee Concept," *Cato Journal* (Winter 1994), pp. 413–445, and Bert Ely, "Regulatory Moral Hazard: The Real Moral Hazard in Federal Deposit Insurance," *Independent Review* (Fall 1999), pp. 241–254.
7. See Michael Keeley, "Deposit Insurance, Risk, and Market Power in Banking," *American Economic Review* (1980), pp. 1183–1200, and Gary Gorton and Richard Rosen, "Corporate Control, Portfolio Choice and the Decline of Banking," *Journal of Finance* (1995), pp. 1377–1420.
8. See Dennis Cauchon, "Federal Workers Earning Double Their Private Counterparts," *USA Today*, August 13, 2010, http://www.usatoday.com/money/economy/income/2010-08-10-1Afedpay10_ST_N.htm.
9. See Ludwig von Mises, *Bureaucracy* (Grove City, PA: Libertarian Press, Inc.).

Chapter 5

1. See studies of the long-term impact of U.S. government housing policy by Alex Pollock, resident fellow at the American Enterprise Institute, including "Comparing International Housing Finance Systems," October 11, 2010, and "The Future of Housing Finance," October 19, 2010, at http://www.aei.org/scholar/88.
2. See Steven A. Holmes, "Fannie Mae Eases Credit to Aid Mortgage Lending," *New York Times*, September 30, 1999.
3. See Edward Pinto, "Government Housing Policies in the Lead-up to the Financial Crisis: A Forensic Study," American Enterprise Institute, Washington, DC, February 5, 2011.
4. Portfolioing means to put the loan on the bank's books as an asset and fund it with deposits or other liabilities.
5. See Center for Responsive Politics, "Lobbying: Top Spenders," 2008, www.opensecrets.org.
6. See Peter J. Wallison and Charles W. Calomiris, "The Last Trillion-Dollar Commitment: The Destruction of Fannie Mae and Freddie Mac," *AEI Outlook Series*, American Enterprise Institute, Washington, DC, September 2008, http://www.aei.org/outlook/28704.

Chapter 6

1. I should note that more than a few modern-day monetary economists working in the Austrian economic tradition defend fractional-reserve banking (but not central banking) as being both moral and stable, and two of them contend that their position is close to that of von Mises; see George A. Selgin and Lawrence H. White, "In Defense of Fiduciary Media—or, We are Not Devo(lutionists), We are Misesians!," *Review of Austrian Economics* (1996), pp. 83–107.

2. The argument that retail investors were misled is also misleading. The vast majority of retail stock investments are made through registered brokers and mutual funds managed by very sophisticated investors. The fact is that when the stock market (or real estate market) is going up, everyone wants to get on the ride. I had dozens of individuals tell me to buy Enron because it was a wonderful investment. When I asked them what Enron did, not a one of them knew. A fool and his money are soon parted. The only way regulators can eliminate the downside risk is to take away the upside opportunity. If you cannot buy the next high-risk internet stock, you also cannot buy Apple. Also, retail investors do not materially impact stock prices. High-volume institutional investors drive stock prices.

Chapter 7

1. Prior to 2007 and after 1896 (when data are first available), U.S. home prices had declined in only 20 years, or just 18 percent of the time, but the last yearly price decline had occurred in 1991, and the one before that in 1941. Thus, present-day Americans did not expect house-price declines, and certainly not for five straight years (2007–2011). For the history, see Robert J. Shiller, *Irrational Exuberance*, 2nd ed. (Princeton, NJ: Princeton University Press, 2005; New York: Broadway Books, 2006), Figure 2.1. For house price data (1896–2006), see http://www.irrationalexuberance.com/Fig2.1 Shiller.xls.
2. The median house price peaked at $230,900 in June 2006, before falling 32 percent to a low of $156,900 in February 2011. The Affordability Index calculated by the National Association of Realtors plunged 30 percent between February 2004 and June 2006, a time when the Greenspan-Bernanke Fed was raising its fed funds rate from 1.00 percent to 5.25 percent.
3. Lehman Brothers filed for bankruptcy on September 15, 2008. The capital markets were still open for healthy banks. WaMu was seized by the regulators and sold to JPMorgan on September 25, 2008. The capital markets for banks closed after the WaMu seizure.
4. In the prior episode of U.S. house-price decline, 4½ years passed between the peak (October 1989) and the trough (February 1994), but the decline was just 8 percent, not 33 percent, as has occurred from the recent peak to the present (July 2006 to March 2011).

Chapter 8

1. Although the United States had last suffered a mild recession in 2001, U.S. house prices didn't decline, but instead kept rising—indeed, by 35 percent from the end of 2000 to the end of 2003.

Chapter 9

1. Since the Fed's founding in 1913, the U.S. CPI increase has averaged 3.4 percent per year and the index has increased 23-fold, so the dollar today is worth only 5 percent of what it was worth in 1913. In the same period prior to 1913

(97 years), when the United States operated largely on the classical gold-coin standard without a central bank, the CPI declined by 0.3 percent per year—a steady drop in the cost of living—and yet the economy boomed. The U.S. dollar was worth more in 1913 than in 1816, thanks to the gold standard. See http://www.measuringworthy.com/datasets/uscpi/result.php.

Chapter 10

1. A number of thrift executives were also very actively involved in the push into commercial real estate lending. They knew that the traditional residential real estate lending business was not viable in competition with Freddie and Fannie. Also, there were a number of crony capitalists (crony socialists) who wanted to leverage government deposit insurance for their own profit. Again, these crony capitalists were fundamentally unethical. They could not have accomplished their goals if there had been separation of business and state (like separation of church and state).

Chapter 11

1. In April 2009, FASB announced the end of its destructive two-year experiment mandating that fair-value accounting apply even when a market isn't trading (http://www.fasb.org/jsp/FASB/FASBContent_C/NewsPage&cid=1176154545286). Significantly, the U. S. stock-price plunge that had begun in October 2007 promptly ended in April 2009.
2. William M. Isaac, "How to Save the Financial System," *Wall Street Journal*, September 19, 2008, http://online.wsj.come/article/SB122178603685354943 .html. FASB didn't drop its strict view of fair-value accounting (FVA) until April 2009, and although the Troubled Asset Relief Program (TARP) was enacted in October 2008, from September 2008 to April 2009, U.S. bank stocks plunged 63 percent as the S&P 500 fell 38 percent. In the next year (post-FVA), banks gained 98 percent as the S&P 500 gained 52 percent.
3. When FASB was created in 1973, it replaced the Committee on Accounting Procedure (CAP) and the Accounting Principles Board (APB), both of which were part of the venerable American Institute of Certified Public Accountants (AICPA). Notably, until 1935, the AICPA was a purely private group, founded in 1887, long before government intervened in the field. The AICPA established accountancy as a profession, distinguished by rigorous education requirements, high work standards, and a strict code of professional ethics. It was not a political group.
4. In corporate finance, Economic Value Added (EVA) became a registered trademark of Stern Steward & Co., a consulting firm founded in 1982 that stressed cash flow accounting instead of GAAP-based accrual accounting and counseled executives to maximize EVA, defined as the value created over and above the true cost of capital, or shareholders' required rate of return. This approach required material changes to unreal GAAP accounting. Upon implementing EVA and tying it to executive incentives, many corporations radically

improved their performance. As cofounder Joel Stern once said, "EVA makes managers think more like shareholders" and "like entrepreneurs, by becoming more cost conscious and aggressively seeking ways to conserve capital and operate more efficiently."

Chapter 12

1. See Bill Gross, "Beware Our Shadow Banking System," *CNNMoney*, November 28, 2007, http://money.cnn.com/2007/11/27/newa/newsmakers/ gross_banking.fortune/.
2. According to Federal Reserve data, during the 1960s, roughly 23 percent of the total loans and investments at U. S. commercial banks consisted of traditional commercial and industrial (C&I) loans, while just 16 percent were in real estate (RE) loans. In the 1980s, C&I loans averaged 26 percent of the total, while RE jumped to 23 percent. In the 1990s, the C&I average was down to 21 percent, while the RE average rose further to 31 percent. By the time U.S. residential real estate prices peaked at the end of 2006, C&I loans made up just 15 percent of total loans and investments, compared to 42 percent for RE loans.
3. There is an interesting aside. When the government took over AIG, it forced AIG to settle its insurance contracts prematurely, that is, before markets had fully recovered. This strategy maximized AIG's losses.

Chapter 13

1. David Henderson, "Are We Ailing from Too Much Deregulation?," *Cato Policy Report*, Cato Institute, November/December 2008, http://www.cato .org/pubs/policy_report/v30n6/cpr30n6-1.html. See also Peter J. Wallison, "Deregulation Not to Blame for Financial Woes," American Enterprise Institute, September 30, 2008, http://www.aei.org/article28701, and Charles W. Calomiris and Peter J. Wallison, "Blame Fannie Mae and Congress for the Credit Mess," *Wall Street Journal*, September 23, 2008, http://online.wsj.com/ article/SB122212948811465427.html.

Chapter 14

1. In the 300 months prior to the latest U.S. recession (which began in December 2007), the United States was in a recession (that is, a correction mode) for only 18 months, or just 6 percent of the time. In contrast, during the previous 300-month period (1957–1982) the United States had been in recession (that is, correcting prior excesses) for 69 months, or 23 percent of the time. Compared to the 1960s and 1970s, Fed policy from 1982 to 2007 was overcommitted to keeping us out of a correction mode.
2. From its high level to its recent low during the last recession (2007–2009), real GDP in the United States declined by 5.1 percent, or more than double the average drop of 2.1 percent seen in 10 prior post–World War II recessions. The 5.1 percent decline was also deeper than the previous worst drop of 3.7 percent (1957–1958). For context, real GDP plunged 27 percent from 1929 to 1933.

3. Loan loss reserves at U.S. commercial banks averaged roughly 2 percent of all loans between 1987 and 1996, but thereafter declined steadily to an average of only 1.2 percent when the latest recession began in December 2007. In 2010–2011, the ratio has averaged 3.4 percent. See http://research.stlouisfed .org/fred2/series/USLLRTL?cid=93.

Chapter 15

1. See Bob Woodward, *Maestro: Greenspan's Fed and the American Boom* (New York: Simon & Schuster, 2000).
2. See Amity Shlaes, *The Forgotten Man: A New History of the Great Depression* (New York: HarperCollins, 2008), and Burton W. Folsom, Jr., *New Deal or Raw Deal? How FDR's Economic Legacy Has Damaged America* (New York: Simon & Schuster, 2009).
3. William M. Isaac, *Senseless Panic: How Washington Failed America* (New York: John Wiley & Sons, 2010).
4. The capital markets remained open for healthy banks after Lehman's failure, but closed after WaMu was seized by regulators and "sold" to JPMorgan.
5. See Peter J. Wallison, "Magical Thinking: The Latest Regulation from the Financial Stability Oversight Commission," American Enterprise Institute, Washington, DC, October–November 2011.

Chapter 16

1. See Thomas E. Woods, Jr., *Meltdown: A Free-Market Look at Why the Stock Market Collapsed, the Economy Tanked, and Government Bailouts Will Make Things Worse* (Washington, DC: Regency Publishing, 2009), p. 95.
2. See Ben S. Bernanke, *Essays on the Great Depression* (Princeton, NJ: Princeton University Press, 2000) and Ben S. Bernanke, "The Macroeconomics of the Great Depression: A Comparative Approach," NBER Working Paper No. 4814, National Bureau of Economic Research, August 1994, http://www.nber .org/papers/w4814.

Chapter 17

1. For a recent popular critique of Keynesian myths, see Hunter Lewis, *Where Keynes Went Wrong—and Why World Governments Keep Creating Inflation, Bubbles and Busts* (Mount Jackson, VA: Axis Press, 2009).
2. Nobel Prize winner Thomas Sargent's research on rational expectations proves this point.
3. For corroboration, see this op-ed by Harvard economics professor Robert J. Barro: "Government Spending Is No Free Lunch," *Wall Street Journal,* January 22, 2009, http://online.wsj.com/article/SB123258618204604599.html.

Chapter 19

1. Steve Forbes, *Flat Tax Revolution: Using a Postcard to Abolish the IRS* (Washington, DC: Regnery Publishing, 2005).

2. Neal Boortz, *The Fair Tax Book: Saying Goodbye to the Income Tax and the IRS* (New York: HarperCollins, 2005).
3. Dennis Cauchon, "Federal Workers Earning Double Their Private Counterparts," *USA Today*, August 13, 2010, http://www.usatoday.com/money/economy/income/2010-08-10-1Afedpay10_ST_N.htm.
4. For further analysis and a well-thought-out plan for privatizing social security by two long-term experts, see Peter Ferrara and Michael Tanner, *A New Deal for Social Security* (Washington, DC: Cato Institute, 1998).
5. For a detailed examination and critique of the Patient Protection and Affordable Care Act (Obamacare), see Michael Tanner, *Bad Medicine: A Guide to the Real Costs and Consequences of the New Health Care Law* (Washington, DC: Cato Institute, 2011).
6. See, for example, Brian Riedl, "A Guide to Fixing Social Security, Medicare, and Medicaid," Heritage Foundation, Backgrounder #2114, March 2008, http://www.heritage.org/research/reports/2008/03/a-guide-to-fixing-social-security-medicare-and-medicaid.
7. Clyde Wayne Crews, Jr., "Ten Thousand Commandments: An Annual Snapshot of the Federal Regulatory State" (Washington, DC: Competitive Enterprise Institute, 2011), http://cei.org/issue-analysis/ten-thousand-commandments-2011.

Chapter 20

1. In the past three years alone, the Fed has increased bank reserves—the fuel for future money growth—from only $46 billion (in August 2008) to $1.6 trillion (in August 2011), an expansion that is absolutely unprecedented in U.S. history.

Chapter 21

1. See "altruism" examined by novelist-philosopher Ayn Rand in *The Ayn Rand Lexicon: Objectivism from A to Z*, ed., Harry Binswanger, introduction by Leonard Peikoff (New York: New American Library, 1986), http://aynrandlexicon.com/lexicon/altruism.html.
2. Ayn Rand, "The Common Good," in *Ayn Rand Lexicon*, http://aynrandlexicon.com/lexicon/common_good.html.
3. Richard M. Salsman, "Altruism: The Moral Root of the Financial Crisis," *Objective Standard* (Spring 2009), http://www.theobjectivestandard.com/issues/2009-spring/altruism-financial-crisis.asp.
4. From the end of May 2007 until March 2009, Citigroup's stock price plunged 98 percent (as did its market value, from $300 billion to a mere $5 billion), compared to a decline of 84 percent in the S&P 500 Financial Sector Index. During this same tumultuous period, BB&T's stock outperformed Citigroup and the sector index by 33 percentage points and 19 percentage points, respectively.

Chapter 23

1. Laurence J. Kotlikoff, "U.S. Is Bankrupt and We Don't Even Know It," *Bloomberg News*, August 11, 2010, http://noir.bloomberg.com/apps/news?pid=newsarchive&sid=aiFjnanrDWVk. Kotlikoff is a professor of economics at Boston University and an expert on U.S. public finance, especially entitlements and intergenerational liabilities. See also Kotlikoff, "Is the U.S. Bankrupt?" *Review*, Federal Reserve Bank of St. Louis, July/August 2006, pp. 235–250, http://research.stlouisfed.org/publications/review/06/07/Kotlikoff.pdf, and "America's Debt Woe Is Worse than Greece's," CNNOpinion, September 20, 2011, http://www.cnn.com/2011/09/19/opinion/kotlikoff-us-debt-crisis/index.html?hpt=hp_t2.

2. See Ayn Rand, "Sense of Life," in *The Ayn Rand Lexicon: Objectivism from A to Z*, ed. Harry Binswanger, introduction by Leonard Peikoff (New York: New American Library, 1986), http://aynrandlexicon.com/lexicon/sense_of_life.html.

3. For a fascinating account of this monumental shift away from our founding political principles between the 1880s and the 1920s, see "America Reverses Direction," Chapter 14 in Leonard Peikoff, *The Ominous Parallels: The End of Freedom in America* (New York: Stein & Day, 1982), pp. 279–296.

4. See Jeffrey E. Paul "The Second American Civil War: Revolution and the Roots of Counterrevolution in American Ideological History," original paper in *Social Philosophy and Policy,* no. 8, Bowling Green State University.

5. See Howard Kurtz, "College Faculties a Most Liberal Lot, Study Finds," *Washington Post*, March 29, 2005, p. Cl, http://www.washingtonpost.com/wp-dyn/articles/A8427-2005Mar28.html. The study, conducted by professors Robert Lichter of George Mason University, Stanley Rothman of Smith College, and Neil Nevitte of the University of Toronto, surveyed 1,643 full-time non-science faculty members at 183 four-year U.S. colleges. A remarkable 72 percent of the professors surveyed described themselves as "liberal," versus only 15 percent calling themselves "conservative," and while 50 percent of them identified themselves as Democrats, only 11 percent said that they were Republicans. The disparity was even wider at "elite" colleges (like the Ivy League), with 87 percent liberals versus only 13 percent conservatives. In contrast, a Harris Poll of the American general public in 2004 found only 18 percent describing themselves as liberal, versus 33 percent describing themselves as conservative.

6. See Mark Kramer, ed., *The Black Book of Communism: Crimes, Terror, Repression* (Cambridge, MA: Harvard University Press, 1999).

7. See Charles Murray, *Real Education: Four Simple Truths for Bringing America's Schools Back to Reality* (New York: Random House, 2008).

Chapter 24

1. "The BB&T Philosophy," available from BB&T, 200 W. Second Street, Winston-Salem, NC 27101.

2. See Ayn Rand, "Reason," in *The Ayn Rand Lexicon: Objectivism from A to Z*, ed. Harry Binswanger, introduction by Leonard Peikoff (New York: New American Library, 1986), http://aynrandlexicon.com/lexicon/reason.html.

3. See Richard J. Herrnstein and Charles Murray, *The Bell Curve: Intelligence and Class Structure in American Life* (New York: Simon & Schuster, 1994).

Index

Acknowledgments

How do you acknowledge all the people who have contributed to a lifetime of work? Let me begin by thanking the many outstanding employees of BB&T who made me "look good." I especially want to thank Ken Chalk, Kelly King, Scott Reed, and Henry Williamson, who were the core of the executive management team that built BB&T. I am proud to have been associated with these individuals based on both their competence and, far more important, their outstanding character.

It is also most appropriate to acknowledge a deep intellectual debt to Aristotle, Ayn Rand, and Leonard Peikoff. I acknowledge Aristotle because anyone who believes in reason and logic must recognize his contributions. He is the intellectual father of Western civilization. Ayn Rand was the author of *Atlas Shrugged*, which radically changed my life. The purposefulness of her heroes and heroines fundamentally energized my worldview. Leonard Peikoff's book *Objectivism: The Philosophy of Ayn Rand* enabled me to integrate Rand's philosophy and use it as a major competitive advantage for myself and for BB&T.

When I was growing up in the 1950s and 1960s, my parents, sisters, grandparents, aunts, uncles, cousins, and the rest of my family were a classic middle-class family. There was not a single banker, lawyer, or doctor among this group. What they lacked in wealth, they made up with a powerful American sense of life.

My grandfather went to work at 13, selling newspapers on street corners to help feed his mother and sisters after his father drank himself to death. He worked for the same newspaper for more than

50 years. On Saturdays, my cousins and I would go with him to the newspaper office, where he taught us some powerful life lessons. On the way home, especially when the weather was cold or when it was raining or snowing, we would drive all over town and buy newspapers from the kids who were selling papers on street corners.

My dad went to work for the telephone company when he was 17 years old. He worked there for 41 years. He fought in World War II in the jungles of New Guinea and the Philippines. He was among the troops preparing to invade Japan. Having fought the fanatical Japanese, he was absolutely certain that dropping the atomic bomb was the right action. My dad almost died of malaria that he got in the Pacific. He would very seldom talk about the war. My father-in-law also fought in World War II in the Battle of the Bulge. His company was the first across the Remagen Bridge on the Rhine River. They suffered more than 100 percent casualties. My father-in-law talked about his combat experience only in the last few years of his life.

My family consisted of hardworking, honest, "get the job done" individuals who would bend over backward to help you if (and only if) you were trying to help yourself. They were the type of people who "hold the earth together" and exemplify the American sense of life.

I owe an unending debt to Gail Flowers, who has worked with me for almost 40 years and has been my executive assistant for 16 years. Gail is world class in her abilities and makes my work possible. She is a great friend and a wonderful person. Richard Salsman assisted with a significant amount of research and provided most of the footnotes. Barbara Honey typed a substantial part of the manuscript from my incredibly bad handwriting. It has also been a pleasure to work with Donya Dickerson and the professional team at McGraw-Hill.

I have three extraordinary children who have been the joy of my life and who constantly teach me important lessons. My partner, best friend, strongest supporter, and soundest critic is my wife, Betty. Anything I have accomplished in life is possible only because of her. We have been married 39 years and counting.

About the Author

 **John A. Allison** is the longest-serving CEO of a top-25 financial institution, having served as Chairman of BB&T for 20 years. He currently serves as President and CEO of the Cato Institute and as a distinguished professor at the Wake Forest University Schools of Business. He is also one of the lead spokespersons for banking and policy reform today, appearing at universities and business groups nationwide and serving on the board of directors of the Ayn Rand Institute. He received a Lifetime Achievement Award from American Banker and was named one of the decade's top 100 most successful CEOs by Harvard Business Review.